ANSELM OF CANTERBURY

VOLUME FOUR

ANSELM
OF CANTERBURY

VOLUME FOUR

HERMENEUTICAL AND TEXTUAL PROBLEMS IN THE COMPLETE TREATISES OF ST. ANSELM

by
Jasper Hopkins

THE EDWIN MELLEN PRESS
Toronto and New York

Library of Congress Catalog Card Number 74-19840
ISBN 0-88946-551-7 (Vol. IV)
0-88946-977-6 (Set of 4 vols.)

First Edition by The Edwin Mellen Press 1976

Toronto and New York

To the international circle
of Anselm-scholars

CONTENTS

PREFACE

Unlike *A Companion to the Study of St. Anselm*,[1] which is addressed to the nonspecialist, the present book is intended for the advanced scholar. Though its scope encompasses the entirety of Anselm's Complete Treatises, its primary focus is upon the *Monologion* and the *Proslogion*. These two treatises, perhaps better than any of the others except the *De Grammatico*, illustrate the complicated relationship between text, translation, and interpretation.

I have seen the claim that Anselm's "ideas and language are clear and simple; the difficulty lies in comprehending the ideas expressed."[2] Now, this is a claim which I do not readily understand. For I do not know what is supposed to be involved in the distinction between Anselm's *ideas* and his *ideas expressed*. Indeed, the only way we have of ascertaining Anselm's ideas is through the ideas expressed. So if the latter are difficult to comprehend, then so too are the former — unless the language in which the ideas are expressed poses special problems by not being clear and simple. That is, if both the ideas and the language are clear and simple, then the ideas expressed cannot be any more difficult to comprehend than are the ideas themselves. In short, the foregoing claim seems itself to be either unclear or incoherent. Let us assume that it is unclear. Then, perhaps what the author is aiming to say is something like the following: "Anselm's meaning is clear enough; the problem comes in evaluating the truth of what is meant." Or: "Anselm's statements are uncomplicated[3] and lucid; the difficulty lies in comprehending their implications." Yet, neither of these claims would be correct. For even apart from the question of implication or of truth-value, Anselm's *meaning* is not always clear — as evidenced starkly (though not exclusively) by *Monologion* 1–4 and *Proslogion* 2–4. What does he mean by "greater"? What is it for something to exist in the understanding? What exactly is meant by thinking the word which signifies the object? What is meant (in the preface to the *Monologion*) by meditating *de divinitatis essentia*? How are we to construe "*Idem namque naturam hic intelligo quod essentiam*" (in *Monologion* 4)? What is meant by "*unum argumentum*" (in the preface to the *Proslogion*) or by "*prolatio*" (in *Reply to Gaunilo* 10)?

The present study seeks to illustrate the difficulty of grasping some of Anselm's ideas. And it purports to show how his simple language is not always clear and how some of his clear ideas are not really simple. In fact, if there is one irony about Anselm's writings, it is the irony that some of his ideas are unclear precisely because his language is too simple, and thus too imprecise, too empty of distinctions. The difficulty of understanding *Monologion* 1–4 arises out of such imprecisions. Accordingly, in the translation of *Monologion* 1–4 there is a risk involved in veering away from Anselm's very sentence-structure, as well as a counter-risk of promulgating opacity by means of a too strictly word-for-word or construction-for-construction rendition. In the revised translation hereto appended,[4] I have tried to steer more deftly between Scylla and Charybdis. This revision reflects a better — or at least a different — understanding of certain aspects of these chapters.

In enjoining vigorous debate with a number of Anselm-scholars, I have frequently taken exception to their interpretations. But I remind the reader (1) that I have criticized the views only of those whom I respect, (2) that I have also criticized some of my own earlier interpretations and translations, and (3) that my criticisms are themselves open to debate.

Chapter IV was originally published as an article[5] in *Analecta Anselmiana* V and is reprinted here, with minor modifications, by permission of Minerva GmbH. I wrote this chapter in the spring of 1973; and I revised it during the ensuing autumn, while spending a sabbatical year in Paris as a fellow of the American Council of Learned Societies. Many of the ideas for the present study date from that time. I therefore express my continuing gratitude to both the ACLS and the University of Minnesota.

The appended bibliography supplements and updates the one which appeared in my earlier study of St. Anselm. Taken together, these bibliographies are extensive, though by no means exhaustive.

The hermeneutical and textual problems which inhere in the writings of St. Anselm have their counterparts in the works of all other medieval Latin authors. The present study is therefore paradigmatic of the difficulties faced by every philosopher, theologian, and historian who must cope with medieval texts. These difficulties — which often go unheralded — testify to the truth of R. G. Collingwood's verdict[6] that the reenactment of past thought and the evaluation of that thought must occur simultaneously.

Jasper Hopkins
University of Minnesota

NOTE: Where, for clarification, words from the Latin text have been inserted into the translations, the following rule has been employed: When the Latin term is noted exactly as it appears in the Latin text, parentheses are used; when the case-endings of nouns have been transformed to the nominative, brackets are used.

The numbering of the Psalms accords with the Douay Version and, in parentheses, with the King James (Authorized) Version.

The symbol ~ indicates negation.

CHAPTER I

ON TRANSLATING ANSELM'S COMPLETE TREATISES

Now that new translations of St. Anselm's Complete Treatises have just been published in a single edition of three volumes,[1] the time is perhaps fitting for the translators to call attention to some special problems attendant upon such an enterprise. For by becoming aware of these problems, a student of St. Anselm's systematic works will more readily discern the interrelationship between interpretation and translation. Indeed, he will recognize why translations cannot be completely free of interpretation and why he must guard against uncritical reliance upon any of them — the above-mentioned ones included.

1. Unlike St. Thomas Aquinas, Anselm neither develops nor works with a technical vocabulary of philosophical and theological expressions. Even though he is called the Father of Scholasticism, he is called this not in view of any "rigid" or "artificial" terminology but in view of his *sola ratione* methodology. The absence of a body of expressions which are used with more or less fixed significations creates the impression that Anselm's Latin is easier to deal with than is Thomas'. But as a matter of fact the looseness of Anselm's use of terms contributes immensely to the difficulty of comprehending his thought. Oftentimes, it is vexing to try to determine whether he is making a distinction or is simply employing another word in order to avoid monotony. For instance, when he switches from "*intelligi*" to "*cogitari*" in *Proslogion* 9 (S I, 108:12–13), he is obviously doing so to avoid repetition. And obviously in his *Reply to Gaunilo* 4 he is making a distinction between *non esse nequit cogitari* and *non esse nequit intelligi*. But what about the use of "*cogitare*" and "*intelligere*" at S I, 130:12–18 and S I, 139:1 (i.e., toward the beginning of *Reply to Gaunilo* 1 and 10 respectively)?

Admittedly, it makes no difference to Anselm whether he says "*intellectu dissolvi potest*" or "*cogitatione dissolvi potest*,"[2] whether he writes "*ille quod patri placiturum intellexit*" or "[*ille*] *hoc quod patri placiturum scivit*."[3] At times "*intelligere*" is best translated as "to understand," at times as "to judge,"[4] "to think,"[5] "to take to be the case,"[6] "to know,"[7] "to include,"[8] "to be plausible."[9] Similarly, in certain places "*intellectus*" is best construed as "understanding"; in other places it is more suitably rendered as "meaning,"[10] "interpretation,"[11] "accurate account,"[12] "intelligence,"[13] "intellect." Finally, "*constituere intellectum*" can be translated as "to signify";[14] and "*in nullo intellectu*" often means "in no respect,"[15] rather than "in no intellect." Anselm's flexible use of "*intelligere*" and "*intellectus*" makes a translator almost totally dependent upon the context in order to determine how narrowly or broadly the term is being employed. For Anselm does not fix upon a "standard" use which exhibits a "standard" meaning, from which occasionally to deviate.

Other examples of fluid terminology abound. In *De Grammatico* he interchanges synonymously "*in sensu*," "*in intellectu*," and "*in sententia*."[16] In *De Concordia* he acknowledges that *spiritus* may acceptably be called *mens* or *ratio*.[17] To signify existing, he uses "*esse*," "*existere*," "*haberi*,"[18] "*subsistere*,"[19] "*habere essentiam*,"[20] "*consistere*,"[21] and "*esse in re*."[22] It would be misleading to translate "*subsistere*" as "to subsist" — thereby suggesting that Anselm was distinguishing subsisting from existing.[23] Moreover, depending upon the context, "*Filius de patre essentiam habet*" may be rendered either as "The Son has His essence from the Father" or as "The Son has His existence from the Father." For Anselm makes no precise distinction between *essentia* and *existentia*. At *Monologion* 62 (S I, 72:17) "*cogitare*" may be rendered as "to perceive," and at *Cur Deus Homo* I, 19 (S II, 85:10) as "to imagine." At *De Veritate* 8 (S I, 186: 31), "*concipitur*" should be translated not as "is conceived" but as "is committed"; whereas at *Cur Deus Homo* II, 19 (S II, 131:4) "*concipio*" means "I receive." Furthermore, Anselm makes no systematic distinction between the meanings of "*potestas*," "*possibilitas*," and "*potentia*." And he interchanges[24] "*oratio*," "*propositio*," and "*enuntiatio*" —

all in the sense of "statement" — even though elsewhere[25] he employs "*oratio*" in the sense of "a phrase."

In short, Anselm's lack of a technical philosophical or theological vocabulary sometimes makes his thoughts difficult to grasp. A final example will suffice to illustrate this point concisely. The word "*argumentum*" can be used to mean either argument or premise. And, indeed, Anselm does use it in both these senses.[26] But when in the *Proslogion* Preface he speaks of propounding *unum argumentum*, does he mean that he has found a single argument-form which suffices to prove that God exists and is whatever we believe about the Divine Substance? Or does he mean he has found a single premise?: viz., the premise "God is something than which nothing greater can be thought." That is, does "*argumentum*" substitute here for "*ratio*" and "*probatio*" or for "*praemissum*" and "*prolatio*" ("utterance")? Only an examination of the entire work, as well as a comparison with the *Monologion* and the *Debate with Gaunilo*, can help one reach a judgment about the matter. But, in last analysis, whichever translation one chooses for "*unum argumentum*" will be a matter of interpretation. Thus, Richard R. La Croix[27] opts for the reading "a single argument" or "a single argument-form." And he accepts Charlesworth's translation of "*prolatio*" (in the second sentence of *Reply to Gaunilo* 10) as "proof." Interestingly, La Croix comes to believe that Anselm's argument-form can be correctly identified only by reference to the *Reply to Gaunilo*; for the *Reply* completes the "incomplete" proof found in *Proslogion* 2 and 3. By contrast, one can maintain (over against La Croix) that Anselm's statements in *Proslogion* 2 do constitute a complete proof without recourse to the *Reply to Gaunilo*, and that what Anselm attempted to undertake in the *Proslogion* was to show how a single consideration (*unum argumentum*) involves a single line of reasoning (*unum argumentum*). This single line of reasoning has different stages to it. The first stage attempts to demonstrate the existence of that being — assumed to be God — than which nothing greater can be thought (Chapter 2). The second stage shows that this being exists so really that it cannot even be thought not to exist (Chapter 3). The third stage purports to establish that this being has the other attributes (omnipotence, eternity, etc.) which are traditionally ascribed to God. On this reading, Anselm actually has a number of arguments in the *Proslogion*; and in the *Reply* he produces new arguments and argument-forms. In last analysis, this dispute over how to translate "*argumentum*" and "*prolatio*" illustrates how translation and interpretation do proceed — and must proceed — *pari passu*.

2. Just as the lack of a technical vocabulary makes it difficult to understand and to translate Anselm's expressed thoughts, so too Latin's lack of definite and indefinite articles conduces to the same difficulty. However, we must be careful in locating the exact source of trouble. Some philosophers suppose that the absence of these articles not only makes various perplexities inevitable but that it also absolutely prevents certain puzzles from arising. For instance, in *Reference and Generality*[28] Peter Geach contends that Latin thinkers *could not* have had a theory of definite descriptions:

> The lack of an indefinite article in Latin did not prevent the development of a theory remarkably similar to the theory expounded in Russell's *Principles of Mathematics* about 'denoting' phrases of the form 'an A'. The lack of a definite article, on the other hand, means that no 'theory of definite descriptions' may be looked for in medieval writers.

Nonetheless there is no basis to this claim.[29] For, like all Latin writers, Anselm had substitute-ways of expressing what in English is expressible by the use of articles. Thus, in *De Grammatico* 13 (S I, 157:30) Anselm writes:

> *Ponamus quod sit aliquod animal rationale — non tamen homo — quod ita sciat grammaticam sicut homo*. ("Let us suppose there is some rational animal — other than man — which has expertise-in-grammar, even as does a man." Or: "Let us suppose there is a rational animal. . . .")

And three lines later he infers:

> *Est igitur aliquis non-homo sciens grammaticam*. ("Therefore, there is something which is not a man but which has expertise-in-grammar." Or: "Therefore, there is a non-human being which has expertise-in-grammar.")

This use of "*aliquis*" to express what in English would be expressed by the article "a" is typical of virtually all medieval writers. Another Latin word which plays the same role as does the indefinite article is "*quidam*" and its variants. Thus, in *De Grammatico* 9 (S I, 154:4–5) Anselm writes:

> *Aristoteles dicit et quendam hominem, et hominem et animal grammaticum*. ("Aristotle says that a man and *man* and *animal* are expert[s]-in-grammar.")

Regarding his knowledge of Aristotle, Anselm is relying upon Boethius' translation of the *Categories*. And frequently Boethius used both "*aliquis*" and "*quidam*" to translate the indefinite τὶς

Similarly, Anselm has substitute-words for the definite article which Latin lacks. One of these substitutes is the demonstrative pronoun; another is the intensive adjective. Thus, in *De Libertate* 6 (S I, 217:25) he writes: "*Sed ipsa tentatio sua vi cogit eam velle quod suggerit*." ("But the temptation by its own force compels the will to will what it is suggesting.") And in *Cur Deus Homo* II, 16 (S II, 119:28–30) he says: "*Virgo autem illa de qua homo ille assumptus est, de quo loquimur, fuit de illis qui ante nativitatem eius per eum mundati sunt a peccatis, et in eius ipsa munditia de illa assumptus est*." ("But the virgin from whom that man (of whom we are speaking) was taken belonged to the class of those who through Him were cleansed from their sins before His birth; and He was taken from her in her purity.") Accordingly, even though it may have been unlikely, there is in principle no reason why Anselm or another of the medieval philosophers could not have raised certain puzzles about definite descriptions, since they had expressions which were equivalent to what *we* call definite descriptions. Indeed, the expression "*id quo maius cogitari nequit*"[30] is tantamount to the definite description: "The being than which a greater cannot be thought."

The trouble-point for understanding Anselm does not occur because he *did not have* a way of saying clearly what can be said in English using the definite or the indefinite article; rather it occurs because he *did not use* these substitute expressions when they were required to disambiguate his Latin sentence. There is no better instance of this than the title of his major work: "*Cur Deus Homo*." Unquestionably, this title is excerpted from three fuller expressions in the text itself: (1) "*Deus homo factus est*," (2) *Deus se facit hominem*," and (3) "*deum fieri hominem*."[31] And these fuller expressions are alternatives to the expression "*Deus incarnatus est*" (or "*Deus incarnatus factus est*"). In fact, in *De Conceptu Virginali* 17 (S II, 158:10–11, 14–17) Anselm poses the question "*Cur necesse fuit deum incarnari*?" and answers it with the words "*Ideo deus factus est homo, quia non sufficeret ad redimendos alios . . . homo non-deus*."[32] Now, as Anselm's theory of incarnation teaches, the Son of God became the man Jesus by assuming *a* human nature. That is, *De Incar-*

natione Verbi 11 (S II, 29:26–30:6) shows clearly that, on Anselm's view, the Son of God did not assume human nature as such — i.e., unindividuated human nature. Accordingly, he was not Man (not even the God-Man) but was a man (viz., the God-man). Hence, the appropriate translation of "*Cur Deus Homo*" is "Why God became a man" rather than "Why God became man." This difference of translation is important. For too often in the past the statement "God assumed human nature" or "God became man" has fostered the mistaken impression that, for Anselm, Jesus assumed universal human nature, so that when *He* paid the debt of Adam's sin, *man* (or human nature as such) made this payment. But, in fact, Anselm's view is that *a* man paid this debt — doing so on behalf of all other men.

If the foregoing fact were not already clear by inference from *De Incarnatione Verbi* 11, it would be clear from the following consideration. If it were the case that through Jesus, man (*homo*) made payment for his sins, then it would be the case that through Jesus human nature (*homo*) made this payment. But human nature was unable to make the payment, even though it ought to have made payment because it was obligated to do so — obligated both in Adam, after the Fall, and in Adam's natural descendants. But in Jesus, human nature was sinless and thus was free of the obligation which resulted from Adam's sin. Hence, Jesus' human nature was, in one sense, not Adam's nature, even though in another sense it was. It was not *numerically* the same as Adam's nature, for otherwise it too would have been guilty. On the other hand, it was of the same species as Adam's nature, because it was derived from Mary, who was descended from Adam. Now, of itself, even Jesus' sinless, individuated human nature was unable to make satisfaction for the sin of the human race (i.e., for Adamic nature, generically speaking). For with respect solely to His human nature Jesus did not have anything which in value exceeded everything other than God. And such was the payment necessary as satisfaction.[33] Therefore, it was not Jesus' human nature which, of itself, made satisfaction; it was rather His divine person. (For it was His divine person which was more valuable than all of creation.) This is what Anselm means when he states:

> *Unde necesse erat, ut deus hominem assumeret in unitatem personae, quatenus qui in natura solvere debebat et non poterat, in persona esset qui*

posset. ("Hence, it was necessary for God to assume a human nature into a unity of person, so that the one who with respect to his nature ought to make payment, but was unable to, would be the one who with respect to his person was able to.")[34]

In other words, when the person Jesus performed a meritorious deed for the honor of God, He may be thought of as having paid with respect to His human nature that which was owed as a debt by every other human nature, though not by His own. Nonetheless, since His human nature was an Adamic human nature, it *ought* to have rendered a meritorious service to God in order to remove a disgrace from upon all human nature. His human nature ought to have done this because for it to do so was fitting, not because it was indebted to do so. Consequently, since a person does not exist apart from his nature: when the person of Jesus made payment, His human nature as well as His divine nature also made payment — making it on behalf of all other human natures (men). Thus, man made satisfaction only in the sense that a man made satisfaction on behalf of all other men.

In sum, *Cur Deus Homo* I, 8 (S II, 60:3–5) speaks of *illum hominem . . . quem filius se ipsum fecit*: that man . . . whom the Son caused Himself to become [viz., Jesus]. The appearance of the phrase "*illum hominem*" is meant to preclude the phrase "*quemlibet hominem*." (Note *De Incarnatione Verbi* 11. S II, 29:6–12.) Since Anselm's use of "*Filius se fecit illum hominem*" is but a consistent expansion and specification of what he meant by "*Deus se fecit hominem*," and since "*Cur deus se fecit hominem*" is but a consistent expansion of what he meant by the title "*Cur Deus Homo*," this title is more accurately rendered with the indefinite article than without it.

Assuredly, Anselm would have helped his interpreters had he entitled his work "*Cur Deus ille homo*," or even "*Cur Deus quidam homo*" or "*Cur Deus Jesus*" or "*Cur Deus incarnatus*." The fact that he did not employ any of these other titles means that his argument must be *understood* before the title of his treatise can be known to be translated accurately. ("*Qui non intellegit res, non potest ex verbis sensum elicere*" was Luther's way of putting the principle behind this point.)[35]

Anselm's refusal to deal explicitly with the problem of universals parallels his imprecise discourse about human nature. Thereby the translator is required to be a student of Anselm's thought. For he is forced to translate Anselm's expressions in one of several ways — any one of which will convey an interpretation. Thus, it is unreasonable to demand that a translator not interpret; indeed, that would be tantamount to asking that he not translate. What must be demanded is rather the following: (1) that he not usurp the role of the exegete by leaning too far in the direction of making Anselm say things more precisely than Anselm in fact does; and (2) that he not saddle any one of Anselm's texts with so many ambiguities and inconsistencies that it becomes more incoherent than is warranted by a full comparison of all the texts.

Similar problems arise elsewhere in the *Cur Deus Homo* and *De Conceptu Virginali*. For instance, in *De Conceptu Virginali* 27 (S II, 170:13–14) Anselm states that *cum peccat persona quaelibet, peccat homo*. One translator has rendered this as: "When any person at all commits sin, man commits sin." And he appends a footnote explaining that Anselm is an ultra realist regarding the status of universals.[36] Yet, Anselm is not an ultra realist; nor is the translation correct. It is simply not the case that for Anselm there is numerically one universal human nature which all men share and which sins when any person sins. On the contrary. The more accurate reading is: "When any person sins, his human nature sins." Like many Latinists, Anselm did not always bother to insert possessive pronouns. In order to recognize that they are required, the translator must apprehend Anselm's position in toto. And to do so requires scrutinizing his complete treatises and formulating a framework in terms of which to elicit his meanings. Obviously, there will be reciprocity: The exegesis of particular passages will help determine the overall position; and the overall position will condition the exegesis of particular passages. Consequently, any student of St. Anselm's thoughts who does not read Latin must come to terms with the fact that in interpreting Anselm he is working from an English text which itself is already an interpretation.

At first, one might think it desirable to adopt the following rule: "If Anselm had an alternative way of saying something and did not say it that way, then he did not mean it that way." This rule might even be generalized: "If any author has a way of saying something and does not say it that way. . . ." Yet, no matter what is supposed about the intrinsic plausibility of this rule, it is questionable whether it can be adopted even as a rule-of-thumb for understanding Anselm. Take, for instance, the single word "*aliud*." Frequently, Anselm and Gaunilo do not use this word even though they intend for the reader to supply it.[37] Normally, this omission is inconsequential. But in some cases a vast difference will result, depending upon whether the reader does or does not supply it. Suppose a reader were to construe Gaunilo's "*illud omnibus quae cogitari possint maius*"[38] as "that which is greater than all that can be thought," instead of as "that which is greater than all *others* that can be thought." And suppose he reasons: "Gaunilo could have included the word "*aliis*" had he wanted to. Therefore its omission was deliberate. Therefore, as construed by Gaunilo the expression means that this being is inconceivable." Such reasoning would be naive precisely because it would not take account of the context of Gaunilo's argument. It would be as simplistic as would be the claim:

> Gaunilo writes "*insulam illam terris omnibus praestantiorem*." But he could have written "*insulam illam terris aliis omnibus praestantiorem*." Therefore, he meant an island which is more excellent than all lands (including itself), rather than an island which is more excellent than all *other* lands.

Likewise, then, simply because Anselm writes "*Cum peccat persona quaelibet, peccat homo*" instead of writing "*Cum peccat persona quaelibet, peccat humana natura sua*," it does not necessarily follow that he did not mean the latter. Indeed, since we know from *De Incarnatione Verbi* 11 and elsewhere[39] that Anselm uses "*homo*" as a substitute for "*humana natura*," and since we are aware of his frequent omission of words like "*eius*," "*sui*," "*aliud*," we cannot determine the correct translation by appeal to the above-mentioned rule. Indeed, if there is any general rule of hermeneutics, it is simply that rules of interpretation must be *elicited* from the texts themselves. And it is easy to find an example of eliciting such a particular rule: In reading Anselm's texts we notice again and again cases of his substituting one word for another without a corresponding change of meaning. In *De Incarnatione Verbi* 2 (S II, 11:10) he uses "*vox*" and "*nomen*" with the same meaning. In *Monologion* 38 (S I, 56:22–23) he interchanges "*significet*" and "*designet*" without any change of meaning. And in *De Concordia* III, 2 (S

II, 265:14–16) he substitutes "*rectitudinem servat*" for "*rectitudinem tenet*." After witnessing a large number of such examples, the reader begins to realize that Anselm is working with a rule of style which runs something like this: "Avoid repeating the same word in close succession." Having grasped Anselm's rule of style, a translator will not be misled into supposing that in *De Veritate* 2 the switch from "*enuntiatio*" to "*oratio*" is made in order to mark some important distinction between a statement and a sentence. Accordingly, he will translate both Latin words by the one English word "statement." Similarly, a passage such as

> *Communis terminus syllogismi non tam in prolatione quam in sententia est habendus. Sicut enim nihil efficitur, si communis est in voce et non in sensu: ita nihil obest, si est in intellectu et non in prolatione. Sententia quippe ligat syllogismum, non verba.*[40]

will be rendered as

> The common term of a syllogism must be common not so much in verbal form as in meaning. For just as no conclusion follows if it is common in verbal form but not in meaning, so no harm is done if it is common in meaning but not in verbal form. Indeed, the meaning — rather than the words — determines a syllogism.

instead of as

> It is not so much in the form of utterance as in its meaning that the common term of a syllogism is to be sought; for on the same grounds as those according to which no proof emerges from a mere verbal identity of terms without identical sense, there is nothing wrong with an identity which is understood although not made explicit. The meaning of the words is what really binds the syllogism together, and not just the words themselves.

3. A further set of problems is produced by certain of Anselm's Latin idioms. In particular, the expression "*verbum alicuius rei*" would ordinarily be rendered in English as "a word for some thing." But in the *Monologion* Anselm's argument trades upon a parallel between "*verbum rei*" and "*verbum spiritus summi*."[41] As "the word of a thing" is not idiomatic English, so "the Word for the Supreme Spirit" distorts Anselm's meaning. Yet, to say asymmetrically "the word for a thing" and "the Word of the Supreme Spirit" fails to capture in English the parallel upon which Anselm is trading in Latin. Moreover, the translation "word for a thing" can also be misleading — for example, in the sentence which would read: "There can be no word for that

which neither was, is, nor will be."[42] But surely, someone might protest, the word "unicorn" is a word for something which never has existed and, presumably, never will exist. S. N. Deane deals with this problem by putting: "To what has not been, and is not, and will not be, there can be no word corresponding." And for "*verbum alicuius rei*" he writes "a word corresponding to some object." Yet, by the logic of Anselm's argument Deane is prevented from construing "*verbum spiritus summi*" as "Word corresponding to the Supreme Spirit." Moreover, since Anselm is talking about images — to which he gives the name "words" — the term "corresponding" is not the most felicitous one. For although images do correspond to things, "correspond" is both vague and artificial. Indeed, the expression "an image of a thing" is much more idiomatic than the expression "an image corresponding to a thing."

In the light of the above considerations, the translation in the Complete Treatises makes use of the phrase "the word [or image] of a thing." This phrase has three advantages. First, it holds before the reader's mind the fact that Anselm is not talking about spoken words but about a special kind of word, viz., thoughts, memories, percepts, likenesses — all of which he calls images. Secondly, this phrase preserves the grammatical parallel with "*verbum spiritus summi*." Finally, in Anselm's argument this phrase seems more natural and less misleading than the others. Admittedly, there may be another equally acceptable way to solve the difficulties engendered by the Latin idiom "*verbum rei*" in *Monologion* 32–33 and 48. But whatever the way, it must be other than simply saying "the word of a thing," "the word for a thing," or "the word corresponding to a thing."

Conclusion. I have highlighted three problem-areas that trouble a translator of St. Anselm's treatises: (1) the lack of a technical vocabulary, (2) the omission of possessive adjectives and of words which substitute for definite or indefinite articles, and (3) the presence of idiomatic locutions not easily capturable in English. Along the way, I have cautioned against approaching the Latin texts with a set of preestablished exegetical rules. And I have illustrated how translation and interpretation are often inseparable.

In last analysis, the reader must not expect from the Complete

Treatises that which no lengthy translation can deliver *except* in principle: viz., a wholly perfect rendering. And he dare not demand what no lengthy translation can deliver *even* in principle: viz., a version free of all interpretation. That is to say, the Complete Treatises are *translations*, not some English substitute for the Latin text.

CHAPTER II

MONOLOGION 1–4: THE ANATOMY OF AN INTERPRETATION AND A TRANSLATION

Both the critics and the admirers of St. Anselm's writings have devoted indefatigable efforts to scrutinizing his reasoning in *Proslogion* 2–3. By contrast, they have paid relatively scant attention to his arguments in *Monologion* 1–4. To some extent, this unbalanced treatment is readily understandable. For, without doubt, the *Proslogion's unum argumentum* possesses a seductive quality which the *Monologion's concatenatio multorum argumentorum* lacks. Indeed, the very fact that the four arguments in *Monologion* 1–4 seem so patently implausible[1] explains why they have usually been dealt with cursorily.[2] However, because of their importance for Anselm's program throughout the *Monologion*, and because of the *Monologion's* centrality for assessing Anselm's overall viewpoint, they do merit a full reexamination. In undertaking this reexamination, I do not aspire to conclude that these arguments are more convincing than has previously been supposed. Rather, I aim to articulate them accurately — i.e., as Anselm articulates them — in order to determine what they tell us about (1) his intellectual relationship to Augustine, (2) his intent to prove the existence of God, and (3) his position regarding the status of universals. In particular, I want to ascertain whether or not in *Monologion* 1–4 Anselm (1) *deplatonizes* Augustine, (2) seeks to establish something only about the *essence* of God, and (3) commits himself to an *ultra-realist* theory of universals. In the first part of this endeavor I shall discuss certain problems of translation; in the second part I shall set out each of Anselm's four arguments; and in the third part I shall examine the bearing of the arguments on the three issues just mentioned.

I

1.1. It is advisable, in setting forth Anselm's premises, to adopt a two-step procedure: viz., to state the premises in Anselm's "own words" (in translation), and then to reformulate them less clumsily. This procedure will minimize the danger of inaccurate paraphrasing. For Anselm's style is so concise — and, in places, so ambiguous — that it conduces to his position's being misinterpreted *in the very process of being translated*. Indeed, three kinds of interpretive problems are posed for a translator. First of all, there is a problem about when to introduce into the translation helping-words not present in the Latin text. For instance, in his translation of *Monologion* 1, S. N. Deane introduces the words "cause" and "quality." And his decision to do so constitutes an interpretation — one with which I myself have no quarrel. But it does settle, for the English reader, the issue of whether Anselm is there appealing to the consideration that justice is a quality; and it does obscure the fact that — for whatever reason — Anselm in the beginning-chapters of the *Monologion* is deliberately shunning the overt language of causation.[3] As a rule-of-thumb, a translator ought to avoid introducing, as auxiliaries, words which function (or may be construed by the reader as functioning) in a technical-philosophical way (in the context at hand). Admittedly, though, he *cannot* always avoid introducing auxiliaries of some sort — be they technical or nontechnical. The problem comes in deciding when to do so and when not to. For example, toward the end of *Monologion* 1 Anselm asks:

> *Quis autem dubitet illud ipsum, per quod cuncta sunt bona, esse magnum bonum?*

The literal translation is:

> But who could doubt that that very thing through which all things are good is [itself] a great good?

Yet, is Anselm here committing himself to the view that all things are good (in some sense of "good")? As evidenced from *De Casu Diaboli* 1, there is no doubt that he does adhere to this view, just as assuredly as does Augustine. But the question is whether or not this metaphysical doctrine plays a role in *Monologion* 1–4. When we look at the passages which precede the one above, we see that Anselm is talking not about *all* things but about *all good things*; and he is asking whether all good things are good through one thing or through more than one thing. Might it be that in the above passage — perhaps for purposes of brevity and style — he simply writes "*per quod cuncta sunt bona*" where he means "*per quod cuncta bona sunt bona*": "that through which all *good* things are good"? Here a translator is forced to make a decision. Perhaps like F. S. Schmitt he will opt for "all things," and unlike Schmitt will add an explanatory footnote. Or perhaps he will choose "all good things" — on the understanding that this, after all, is Anselm's meaning, and that to say "all things" would be to distort Anselm's argument. Or perhaps he will write "all [good] things," thereby signaling the reader that he has made an interpretation. The point is that the translator will have to settle upon some rendering or other. Moreover, his choice of a rendering will be governed either by his understanding of the particular text, in comparison with other relevant texts (whether by the same author or from the same period or however), or else by the a priori rule that a word-for-word translation is always preferable. Now, there are obvious virtues to word-for-word translations. But to suppose that such a translation can never be misleading or mistaken would itself be mistaken. And the fact is that in *Monologion* 1 Anselm's argument does not proceed from the consideration that all things are essentially good. Instead, it proceeds both from the claim that "all men seek to enjoy only those things which they consider good" and from the empirical observation that they do not consider all things good and thus do not seek all things. In the above passage, therefore, it is as misleading[4] to employ the translation "that very thing through which all things are good" as it is obvious that "*illud ipsum per quod cuncta sunt bona*" is simply a stylistic abbreviation. And the latter fact *is* obvious from the context of the argument.

1.2. A second kind of interpretive problem arises in regard to the translation of individual words.[5] For instance, in *Monologion* 3 how ought one to render the phrase "*minus est*" in Anselm's maxim?:

> *Quidquid est per aliud, minus est quam illud per quod cuncta sunt alia, et quod solum est per se.*

Does Anselm mean that whatever exists through something other [than itself] *exists less* than that which alone exists through itself and through which all other things exist? Or does he mean that whatever exists through something other [than itself] *is something less* than that which alone exists through itself . . .? Here the Latin does not help us to decide, since "*minus*" may be either an adverb or a neuter adjective. So we search for other relevant passages. And in *Monologion* 4 we find:

> *Quidquid enim per aliud est magnum, minus est quam id, per quod est magnum.*

This passage is best translated as: "For whatever is great through something other [than itself] is something less than that other through which it is great." For the sentence preceding it was

> *Si vero id, per quod plures ipsae naturae tam magnae sunt, aliud est quam quod ipsae sunt, pro certo minores sunt quam id, per quod magnae sunt.*

And the word "*minores*," an adjective, serves as the clue to construing the subsequent "*minus*" adjectivally.

Similarly, in *Monologion* 6 we read:

> *Sed quidquid aliquo ex his tribus modis est: per aliud est et posterius, et aliquomodo minus est eo, per quod habet ut sit.*

Here the previous difficulty recurs. For ought we to translate the passage as?:

> But whatever exists in any of these three modes exists through something other [than itself] and *is* later and somehow *less* than this other through which it has its existence.

Or ought we rather to say?:

> But whatever exists in any of these three modes exists through something other [than itself] and *exists* later and somehow *less* than this other through which it has its existence.

Once again, the proximate Latin passage instructs us how to decide:

> *At summa natura nullatenus est per aliud nec est posterior aut minor* . . . .

Here too the occurrence of the adjectives "*posterior*" and "*minor*" evidence that in the previous sentence the words "*posterius*" and "*minus*" were meant to be adjectives rather than adverbs. Hence, the first of the two translations is the correct one.

So are we now in a better position to determine the reading of "*minus est*" in *Monologion* 3? Is it made more likely — by virtue of comparison with *Monologion* 4 and *Monologion* 6 — that in

Monologion 3 "*minus*" is to be construed adjectivally? Is not Anselm in *Monologion* 3, 4, and 6 subscribing to the unitary axiom that whatever exists through something other than itself *is something less* than that which exists through no other than through itself? In short, does not the Latin wording itself allow this uniform reading, and do not the other relevant passages support it? Well, yes, of course. But the question is how heavily to weight the further consideration that *Monologion* 3 *differs* from *Monologion* 4 and 6 in that it deals primarily with the theme of existing-most-greatly (*maxime est*) and only secondarily with the theme of being-the-greatest-of-all-things (*maximum est omnium*). Since the immediate context must be given preponderance, Anselm's point in *Monologion* 3 seems to be that what exists through something other than itself *exists less* than that which exists through no other than through itself. And thus in *Monologion* 3 he makes use of an axiom which is different from — but not unrelated to — the axiom employed in *Monologion* 4 and 6. This reading of *Monologion* 3 is supported by the fact that in *Monologion* 31 Anselm does clearly teach the doctrine of degrees of existence.

An example of how this second kind of interpretive problem is sometimes interconnected with the first kind can be observed in the case of the word "*per*," which in *Monologion* 1 is generally translatable as "through." Yet, in certain sentences this translation does not make sense in English. For instance, the sentence

> *Cum enim* [*equus*] *dici videatur bonus per fortitudinem et bonus per velocitatem, non tamen idem videtur esse fortitudo et velocitas*

does not sensibly come over into English as

> Although, ostensibly, a horse is called good through strength and good through swiftness, nevertheless strength and swiftness are seen not to be the same thing.

For, in proper English, a thing is not called something *through* something. Rather, it is called something *with respect to* something or *on account of* something or *by virtue of* something. Thus, it seems, a translator cannot consistently have recourse to the word "through," as Anselm can to the word "*per*." In deciding upon how to construe "*per*" in the above passage, the translator will attempt to grasp the movement of Anselm's argument in order to give a rendering which will not obscure it.[6] Suppose that because of his grammatical sense, the translator fixes upon the phrase "with respect to": a horse is called good with respect to strength. At first, Professor Richardson and I chose this translation. Later we were moved, by the following consideration, to say "on account of": In the sentence prior to the one cited, Anselm surmises that a horse is called good *because* it is strong; and his use of the word "because" ("*quia*") suggests the advisability of preserving, in the cited sentence, the "because sense" of "*per*": a horse is called good on account of strength.

But at this juncture a further possibility occurred to us: It would be possible to preserve the consistent translation of "*per*" as "through" provided we construed "*dici*" as "to be said to be" rather than as "to be called." That is, if we were to take Anselm as having written "*dici*" where he meant "*dici esse*" (*as in Monologion* 1 he had written "*putari*" in place of "*putari esse*,"[7] "*consideretur*" in place of "*consideretur esse*,"[8] "*intelligi*" in place of "*intelligi esse*,"[9] and "*aestimatur*" in place of "*aestimatur esse*"[10]), then we would be able to use the rendition:

> Although, ostensibly, a horse is said to be good through strength and good through swiftness, nevertheless strength and swiftness are seen not to be the same thing.

Moreover, we would be able to use a similar rendition for all other appearances of "*dicitur . . . per*," including the long sentence which opens the argument of *Monologion* 1.[11] Yet, prima facie, there seemed to be two prominent reasons for not following this route. First, Anselm nowhere in *Monologion* 1 writes "*dicitur esse . . . per*." By comparison, in *Monologion* 16 he does have "*dicitur esse iusta per iustitiam*" and "*iusta per se dicitur esse*."[12] This fact shows that he did not regularly omit "*esse*" and suggests that the omission *in the similar context* of *Monologion* 1 is deliberate. But since Anselm is no slave to style, this consideration by itself remains untelling. So in *Monologion* 1 the translator is thrown back, as he is so often elsewhere, upon the rationale of the argument. Does Anselm mean?:

> (1) Whatever things are called [*dicuntur*] something [e.g., good] . . . are called [*dicuntur*] it on account of something which is understood to be identical in the different things . . .

or

> (2) Whatever things are said to be something [e.g., good] . . .

> are said to be it through something which is understood to be identical in the different things. . . .

This is a question about the intent of the argument and about the syntactical scope of the verb "*dicuntur*" in its second occurrence. Does Anselm mean?:

> (1′) x, y, and z are called good; and the reason for calling them good is that there is something identical in them,

or

> (2′) x, y, and z are said to be good; moreover, they are said to be good through something identical in them.

The problem is not simply one of deciding whether to construe "*dicuntur*" as "are called" or as "are said to be." If one chooses to, he may use "are said to be" in both Propositions 1 and 2. For this phrase will be semantically consistent with either reading of "*per*," whereas the word "called" will not be semantically consistent with the reading of "*per*," as "through." So the priority of decision-making runs something like this: First, one must determine the syntactical scope of the second "*dicuntur*." This determination will tell him how to translate "*per*." For he knows that if he translates "*per*" uniformly as "through," he will be semantically precluded from taking "*dicuntur*" as "are called" — whereas if he translates "*per*" sometimes as "on account of," he will be semantically free to make use of either reading of "*dicuntur*." But how will he make the initial syntactical determination? Well, he must everywhere try both readings of "*per*," in order to ascertain whether in some sentence or other, the one reading is clearly the more plausible. For instance, what is the better reading for?:

> *Per aliud enim videtur dici bonus equus quia fortis est, et per aliud bonus equus quia velox est.*

At this stage in our reflections, Professor Richardson and I were convinced (1) that the primary sense of the passage is that the horse is called good and (2) that the *quia*-clause tells why the horse is called good. Accordingly, we construed "*per*" as "on account of":

> For on account of one thing a horse seems to be called good because it is strong, and on account of another thing it seems to be called good because it is swift.

Yet, further deliberation did not preclude, as implausible, the other alternative:

> For, ostensibly, a horse is said to be 'good through one thing because it is strong,' and is said to be 'good through another thing because it is swift.'

And after much hesitancy, we finally chose this last rendering, together with comparable ones elsewhere. In so doing, we were induced by four factors. First, S I, 33:20–21 (in *Monologion* 18)[13] suggested to us that "*dicitur*" in *Monologion* 1 does not signify an actual speech-act but functions rather like the verbs "*aestimatur*," "*consideratur*," "*putatur*," and "*intelligitur*" — all of which occur in this first chapter. That is, it signifies not what every single person actually says but what is accustomed to be said. Secondly, we remembered that the analogous passage in *Monologion* 16 corresponds to the above translation. In particular, Anselm says in Chapter 16: "*Summa natura non est iusta nisi per iustitiam*" (S I, 30:9). And a few lines later he writes: "[*Summa natura*] *dicitur esse iusta per iustitiam*." The second sentence — when taken in the light of the first sentence — can only plausibly be rendered: "[The Supreme Nature] is said to be just through justice." Now, if this is the meaning in *Monologion* 16, then presumably the meaning is similar in the analogous passages in *Monologion* 1— on the assumption that Anselm intended for the verb "*esse*" to be supplied in *Monologion* 1. Thus, the scope of "*dici*" seems to be the longer one. Thirdly, at S I, 14:25–27 Anselm writes:

> *Et quidem nihil solet putari bonum nisi aut propter aliquam utilitatem . . . aut propter quamlibet honestatem . . . .* ("Indeed, ordinarily, nothing is thought to be good except because of a certain usefulness . . . or because of some kind of excellence. . . .")

In this sentence "*putari*" replaces "*dici*," and "*propter*" replaces "*per*." Now, "*propter aliquam utilitatem*" and "*propter quamlibet honestatem*" do not give the reason for our thinking that x is good; rather, they give the reason that x is good." What is thought is "X is good because of a certain usefulness." That is, the scope of "*putari*" includes the "*propter*" phrase. Similarly, then, since "*putari . . . propter*" replaces "*dici . . . per*," the scope of "*dici*" includes the phrase governed by "*per*." Lastly — and this must necessarily be the least significant of the four reasons — the reading of "*dici . . . per*" finally chosen by Professor Richardson and me allows "*per*" to be translated (everywhere in *Monologion* 1–4) consistently as "through"; thus, it better displays the wording of Anselm's Latin.

The puzzle over whether to translate "*per*" always as "through" or sometimes as "on account of" turned out to be related to the question of whether or not to construe "*dici*" as shorthand for "*dici esse*." Now, as a general rule, wherever a translator does not understand an argument, he ought to translate word-for-word, provided his doing so does not produce meaninglessness. In the foregoing case, however, this general rule is inapplicable, since "with respect to" and "on account of" and "through" are each word-for-word translations of "*per*," and since (in some contexts) for a writer to say "*dici*" amounts to his having said "*dici esse*." Since any one of these translations will modify the meaning of Anselm's argument, a translator has only two guidelines: the capacity of the translation to reflect the internal coherence of the entire line of reasoning, and the consistency of the translation with the totality of the relevant Latin texts. Where the reasoning is incoherent or where the texts are inconclusive, a translational indeterminacy will result. And in medieval Latin this indeterminacy occurs less rarely than could be wished.

1.3. A third kind of interpretive problem arises in regard to the temptation to restructure Anselm's sentences — to style them, to streamline them, to make them more readable. In this effort to achieve at least a minimal literary appeal there are obvious merits; yet there are also hidden dangers. For example, in *Monologion* 6 Anselm writes:

> *Quod enim dicitur esse per aliquid, videtur esse aut per efficiens aut per materiam aut per aliquod aliud adiumentum, velut per instrumentum.*

And it is tempting, for stylistic reasons, to translate this passage somewhat freely as:

> For what is said to exist through something is seen to exist through it either efficiently or materially or *instrumentally* (i.e., in such way that the other is a kind of *aid*).

This version restructures Anselm's sentence by switching "*per adiumentum*" and "*per instrumentum*" — doing so in order to render "*per efficiens*," "*per materiam*" and "*per instrumentum*" adverbially. For "*per adiumentum*" cannot be rendered adverbially as felicitously as can "*per instrumentum*." At first, it may seem that none of Anselm's meaning has been lost and that, consequently, the stylizing does no harm: he is — is he not? — distinguishing three kinds of causes. But, in fact, the restructuring has obscured Anselm's position in a way that the following more literal translation would not:

> For what is said to exist through something is seen to exist either through something efficient or through matter or through some other *aid*, as through an *instrument*.

One sees readily how important the word "other" ("*aliud*") is — a word which is misconstrued in the free translation. Clearly, Anselm is distinguishing only *two* kinds of causes; viz., efficient and auxiliary (or instrumental) causes. For he is regarding material causes as a subclass of auxiliary causes — a distinction which coincides with Cicero's distinction in his *Topics*. Thus, Anselm is merely repeating Cicero's view rather than modifying it; but on the basis of the free translation he seems to be modifying it by regarding a material cause as something other than a variety of auxiliary cause

The foregoing example strongly suggests that the translating of philosophical arguments ought to proceed differently from the translation of descriptive prose, of poetry, or of prayer. In particular, translations for the last two genres are likely to need some measure of restructuring in order to preserve their emotive richness and affective style; by contrast, a philosophical argument is more likely to be endangered by any restructuring and to lose something essential. Poetry and prayer can only be effectively expressed when expressed freely, whereas argumentation can only be safely expressed in inverse proportion to the degree of freedom. In some cases, however, Anselm's translators must steer a *via media* between preserving the fervor of pious breathings and adhering to the systematic movement of a line of thought. Thus, any acceptable translation of *A Meditation on Human Redemption* will have to combine both features. For Anselm therein summarizes the argument of the *Cur Deus Homo*, clothing his summary in the language of devotion. The attempt to paraphrase the argument for the sake of preserving the devotional style may lead to an inaccurate[14] presentation of the reasoning. George Stanhope's translation of 1701, for instance, *intensifies* Anselm's expressions in order to gain in English an impact more strongly emotive than the impact of Anselm's own words on his Latin readers. Thus, Stanhope's translation reads "most wretchedly of all slaveries" instead of "wretched slavery"; "agonies unspeakable'' instead of ''agonies''; ''infinitely greater than'' instead of ''more precious than''; ''O my dearest Lord'' instead of ''O Lord''; and so on. By contrast with Stanhope's translation, any more literal and reliable translation will seem ''pedestrian.'' In fact, Richard Campbell (in *Theology*, August 1975, pp. 442–443) uses this very term in comparing the translation presented in the Complete Treatises with the translation from 1701. Yet, Campbell should point out that Stanhope's translation is vigorous because it is inflated. And he should note the various mistakes which Stanhope makes in the process of rearranging and paraphrasing. Thus, at a crucial juncture in Anselm's argument, Stanhope presents the incorrect (and inelegant) translation: ''Reason and the eternal rules of equity require, that the sinner should make God amends for the injury done to his honour, by restoring in lieu of it somewhat greater and more valuable, than all that can be, which is not a sufficient compensation for dishonouring him.'' And his method of paraphrasing altogether eliminates the following important sentence: ''For if putting Him to death [is a sin which] surpasses the multitude and magnitude of all conceivable sins which are not against the person of God, clearly His life is a good greater than the evil of all those sins which are not against the person of God.''

1.4. In the *Monologion* Anselm sets out to honor his fellow-monks' request for a nontechnical discussion of the Divine Being. He therefore deliberately shies away from philosophical terminology and from elaborate argumentation. But in his effort to fashion a simplified line of reasoning, he engenders a host of interpretive difficulties. Ironically, these difficulties make his thinking elusive — elusive for his own Latin-speaking students as well as for his twentieth-century translators and commentators.[15] I have cited three kinds of problems which make the task of understanding Anselm more complicated than anyone would initially have imagined. Along the way, I have alluded to four rules-of-thumb which a translator needs to remember:

(1) Avoid introducing, as auxiliaries, words which function (or may be construed by the reader as functioning) in a technical-philosophical way (in the context at hand).
(2) In translating an apparently incoherent or an apparently implausible argument, aim for a very literal rendering.
(3) In translating the premise of an argument, avoid deliberate

syntactical restructuring. Where restructuring seems necessary, use a footnote to indicate to the reader what is happening.

(4) Look to the genre to determine how literally to translate. Philosophical arguments must be rendered more literally than must narrative or prayer.

Rules of this sort are flexible and cannot be given a priori weights relative to one another. That is, the relative weighting must always depend upon the particular author and upon the matrix of his thinking.

A translator's question, then, is not *whether* to interpret; it is rather *what kinds of* interpretations are legitimate and what kinds are illegitimate.[16] To a lesser extent, this same question besets even the paleographer. Thus, in the last sentence of *Proslogion* 20 F. S. Schmitt puts "*tibi*" in place of "*ibi*" — even though the best manuscripts have the latter.[17] But he is a long way from subscribing to Bentley's dubious principle: "*Nobis et ratio et res ipsa centum codicibus potiores sunt*."[18]

II

Having become sensitive to the fact that many exegetical dangers are lurking in *Monologion* 1–4, we must approach with caution the argument contained in each chapter. In the case of the first argument, the best procedure will be to state the steps in Anselm's "own words" before indulging in any reformulation.

2.1. *Argument I.*

(1) Whatever things are said to be something in such way that they are said to be it either in greater or lesser or equal degree in relation to one another, are said to be it through something which is understood to be identical in the different things (rather than through something different in the different things), whether it is observed in them in equal or in unequal degree.

(2) If compared with one another, all good things are either equally or unequally good.

So: (3) All [good] things are good through something which is understood to be identical in these various goods. (1) (2)

(4) That through which all [goods] are good is [itself] a great good.

So: (5) That through which all [good] things are good is good through itself (since every [good] thing is good through it). (3) (4)

So: (6) All other [good] things are good through something other than what they are, and this other alone [is good] through itself.

(7) No good which is good through something other [than itself] is equal to or greater than that good which is good through itself.

So: (8) Only that which alone is good through itself is supremely good. (6) (7)

(9) What is supremely good is also supremely great.

So: (10) There is one thing which is supremely good and supremely great — i.e., which is the highest of all existing things. (8) (9)

Step 1 is clarified by an example:[19] "Whatever things are said to be *just* in relation to one another — whether they are said to be equally just or whether some are said to be more just and others less just — can be understood to be just only through justice, which is not something different in these different things." As it stands, this statement is not an exact substitution-instance of the first premise; for after the dashes there is no repetition of the word "*dicuntur*." Thus, although the first premise is expressed as ". . . are said to be it [e.g., just] through something which is understood to be identical in the different things," the example has ". . . can be understood to be just only through justice, which is not something different in these different things." This elimination of "said to be" suggests that reference to our practice of calling things good is not an essential aspect of Anselm's argument. This suggestion is corroborated by the fact that no other premise of the argument employs the verb "*dicere*." Why, then, does Anselm begin his argument with reference to the practice of calling things comparatively good? Presumably, he does so in order to begin with an uncontroversial premise — a premise which, in conjunction with others, will entail (Anselm believes) an incontrovertible conclusion. By commencing with a practice which is so familiar, he hopes to render his derivation all the more undeniable.

Of course, if various objects are *truly* said to be good through one thing, then it follows that they *are* good through one thing. And this fact undoubtedly explains why Anselm does not bother to articulate the example exactly as he does the premise.

It is possible to elicit from this first premise a number of subtle points. First, there is no begging the issue of whether or not the one thing is a substance or a quality or, in some sense, both.[20] In *Monologion* 16 he calls justice a quality; but the substance/quality distinction does not play an explicit role in the argument of *Monologion* 1. Secondly, the words "in the different things" are not meant to *exclude* the possibility that the one thing exists independently of the many things.[21] In *Monologion* 14 Anselm maintains that the Supreme Being is in all other things, without denying that it transcends all other things. Similarly, in *Monologion* 1 the statement that the one thing is *in* the different things is intended to leave open the question of whether or not it also transcends them. Thirdly, the identity referred to in the initial premise is numerical identity. Anselm is not dealing explicitly with the problem of universals and hence does not even mention identity of species in contrast to numerical identity. In fact, we must be wary of using *Monologion* 1–4 as a basis for determining Anselm's position regarding universals; for the reasoning contained in these chapters is too concise to yield much information about topics *not* dealt with there. The better strategy would be to look elsewhere in the *Monologion* for indications of Anselm's position and then to look again at *Monologion* 1–4 to make certain that it is not incompatible with the interpretation arrived at.

In sum, it seems safe to reformulate Premise 1 by streamlining it into: Whatever things are either equally or unequally *x* in comparison with one another, are *x* through something which is identical in the different things.

Step 2 is intended as an instantiation of the first part of Premise 1. Anselm leaves aside the illustration about just things and turns to considering good things. For they too are apprehended as being either equally or unequally something in comparison with one another.

This step may be restated as: All good things are either equally or unequally good in comparison with one another.

Step 3 is derived from the first two. There is a noteworthy difference between it and the example which Anselm uses to illustrate and support the first premise (viz., the example of just things). In the example he states that all just things are just through justice; but in the third step he does *not* state that all good things are good through goodness (*bonitas*). To put the point the other way around: in Step 3 he states that all good things are good through some one thing (without concluding immediately that this one thing is good, or without calling it goodness);[22] but in the example he does not say merely that all just things are just through some one thing. Why, then, does he avoid the term "*bonitas*" but not the term "*iustitia*"?[23] Why does he not preserve the parallel with the example of justice by here inferring?: "Therefore, all good things are good through goodness, which is not something different in these different things." Is it because he wants to avoid saying, in Step 4, that goodness is a great good? Well, in fact, he does not say in Step 4 that *bonitas bona est*, or that *bonitas bonum est*. Rather, his argument proceeds without *assuming* that the one thing through which all good things are good is itself either goodness (*bonitas*) or a good (*bonum*). That is, Anselm is not developing an argument which has recourse to self-predication or to Platonism.[24] Although he subsequently proves[25] that that through which all good things are good is itself supremely good[26] and is Supreme Goodness,[27] these considerations play no role in Steps 3 and 4. Moreover, even these subsequent statements do not involve self-predication. In fact, Anselm nowhere explicitly utters the statement "(Supreme) Goodness is good." *Monologion* 16–17 suggests that he would construe the statement "The Supreme Nature is good" as tantamount to the identity statement "The Supreme Nature is Goodness." And thus, were he to say "(Supreme) Goodness is good," presumably this statement, too, would be one of self-identity. Now, I cannot imagine that Anselm would object to the statement "Supreme Goodness is good" or to the statement "Supreme Goodness is good through itself"; for he does not object (in *Monologion* 44) to the statement "Supreme Wisdom is always wise through itself."[28] The fact that his Latin sentence here employs the verb "*sapere*" instead of the predicate "*est sapiens*" is inconsequential. In *Monologion* 16 he uses the predicate "*est iusta*" (there being no corresponding verb) when he comes close to saying "Supreme Justice is just," but actually says: "This [Supreme] Nature (which is justice itself) is just."[29] As by the latter statement he means that the Supreme Nature is essentially justice, so by the former he means that Supreme Wisdom is essentially wisdom. Presumably, he would agree with Augustine's verdict in *De Trinitate* 7.1.2: "As it is absurd to say that whiteness is not white, so it is absurd to say that wisdom is not wise."[30] And yet the argument of *Monologion* 1 unfolds in such a way as not to require this kind of premise.

Bearing in mind the significance of Step 3, we may reformulate it more concisely as: Therefore, all good things are good through something which is identical in the different good things.

Step 4 is presented independently of any justification; and, indeed, it is intended as axiomatic. It is not supposed to be inferred from the (false) assumption that every cause must resemble its effect. (A knife does not resemble a wound.) Rather, Anselm simply finds inconceivable the view that that through which all good things are good would not itself be a good thing.

Step 5 is the inference that the one thing under discussion is good through itself (*per se*). This inference is based upon the previous concession that all good things — of which it is one — are good through it. That Step 5 is *inferred* shows that it is different from the analytic proposition "Goodness is good through itself," which would not need to be inferred. And it confirms the previous observation that Anselm's argument does not involve self-predication.

Step 6 simply makes explicit what is implicit in Step 5. This move brings into perspective the fact that the one good thing is an independent good. For what is good *per se* cannot be identical with what is good *per aliud* (i.e., good through something other than itself). Here a distinction must be noticed. Anselm is not yet trying to prove that what is good *per se* either could or would continue to exist if what is good *per aliud* perished. That is, he is not yet arguing that the former *exists independently* of the latter. Rather, he is inferring that the former *is independently good*, whereas the latter are dependently good.

We may reformulate this step as: Therefore, all other [good] things are good through something other than themselves, and this latter alone [is good] through itself. For the unreformulated clause "All other [good] things are good through something other than *what they are*" does not imply that the one thing is other than the many good things with respect to being good. Rather, the phrase "other than what they are" implies that the one thing is a different being from any of the other beings.

Step 7 is regarded as introducing a self-evidently true premise, since the maxim "to be independently good is better than to be dependently good" is regarded as self-evidently true.

Step 8 is a straightforward inference which establishes that there is only one supremely good thing.

Step 9 is true because whatever is supremely good is supremely excellent, and because by "great" Anselm here means "excellent."

Step 10 concludes the argument, doing so by means of the inference that there exists a being which is supremely good and supremely great.

In retrospect,[31] the soundness of the argument can be seen to turn, above all, upon the meaning and the truth-value of its first premise. Although Anselm explains and supports this premise by way of examples, these few examples do not constitute a sufficient context for adequately interpreting the premise; nor do they furnish sufficient evidence for its truth. Perhaps this first premise seemed to him more commonsensical than it does to us, so that he did not feel the need for prolonged debate. Once we grant that there is one thing existing "in" the many things, the argument can continue plausibly, until it has determined that this one thing is the Supreme Good.

But does this Supreme Good exist independently of the many things, even as it is good independently of them? Anselm turns to this topic in Chapter 3. However, before doing so, he sketches (in Chapter 2) an alternative argument to the one just considered.

2.2. *Argument II*.

Accordingly, *Monologion* 2 indicates that the conclusion to Argument I can be established by beginning with the observation that some things are great, instead of with the observation that some things are good. Anselm does not actually bother to state this second argument fully since its steps correspond to those of the first argument — as evidenced by substituting "great" or "great thing" for "good" in Steps 1–8. Step 9 is stated as "Only what is supremely good can be supremely great." (This is meant as the converse of the corresponding statement in the previous proof.)[32] And Step 10 may be shortened to: Therefore, there is one thing which is supremely great and supremely good.

So Anselm is not really opening up a new line of reasoning here. And this is why he entitles the chapter "The same topic continued." By contrast, he does in Chapter 4 open a line of reasoning different from that in Chapter 3 — and does so in spite of the fact that he entitles Chapter 4 "The same topic continued."

2.3. *Argument III.*

On the basis of *Monologion* 3 and 4 — and not on the basis of *Monologion* 1 and 2 — Anselm has generally been thought to be aiming, in the *Monologion*, at proving God's existence. Those who like Karl Barth and F. S. Schmitt deny that this is his aim, must therefore focus their denial on Chapters 3 and 4.[33]

For convenience, Argument III may be divided into three sections — of which the first section is the longest.[34]

2.3.1 *Section A.*

(1) Whatever exists exists either through something or through nothing.

(2) That anything exists through nothing is inconceivable.

So: (3) Whatever exists exists through something. (1) (2)

(4) This something through which all existing things exist is either one or many.

Assume: (5) That through which all existing things exist is many.

(6) Either (a) these many are traced back to some one thing through which they exist, or (b) each of the many exists through itself, or (c) they exist mutually through one another.

(7) If *a* is the case, then [in last analysis] everything exists through the one thing through which the many exist.

(8) If *b* is the case, then there is some one power (or nature)-of-existing-through-itself which the many have in order to exist through themselves. And the many exist through this one thing through which they have the fact that they exist through themselves. And thus all things exist through this one thing more truly than through the many things which themselves are not able to exist without this one thing.

(9) Since the thought that a thing exists through that to which it gives existence is irrational, *c* is not the case.[35]

So: (10) It is not the case that that through which all existing things exist is many. (6)-(9)

So: (11) That through which all existing things exist is one thing. (4) (10)

Section A actually presents an argument for Proposition 11; whereas in the first proof there is no comparable argument for Proposition 3, which corresponds to Proposition 11 here. Or, to state the contrast somewhat differently: Proposition 3 of the first proof is argued solely from examples.

Now, in Section A the crux of the reasoning is Step 8. And we see immediately that this step is reminiscent of Step 1 in the first proof. Here, perhaps, we find another reason why Anselm began his *concatenatio multorum argumentorum* with a consideration of the good. For it is somehow more plausible to say "All good things are good through something which is identical in the different good things" than it is to say "There is some one power-of-existing-through-itself which the many have in order to exist through themselves."[36] (To say that the many "have" this power is tantamount to saying that this power is "in" them.) So Anselm is relying upon his considerations in the case of the good to lend credence to his analogous point here.

2.3.2 *Section B.*

(12) This one thing through which all existing things exist exists through itself. (3) (11)

Thus: (13) All existing things other [than this one] exist through something other [than themselves]; and this one alone exists through itself. (12)

(14) Whatever exists through something other [than itself] exists less than that which alone exists through itself and through which all other things exist.

So: (15) That which exists through itself exists most greatly of all. (13) (14)

So: (16) There is some one thing which alone exists most greatly and most highly of all. (12) (15)

Section B continues the parallel with Argument I in obvious ways.[37] Moreover, it shows that the one thing under discussion exists independently of all else. For since it exists *per se*, whereas all else exists *per ipsum*, it can exist without these other things, which cannot exist without it. Accordingly, if it exists "in them," it must also transcend them.[38] In proving the *independent* existence of this one thing, Anselm gives what he will deem in retrospect (i.e., once he has derived the other attributes) to be a proof of the existence of God.[39] For to prove God's existence is to prove the independent existence of a being that has the attributes God is traditionally described as having. Thus, in the course of reflecting upon existing objects Anselm believes that he discerns reasons which necessitate the inference that a Supreme Being exists. And, as supreme, this Being is not simply one object among others.

2.3.3. *Section C*.

(17) That which exists most greatly of all and is that through which exists whatever is good and great and whatever is anything at all, is supremely good, supremely great, the highest of all existing things.

So: (18) There is something which is the best and the greatest and the highest of all existing things. (16) (17)

Section C claims that what exists supremely is also what is supremely good and supremely great. But what is the basis for this identification? Does Anselm regard the identification as self-evidently true? Or does he suppose that it somehow follows from an assumption which is self-evidently true? — for instance, the assumption that that through which all good things exist must also be that through which all good things are good. Now, since Proposition 17 does not seem to me to be self-evidently true, I am tempted to think that Anselm implicitly derived it from the foregoing assumption together with Steps 4–9 from Argument I. However, the assumption does not seem to me to be self-evidently true either. So I have to ask myself: Could not all good things be good through one thing and exist through another thing? Well, maybe in denying that they could, Anselm would reason as follows: "Assume that all good things are good through one thing and exist through another thing. Then, the one thing through which they are good would itself be a great good (cf. Argument I) and so would exist through the one thing through which all good things exist. But that through which all good things exist would also be a great good, since it would be the cause of so great a good (cf. *Monologion* 6).[40] Thus, by hypothesis, that through which all good things exist would be good through that through which all good things are good. But that through which all good things are good could not exist through that through which all good things exist unless the latter were good logically prior to the former. Hence, the latter could not be good through the former. Hence, either it is not the case that all good things are good through one thing or else that through which all good things are good is also that through which all good things exist. But it *is* the case that all good things are good through one thing (Argument I, Step 3). Therefore, that through which all good things are good is also that through which all good things exist."

Now, the foregoing reasoning seems too complicated to serve

as an *explication* of Section C of Argument III. For if Anselm did not regard as self-evidently true either Proposition 17 or the assumption that "that through which all good things exist must also be that through which all good things are good," then he would surely have expanded his reasoning in Section C. And so we may conclude that however unintuitive Proposition 17 or the above assumption may seem to us, they did not appear unintuitive to Anselm. Probably, then, he accepted one or the other of these as self-evident — unless perhaps there remains some different assumption which he might have been making.

Anselm's reflective meditation is now well underway toward rationally deriving the other attributes of this one Being. This reflection will reach a focal point in Chapter 6, and another in Chapters 15 and 28, before turning to meditate upon the fact of triunity. But in order to leave no doubts about the fact that he is building upon a (supposedly) solid foundation, Anselm will set forth an alternative proof in *Monologion* 4.

2.4. *Argument IV.*

For convenience this long argument can also be divided into three sections. Its very complexity manifests why Anselm kept seeking to formulate a simpler one — until he finally struck upon the *Proslogion's* formulation.

2.4.1. *Section A.*

	(1)	Some natures are more excellent than others.
	(2)	[Either such a division of gradation is limitless or it is not.]
Assume:	(3)	Such a division of gradation is so limitless that for each grade a higher grade can be found.
Then:	(4)	The number of these natures is boundless — an absurdity.
So:	(5)	The division of gradation is not limitless. (3) (4)
So:	(6)	There is a nature which is so superior to others that there is no nature to which it is ranked as inferior. (3) (5)

Section A begins with the allegedly commonsensical[41] observation that some natures are more excellent than others, and that these different natures can be ordered serially in accordance with their respective grade of excellence. By "a nature" Anselm here means what, at times, Augustine means: viz., an existent, a being, a substance (e.g., a tree, a horse, a man). To say that one thing is better, or more excellent, than another is sometimes to say that the one has more perfections — i.e., more compatible perfections — than does the other. For example, both a tree and a horse have the perfection of being alive; and in this respect they both are superior to a stone. But a horse also has the perfection of sensation; and in this respect it is superior to the tree. In fact, however, the issue is not just about having more perfections — as one man might be both wise and strong, whereas another might be only strong. Anselm thinks of some perfections as being greater than others. Thus, to be able to reason is a greater perfection than merely to be able to sense. In the present case, then, he is not so much thinking about the fact that some individual men (or some individual trees, etc.) might be more excellent than other individual men (or individual trees, etc.) as he is supposing that some *species* are more excellent than others. Now, not all metaphysicians would be willing to agree that it makes sense to assert that a bird is more excellent than a flower. Some birds, they say, are better (because stronger, or swifter, or more intelligent, etc.) *birds* than are others; and some flowers are better (because prettier, etc.) *flowers* than are others. But a flower is neither better nor worse, *simpliciter*, than a bird. However, Anselm does not subscribe to this viewpoint. Like Augustine, he finds it just as intelligible to compare species as to compare individuals of the same species. And he believes that what legitimates these value-judgments about species is the fact that (in some sense) every nature is essentially good. This assumption — actually propounded as a doctrine in *De Casu Diaboli* 1 — underlies the present argument. Augustine explicitly mentions this same assumption — though only in passing — in *De Trinitate* 8.3.4, where he remarks that unless the soul were something good by the very fact that it is a soul, then it could not be called better than the body.

So in *Monologion* 4 Anselm is tacitly maintaining that one being (or one kind of being) can be better than another because every being is essentially good. But this principle is not operative in *Monologion* 1, where he is not dealing with a *hierarchy* of all beings but is only observing that we regard some things as goods. Thus, if I want a good horse, I want one which is swift and strong, not one slow and frail. Of course, Anselm believes that even a frail horse is essentially good. But this latter point plays no role in *Monologion* 1. (Similarly, in *De Trinitate* 8.3.4 Augustine is discussing not what it is to be essentially good but what it is to be a good thing of such and such kind: A good farm is fertile and level; a good house is symmetrical and spacious; good food is tasty and healthful, etc.)[42] Accordingly, in *Monologion* 1, Anselm groups all good things together (nonhierarchically) in order to infer that all of them are good through one thing.

In the present section Anselm does not attempt to *prove* that the progression of graded beings must be limited. In fact, he does not know how to go about proving this. Within his metaphysical system the foregoing proposition is so basic as to be deemed self-evident. Accordingly, it does not admit of proof, but is an axiom — by appeal to which other propositions are subjected to proof.

2.4.2. *Section B.*

	(7)	Either this nature which is thus superior is singular; or else there is more than one nature of this kind, and they are equal.
Assume:	(8)	There are many of these natures, and they are equal. (That is, assume that there is more than one nature which is so great that it is inferior to no other, though it is equal to some other.)
	(9)	These equally great natures can only be equal through the same thing. (Argument I, Step 1)
	(10)	The one thing through which these natures are equally so great either is the same thing which they are (i.e., is their essence), or else it is something other than what they are.
Assume:	(11)	This one thing is the essence of the natures.
So:	(12)	The essence of the natures is one essence. (11)
	(13)	*Idem naturam hic intelligo quod essentiam.*
So:	(14)	The natures are one nature. (12) (13)
Assume:	(15)	This one thing is other than what the natures are (i.e., it is not their essence).
	(16)	Whatever is great through something other [than itself] is less than that other through which it is great.
So:	(17)	The many equally great natures are less than that through which they are great. (15) (16)
So:	(18)	The many equally great natures are not so great that nothing else is greater than they. (This contradicts the assumption in Step 8.) (15)-(17)
So:	(19)	It is not the case that there is more than one nature which is so great that it is inferior to no other, though it is equal to some other. (7)-(19)
So:	(20)	There is only one Nature which is so superior to [all] others that it is inferior to none. (6) (7) (19)

Section B continues cautiously. Since there are often many beings of the same kind, perhaps there are many beings which, in kind, are such that no other being is inferior to them; and perhaps these beings are all equal.

Steps 8-14 are subject to various interpretations. For in its simple style the argument is so elusive that it almost defies comprehension. In particular, Step 13 is subject to various construals, each of which will lend a different focus to the argument. Consider, for instance, the following construals:

(a) Here I take "*natura*" to mean the same thing as "*essentia*."
(b) Here I understand a nature to be the same thing as an essence (or: as a being).
(c) Here I understand the nature to be identical with the essence.

Apart from all context, each of these construals would constitute an accurate translation of Proposition 13. Only the context will determine which reading is the preferable one. And, in the case of a sound argument, the reading which would make the argument proceed logically would be the preferable reading. However, in the case of an unsound argument, an interpreter may not see — within the limited alternatives open to him — any way in which the argument could proceed logically. Accordingly, he will not be able to rely upon a ready sense of how the argument works. Instead, he will be cast back upon the more murky enterprise of trying to find the most *plausible* reading. But *then* he is confronted with the question: what are the criteria for determining the most plausible construal of such-and-such premise in the unsound argument? And no rigid answer will be acceptable a priori. There will be, rather, only the rule-of-thumb: Choose the reading which tends to advance the line of reasoning. This rule entails such sub-rules as: Where there are two readings — one of which will render the argument more coherent than will the other — choose the more coherent interpretation. Now, here in the first part of Section B arises just such a problem of coherence. And we must presume that Anselm was too keen a thinker to reason in an egregiously incoherent way.[43] With the sub-rule and the presumption as our only guidelines, let us examine the logic of the argument in relation to the three construals above.

Construal a. If in Section B Anselm is taking "*natura*" to mean "*essentia*," then an incoherence occurs. This incoherence can be exhibited from a number of angles. For instance, in Proposition 11 "nature" would be substitutable for "essence," and vice-versa. But as a result of this substitution Proposition 11 either would become senseless or else would contain equivocal instances of the same term. For, on the one hand, to say "This one thing is identical with the essence of the essences" would be senseless. And, on the other hand, to say "This one thing is identical with the nature of the natures" would involve equivocation. For "nature" would mean *what a thing is*; whereas "natures" would be *things which are*, i.e., beings. Although this equivocation would not present a logical difficulty in Proposition 11, it would pose a difficulty for the movement of the argument. For Proposition 13, in conjunction with Proposition 12, would no longer serve as the *reason* for Proposition 14. That is, the reason the natures are one nature cannot be that "nature" means "essence," and that the essence is one essence. Indeed, in Proposition 14 "natures" means "*things which are*."[44] And so it would be non sequitur to think that the reason 14 follows from 12 is that "nature" means "essence," or "*what a thing is*."

Construal b. But perhaps Anselm is also equivocating on the word "*essentia*," which, after all, can mean either "an essence" or "a being." And perhaps these two senses correspond to the two senses of "*natura*." Given construal *b*, this equivocation would seem obvious. For on this construal Anselm is saying that the natures are one nature because the *essentia* is one *essentia* and because a nature is an *essentia*. Since he has previously been using "a nature" in the sense of "a being": when he says now that a nature is an *essentia*, he must mean that a nature is a being (*essentia*) — not that it is an essence (*essentia*). But if so, then his conclusion in Step 14 is non sequitur because "*natura*" there means something different from what "*essentia*" means in Step 11.

Yet, perhaps Anselm simply recognizes no sharp distinction between the two different senses of "*essentia*," so that (strictly speaking) he blurs the distinction rather than equivocating. After all, he does not emphasize, as does Thomas, the sharp difference between what a thing is and the fact that it is. (Even in *Monologion* 34 he does not say that what-a-thing-is, i.e., its essence, exists in the Supreme Spirit's Word; he says, rather, that that *thing* exists in the Supreme Spirit's Word.)

Construal c. This last construal seems to render Section B more plausible.[45] And, in last analysis, this fact furnishes our only justification for selecting *c* in preference to *a* and *b*. In Section B Anselm is trying to show, regarding the natures and the one thing through which they are equally great, that

> (A) If this one thing is their essence, then the natures are really one nature;
> (B) If this one thing is not their essence, then the natures are less great than it is.

And in order to establish the first of these points, he reasons (in effect) as follows:

> Assume that this one thing is identical with the natures, i.e., is their essence. Then, just as their essences are one essence, so the natures are one nature. For here I am understanding the nature to be (numerically) identical with the essence.

On this interpretation, Anselm is not maintaining that in Section B "nature" and "essence" are used synonymously. Nor is he claiming that in this section he is regarding a nature as an essence. Nor do either of these considerations constitute — either in full or in part — his *reason* for concluding that there is only one nature of the kind under discussion. Instead, he begins by hypothesizing that the essence of the natures is one essence. And he concludes by inferring that the natures would really be only one nature, since the nature would be identical with the essence. Now, someone might suppose that this "since" statement provides only a partial reason for the conclusion; for it is possible to ask why the nature would be (numerically) identical with the essence. Thus, he might seek to push the interpretation in the following direction:

> Presumably, Anselm is relying upon an "Aristotelian" assumption, viz., that if there is only one essence (i.e., one essential form), then there can be only one nature (i.e., one being). For it is not the case that many beings share *numerically one* form. If they do in some sense have one common form, then it is common in species, not in number. But in Section B Anselm is dealing not with oneness of species but with oneness of number. From S I, 17:13 it is clear that "*per idem aliquid*" means "*per aliquid unum*."[46] Indeed, throughout *Monologion* 1-4 the sense of "*idem*" and "*idipsum*" is that of numerical sameness. And in fact, this is the only sense which makes sense. For Anselm presumably understood "*idem*" to mean either "sameness of genus," "sameness of species," or "sameness of number."[47] And neither of the first two senses cohere with his reasoning.

Accordingly, the first part of Section B advances along Aristotelian lines. Were Anselm making Platonistic or ultra-realist assumptions, he would not be able to infer that because there is one essence there is one nature, or being. For a Platonist or an ultra realist finds nothing objectionable in the view that several beings can all have numerically one essence.[48] Moreover, a Platonist would infer immediately that these natures are equally great through greatness, which is their essence. By contrast, Anselm entertains the possibility that the one thing is not the essence of these natures; and he does not conclude immediately that this one thing is greatness.

Although someone might plausibly interpret Anselm's position along these lines, this reasoning does not seem to me to explicate Section B of Argument IV. For it is an interpretation which is too complicated — which involves too many adventitious metaphysical assumptions — to be supported by Anselm's own statement of his argument. As I see it, Anselm is not here *endorsing* any position. He is simply hypothesizing about a possible alternative. Indeed, the sense of "*intelligo*" in Proposition 13 might well be: "[For here] I am hypothesizing that . . . ." At any rate, it would be an exegetical mistake to attempt to wrest from Section B the view that Anselm's theory of universals is Aristotelian. (Similarly, it would be mistaken to infer, on the basis of *Monologion* 1,[49] that Anselm is either an ultra realist or a Platonist.) Instead, the simplicity of Anselm's point must be preserved in the interpretation of Section B. Is he not reasoning along the following lines?: "There is one thing through which these natures are equally so great. Either the natures are this one thing (i.e., it is their essence) or they are not. If they are this one thing, then they are not many natures but are only one nature. For here I am hypothesizing that the nature and the essence are the same thing. On the other hand, if they are not this one thing, then . . ., etc." Paradoxically, Anselm's point is so simple that it can easily be missed. For his language misleads us. In particular, the phrase "*quod ipsae sunt*" (S I, 17:14 and 15), together with the appearance of the word "*essentia*," suggests an Aristotelian or a Thomistic distinction between *what* an individual thing is and *the fact that* it is. And this distinction leads us to view Anselm's argument in a tendentious way. Yet, the meaning of "*quod ipsa sunt*" in *Monologion* 1 (S I, 15:7), together with the recognition that "*essentia*" is not a technical term for Anselm, should have forewarned us against this tendency.

2.4.3. *Section C.*

(21) That which is so superior to all others that it is inferior to none is the greatest and the best of all existing things.

Thus: (22) There is a Nature which is the highest of all existing things. (20) (21)

(23) That which exists through itself and through which all other things exist is the highest of all existing things. (Argument III, Steps 15-17)

So: (24) Either that which is the highest of all exists through itself and all other things exist through it, or else there are many supreme beings. (22) (23)

(25) There are not many supreme beings. (20)

So: (26) Through itself this Nature is what it is, and through it all [other] existing things are what they are. (22) (24) (25)

So: (27) There is a Nature (i.e., a Being) which through itself is good and great, and through itself is what it is; and through this Nature exists whatever truly is good or great or something. And this Nature is the Supreme Good, the Supreme Greatness, the Supreme Being. (22) (26)

Section C, the last phase of the extended argumentation, needs only a brief word of clarification. Step 22 concludes that there is a Nature which is the highest of all existing things. Now, Argument III already established that there is a Being which exists through itself, through which all other things exist, and which is the highest of all existing things (Steps 13 and 16). So (in Argument IV) the Nature which is the highest of all existing things is identical with the Being (in Argument III) which exists through itself, through which all other things exist, and which also is the highest of all existing things; or else, there are two Supreme Beings. But since it has been established that there is only one Supreme Being, the identity must obtain. And so now Argument IV can conclude in the same way as does Argument III.

It will be useful to summarize the more important points to be gleaned from examining Arguments I-IV.

a. There is no instance of self-predication.
b. There is no immediate inference from x to x-ness.
c. Whereas Arguments I and II are similar to each other, Arguments III and IV are dissimilar to them and to each other.
d. Each argument has a greatness-assumption:
   I and II: No good which is good through something other [than itself] is equal to or greater than that good which is good through itself.

III: Whatever exists through something other [than itself] exists less than that which alone exists through itself and through which all other things exist.

IV: Whatever is great through something other [than itself] is less than that other through which it is great.

e. Neither singly nor collectively do the arguments seem to afford any insight into Anselm's theory of universals.

f. After Proposition 9 of Argument IV Anselm cannot continue as he had after Proposition 3 of Argument II. For since Section B of Argument IV deals only with a subset of great things, there is no basis for inferring that *all* great things are great through one thing, which is great through itself.

III

We are now in a position to explore more fully the three questions posed earlier: viz., Does Anselm in *Monologion* 1-4 (1) *deplatonize* Augustine, (2) seek to establish something only about the *essence* of God, and (3) commit himself to an *ultra-realist* theory of universals?

3.1. According to F. S. Schmitt Anselm's reasoning in *Monologion* 1 is motivated by Augustine's in *De Trinitate* 8.3. Furthermore, says Schmitt, when we compare the two arguments we find that Anselm deliberately omits three aspects of Augustine's approach: that the concept *good* is impressed upon the mind, that the Good itself is seen, and that good things *participate* in the Good.[50] Regarding these omissions Schmitt judges:

> These three lines of thought are exactly what constitutes Augustine's Platonism. When Anselm omits them, his doing so is no accidental silence. For the place for them would have been in the *Monologion*. Thus, we cannot speak of a (Neo-)Platonism in Anselm if the essential elements of this philosophical direction, as he found them in Augustine, are lacking in him. On the contrary, we must assume that he was intentionally attempting to deplatonize Augustine.[51]

Is this interpretation correct? Well, not on the whole. Only if Anselm were significantly influenced by the argument in *De Trinitate* 8.3 would it make sense to speak of him as deliberately leaving parts of it behind. But, in fact, his argument in *Monologion* 1 is vastly different from Augustine's. Anselm is not modifying Augustine's argument: he is proposing an alternative one. And so there can be no question of his selecting out some parts of the Augustinian version while leaving out others: Instead he leaves behind the whole argument, while holding only to Augustine's topic. True, both Augustine and Anselm begin their reasoning with the observation that we desire only what we consider to be good; and both somehow conclude therefrom that there is a sole Supreme Good. But they travel completely different routes — from the point of their initial observation to the point of their concluding inference. Not only does Anselm "leave behind" the three doctrines mentioned by Schmitt, but he also omits four other essential items: (a) the *proof* — on the basis of the soul's relation to the Good — that the Good is unchanging and unchangeable; (b) the explicit distinction between the soul's being good insofar as it is a soul and its being good by virtue of having a good will; (c) the statement that in the Supreme Good we live and move and have our being; (d) the statement that a good cannot be decreased or increased unless it is a good which is good from another good. In short, Anselm's proof is so different from Augustine's that there is no point in singling out, as does Schmitt, only three items of significant difference. To say simply that Anselm did not utilize Augustine's proof would be more accurate than to suggest that he borrowed part of it and discarded part of it. *De Trinitate* 8.3 may have "influenced" Anselm in the reduced sense that it suggested to him a heuristic starting point. But there is no more extensive connection between *Monologion* 1 and *De Trinitate* 8.3 than there is between *Monologion* 2 and *De Trinitate* 5.10.

About the three points singled out by Schmitt, as well as about the points which he neglected to single out, one and the same question must be asked: Do we have, from elsewhere, any reason to believe that Anselm either did accept these points or would have accepted them? Well, he obviously accepted the view that the (Supreme) Good is unchanging, as well as the view that the soul is good in two different respects. And presumably he would have granted that only what is good *per aliud* can become more or less good. Moreover, he obviously agrees that in the Supreme Good (i.e., in God) we live and move and have our being. For in *Proslogion* 16 he cites the very same verse as does Augustine in *De Trinitate* 8.3 (viz., Acts 17:28). By contrast, the *proof* that the Good is unchangeable, and therefore eternal, raises doubts. It does remind us of Anselm's proof, in *De Veritate* 13, that rightness does not change when a statement ceases to be correct. But we have no basis for speculating further — except to affirm that the proof is not incompatible with any of his teachings.

But what about the three doctrines mentioned by Schmitt? Well, clearly, in *Reply to Gaunilo* 8 Anselm does embrace the doctrine that the Good itself is seen. For by "perceiving the Good" Augustine means "understanding, or conceiving, the Good,"[52] seeing the Good with the mind's eye. And in the *Reply* Anselm describes how it is that the Supreme Good can be conceived. We must remember, too, that the first part of *Monologion* 1 alludes to turning the "mind's eye to investigating that thing from whence are derived these goods . . . ." Schmitt makes much out of the fact that Augustine's reflection moves immediately from the many good things to seeing the Good itself, whereas Anselm employs intermediate steps to arrive at the Supreme Good. This observed difference supposedly manifests deplatonization. Yet, in *Proslogion* 24 and 25 Anselm's own reflection moves immediately from the variety of good things to the simple Good.[53] Had Anselm in *Monologion* 1 deliberately omitted Augustine's immediate inference in order to deplatonize, then he would not have reintroduced it subsequently in the *Proslogion*. (Or would he be replatonizing?) This consideration shows that Schmitt is under the spell of a problematical assumption: viz., that in *Monologion* 1 Anselm's silence regarding certain points found in *De Trinitate* 8.3 necessarily results from *disagreement* with Augustine. Yet, in reality, there are many possible reasons for someone's silence — of which disagreement may not always be the most plausible. Certainly, where a philosopher later sanctions a point which earlier he had passed over in silence: either his initial silence had nothing to do with disagreement or else during the interval he changed his position. Now, there is no reason to believe that — with respect to Platonism — Anselm changed his mind in the interval between writing the *Monologion* and writing the *Proslogion*. So there is no reason to suppose that his silence resulted from disagreement.

In the Anselm corpus no passage corresponds to Augustine's statement that the concept *good* is impressed upon the human mind. Yet, how can one seriously believe that Anselm would have repudiated this doctrine? In *Monologion* 10 he adheres to Augustine's view — in *De Trinitate* 8.6.9 — that an *image* of a thing is a *word* of that thing; and with Augustine he distinguishes the spoken word, the silent word, and the conceptual word (DT 9.10.15; 15.10.19). Augustine regarded the last kind of word as impressed upon the mind (DT 9.10.15). And we may infer from *Monologion* 33 and 62 that Anselm agrees. Even though Anselm does not anywhere mention *boni impressa notio*, and even though nothing that he actually states commits him to this doctrine, nevertheless the doctrine is compatible with the totality of his statements. Perhaps because in *Monologion* 1 he is presenting a concise chain of arguments which have a definite aim, he does not allow himself the leisure to make extraneous remarks. Moreover, he is attempting to build upon a solid basis of certainty. And so it is necessary for him (1) to eliminate all that could give rise to needless debate and (2) to keep his assumptions to a minimum. His initial, and apparently commonsensical, claim that "all men seek to enjoy only those things which they consider good" tells us why he commences his line of reasoning with Argument I rather than Argument III. By beginning with the desires familiar to everyone, he hopes to find a common ground for enjoining debate with unbelievers. Since this claim is not itself a proper part of Arguments I–IV, he does not need to trouble the reader with the worry about whether or not good things can be recognized only because the notion of the good has been impressed upon us prior to our encountering them. Furthermore, Augustine's statement to this effect provokes the query: impressed by whom or by what? And in terms of Anselm's approach it would be premature to answer "by God" or "by experience." It seems to me that some such considerations — though not necessarily these — explain why Anselm here remains silent. And I am inclined to believe that he agrees with Augustine that the concept *good* is an a priori concept impressed by God upon the human mind. I do not know of any texts which will demonstrate this agreement. But I think that the burden of proof is upon Schmitt to show that Anselm rejected this position. By itself, Schmitt's appeal to silence can scarcely count as evidence of disagreement between Augustine and Anselm — especially since there seem to be other plausible explanations of the silence, and since Anselm's silence in the previous case (viz., re seeing the Good) was not the silence of disagreement.

Schmitt's third claim is more difficult to assess. He acknowledges, for instance, that in *Monologion* 16 Anselm openly advances the view that just things participate in the *quality* of justice. But he argues that this notion of participation differs from the Platonistic and Neo-Platonistic conceptions; for these latter, he says, take participation to be the participation of substances in a *substance*.[54] Furthermore, Schmitt regards *Monologion* 9 as propounding the doctrine that created things participate in the Idea which God has of them. But he argues that this is a reduced sense of "participation"; for the fuller Platonistic sense is that of really existing things participating in the Supreme Good.[55] Schmitt reasons: in *De Trinitate* 8.3 Augustine's notion of participation is that of participation in the Supreme Good, i.e., in God; and, in *Monologion* 1, by not mentioning participation at all, Anselm is rejecting this substantival view of participation, and is thus deplatonizing Augustine.

Now, in a number of ways Schmitt is reasoning curiously. First of all, he does *not* find it implausible to claim that in *Monologion* 9 Anselm is subscribing to an attenuated doctrine of participation even though the word "participation" does not occur either there or in any other passage where the context is the same. By contrast, Schmitt advances the fact that the word "participation" does not occur in *Monologion* 1 as the main reason for inferring that Anselm rejects the fuller Augustinian version of this doctrine. Secondly, it is not clear why Schmitt places so much emphasis upon the contrast between a created thing's participating in the Idea which God has of it and a created thing's participating in the Supreme Good. Presumably, Schmitt here means to contrast the Supreme Good with God, and to regard it as existing independently of the mind of God, as does Plato in the *Republic*. For if this were not his intent, then his distinction between the two kinds of participation — the reduced sense and the Platonic sense — would be unclear.

To put the issue differently: If in *Monologion* 1 Anselm is leaving behind the view that things participate in the Supreme Good — where the Supreme Good is not identified with God — then Anselm could not be deplatonizing Augustine, because Augustine himself does not hold Plato's view. On the other hand, if the Supreme Good *is* identified with God, then either (1) there is a difference between participating in an Idea in the mind of God, who is the Supreme Good, and participating in God Himself, who is the Supreme Good, or else (2) Anselm's silence in *Monologion* 1 does not indicate deplatonization because in *Monologion* 9 there would be replationizationization. But what exactly could be the difference between the two kinds of participation — the substantival sense and the "reduced" sense — given that an Idea in the mind of God cannot be essentially different from the mind of God? Whatever the difference — if any at all — Schmitt has called attention to an important fact: viz., that in *De Trinitate* Augustine speaks repeatedly of participation in God Himself,[56] whereas in the *Monologion* Anselm does not once employ a comparable[57] expression. We shall have to postpone until the next chapter the question of whether or not Anselm here disagrees with Augustine. For it is an issue which thrusts us beyond the limited scope of *Monologion* 1–4. Let it suffice to realize that Argument I (as well as Argument II) is neutral with respect to so-called *substantival* participation. Steps 6 and 7 — the only steps where participation could consistently play a role — may indeed consistently be interpreted as follows:

So: (6) All the other [good] things are good through participation in something which alone [is good] through itself.
(7) No good which is good through participation is equal to or greater than that good which is good through itself.

Yet, they need not be interpreted this way. For the *per se/per aliud* distinction is not equivalent to the *per se/participatio* distinction. If something is *x* by participation, then it is *x per aliud*, as *Monologion* 16 makes clear. But it may be *x per aliud* (e.g., through creation) without being *x* by participation, as Boethius' *De Hebdomadibus* indicates. So we do not know, on the basis of *Monologion* 1–2 alone, what Anselm's position is with respect to participation of substances in a substance.

In *Monologion* 1 the statement that just things can be understood to be just only through justice is intended only as heuristic. If we were to take it to involve an implicit reference to participation in any sense, but especially in the sense of *Monologion* 16,[58] then the argument of *Monologion* 1 would collapse. For if what the example of justice illustrates in *Monologion* 1 were the same thing it illustrates in *Monologion* 16, then Step 1 would have to be interpreted as: "Whatever things are either equally or unequally *x* in comparison with one another, are *x* through participation in something which is identical in the different things." And if so, then Step 3 would have to be: "Therefore, all good things are good through participation in something which is identical in the different good things." Thus, in accordance with *Monologion* 16, it would follow that all good things are good through participation in the *quality*[59] of goodness. Step 4 would then mean: "That thing through participation in which all good things are good is itself a great good." And Step 5 would become: "Therefore, the quality of goodness is good through participation in itself (since all good things are good through participation in it)." But the argument will now have become incoherent for three reasons. First, it is now inconsistent with Anselm's aim to prove something not about a quality but about a "Substance." Secondly, it involves self-predication, as the literal version of *Monologion* 1 obviously does not. And thirdly, to say that a thing is good through participation in itself is not tantamount to saying that it is good through itself. For to say the latter is to say that it is good other than through participation — including participation in itself.

So Schmitt is right, it seems to me, in maintaining that by itself *Monologion* 1–4 does not *commit* Anselm to the doctrine of participation in *any* sense. But he is wrong in supposing that *Monologion* 1–4 is necessarily *incompatible* with the notion of participation found in *De Trinitate* 8.3. Indeed, since *Monologion* 1–4 is neutral with respect to this version of participation, we must look elsewhere to determine, if possible, Anselm's attitude toward it.

In last analysis, Schmitt's claim about deplatonization rests upon three questionable assumptions:

(a) That Anselm borrows from Augustine's argument.
(b) That Anselm's silence necessarily indicates disagreement with Augustine.
(c) That the *Monologion* would have been the appropriate place for Anselm to take account of Augustine's points.

We have seen (a) that Anselm borrows only Augustine's topic, (b) that — in one clear case at least — his silence does not indicate disagreement, and (c) that the approach of *Monologion* 1 renders superfluous the mention of the three doctrines pointed to by Schmitt. Indeed, throughout the *Monologion* there are places where it would not, strictly speaking, be inappropriate for Anselm to introduce other considerations from *De Trinitate*. For example, although he discusses perception, he does not mention many of the basic points in *De Trinitate* 11, even though mentioning them would not be inappropriate. Nor does he allude to the Augustinian distinction between inner man and outer man — though *Monologion* 66 would have been an appropriate place to do so. It seems, a priori, unlikely that he disagrees with these views. Still, he does not mention them, in spite of the fact that "the *Monologion* would have been the place for them" — whatever, exactly, this phrase of Schmitt's is suppose to connote.

3.2. According to the traditional view Anselm intended to prove the existence of God in *Monologion* 1–4. In more recent times, however, this interpretation has come to be impugned. Karl Barth, in his *Fides quaerens intellectum*, alleges that in the *Monologion*, unlike in the *Proslogion*, the existence of God is never taken as a special problem: it is simply an article of faith. Barth sees the *Monologion* as deducing truths about God's nature, whereas the *Proslogion* purports to show both "*quia es sicut credimus, et hoc es quod credimus*": "that You exist, as we believe, and that You are what we believe You to be."[60]

3.2.1. In the case of F. S. Schmitt we find a progressive change of thought until he finally comes to agree with Barth. Schmitt begins by accepting the traditional view. In the preface to his German translation (1964) of the *Monologion* he writes:

> The *Monologion's* proofs of God are much less the object of discussion [by Anselm] than is the argument of the *Proslogion*. In contrast to the a priori ("ontological") proof (whose validity will long continue to be called into question) the *Monologion's* proofs proceed from experience (viz., from the good things of this world — things which everyone knows and acknowledges). Thus, they usher in the proofs of God — especially the "five ways" of Thomas Aquinas — on the part of subsequent Scholasticism. But whereas Thomas takes his proofs entirely from his predecessors — (The well-known fourth way, viz., from the gradations of being, stems from the fourth chapter of the *Monologion*) — the proofs of St. Anselm are original. Only the first one was suggested by Augustine.[61]

By 1966 Schmitt had already begun to express qualifications.[62] And in 1969 he no longer regarded the *Monologion* as attempting to prove God's existence.[63] His defense of this position warrants detailed examination, since it is stated more fully than Barth's. The *Monologion*, according to Schmitt, does not aim to demonstrate that a Supreme Being exists as the cause of everything; rather, it seeks to establish that the cause of everything — a cause whose existence is presupposed — is a Supreme Being.[64] In defense of this thesis Schmitt advances three considerations. First, the *Monologion* Preface states that Anselm's fellow-monks asked him to prove something about the essence (*essentia*)[65] of God; in accordance with this request the first chapter opens with a discussion of the essence of the Supreme Nature. Secondly, each of the four proofs has three steps[66] in common. These steps establish something about the essence of the Supreme Nature. And in Arguments III and IV they take precedence over an initial "existence proof," whose presence Schmitt acknowledges, while reasoning: "Since the first two chapters do not have this existence-proof, it is clear that this proof is not essential and that in Chapters 3 and 4 it is thought of only as a preliminary."[67] Thirdly, each of the four chapters concludes with a statement about the *essential* determination of God as the highest of everything that is; and the titles of the chapters bespeak this same fact.

Now, Schmitt's three-point defense engenders certain qualms. To begin with, Anselm's word "*essentia*" in the first sentence of the *Monologion* Preface need not mean "*Wesen*," or "*Wesenheit*," in contrast to "*Existenz*" and "*Dasein*." Indeed, "*essentia*" regularly substitutes for "*existentia*."[68] (Thus, Gaunilo can speak of proving the *essentia* of an island.) So when Anselm alludes to meditating on *divinitatis essentia* he does not necessarily mean to restrict himself to dealing with the essence of God, i.e., with what God is. He meditates on the *being* (*essentia*) of God; and this can involve meditating upon both the existence and the essence of God. The phrase "*divinitatis essentia*" does not preclude the intent to prove *quia divinitas est*, in addition to determining *hoc quod divinitas est*. Thus, Schmitt's semantic appeal is inconclusive. By itself, it does not indicate any difference between the goal of the *Monologion* and that of the *Proslogion*. Accordingly, Schmitt's whole case must rest upon his other two defenses.

Now, the second defense contains several curious features. Although Schmitt speaks of existence-proof (*Existenzbeweis*) in the singular, he knows that the opening steps of Chapter 3 are very much different from the opening steps of Chapter 4, and that consequently there are really two different *Existenzbeweise*. In

Arguments III and IV, then, he takes the respective proofs to consist of the steps which *precede* the argument to establish the *singularity* of the cause. So in Argument III this proof consists of Steps 1–3, and in Argument IV of Steps 1–6. But it is bizarre to term Steps 1–3 of Argument III, by themselves, an *Existenzbeweis*; and it is false to describe Steps 1–6 of Argument IV as inessential.

In fact, it is fundamentally misconceived to fragment Arguments III and IV into two parts: *Existenzbeweise* and *Wesensbestimmungen*. Schmitt does so in order to mark off a difference between these arguments and Arguments I and II. What all the arguments have in common, Schmitt says, are certain premises about the divine essence. Arguments III and IV differ from I and II by virtue of their different beginnings. Since these beginnings precede the steps which Arguments III and IV have in common with Arguments I and II, Schmitt does not view them as essential to the common conclusion reached by each of the arguments independently. They are, therefore, alleged to be *Existenzbeweise* — and not very serious ones at that.

A judgment about Schmitt's interpretation will depend upon determining both the nature of the four arguments and the relationship they bear to one another. As I see it, all four arguments are intent upon establishing the *existence* of a Being which is the greatest, the best, and the highest of all. They purport to do so by various routes. Each of the routes tries to show why, on the basis of considerations about existing things, the inference to the existence of a supremely good and great Being is rationally necessary. So in each of the four cases the *whole proof* is the existence-proof. And it is a putative existence-proof even though it does not first attempt to establish — other than by appeal to perception, common sense, and inconceivability — that there are existing things, or that they exist through something, or that some of them are good, or that some of these good things are better than others. It is strange for Schmitt to maintain that these arguments are intended to deal only with the divine *essence*. For in showing the rational necessity of inferring — in Argument III, for example — that that through which all things exist is a *single* Being which is *supremely good* and *great*, Anselm is showing that such a being *exists*. True, he "assumes" that everything exists through something. But he does not assume that this something is something one or that it is something other than these things themselves. Curiously, Schmitt labels as an *Existenzbeweis* Anselm's *axiom* that something cannot exist through nothing. But he ought rather to see that the *Existenzbeweis* is the entire proof and cannot be separated from the *Wesensbestimmung*.

Similarly, Argument I also aims to prove the *existence* of a supremely good and great Being. The difference between Argument I and Argument III is not that the latter has a preliminary and unessential *Existenzbeweis*. The difference is rather that Argument I proves the existence of a Being which is *independently* (and supremely) *good* and great, whereas Argument III establishes, in addition, that the Being *exists independently*. That is, Argument I does not settle the question of whether the supremely good, great, and existent Being can continue to exist in the absence of those things which are good through it. Might it exist "in them" but not "apart from them"? Or might it exist apart from some of them but not apart from all of them? Argument III furnishes the required answer.

Argument III differs from Argument I in another important way: It furnishes more support for the proposition that all things exist through something one than Argument I provides for the proposition that all good things are good through something one. Similarly, Argument IV offers relatively elaborate considerations to undergird the proposition that there is only one Nature which is so superior to all others that it is inferior to none. And this fact explains why, in the past, interpreters of Anselm have put more weight upon these last two arguments. They have been called existence-proofs not to distinguish them from the first two but to indicate that they go farther, are more fully argued, are stronger, more plausible, etc.

As Schmitt fails to call attention to the advance that Argument III represents over Argument I (in terms of proving independent existence), so he fails to mention the overlap between Arguments III and IV. (For Section C of Argument IV appeals to Steps 15–17 of Argument III.) And he does not see the possibility that Argument III draws implicitly upon Steps 4–9 of Argument I. Thus, he gives the impression that each one of the four arguments is totally self-contained.

In last analysis, Schmitt seems to have a mistaken notion of what Anselm regarded as a proof of existence. For, thinks

Schmitt, in *Monologion* 1–4 Anselm (1) presupposes that *eine Ursache des Alls* exists and (2) aims to demonstrate only that this Cause is a Supreme Being.[69] Does Schmitt mean that Anselm presupposes (a) that a Cause of the cosmos (*das Weltall*) exists or (b) that a Cause of all things (*alles Seiende*), including itself, exists? If he means the second, then his claim is misleading because it implies that Anselm believed the cause of all things to be the cause of itself; but, in fact, Anselm explicitly denies in *Monologion* 6 that the Supreme Nature is the cause of itself.[70] If Schmitt means the first, as he seems to, then his claim is misleading because it gives rise to the query: "Need the cosmos have a cause?" And this question, in turn, leads Schmitt to say that Anselm *assumes* that the cosmos has a cause, rather than *proving* that it has a cause. But Anselm's axiom "Whatever exists exists through something" does not automatically imply that the cosmos has a cause. For each part of the cosmos might have a cause without the cosmos itself having a cause. Anselm recognizes this possibility. And this recognition explains his premising that the something through which everything exists might be plural rather than singular. For if it were plural, then the different parts of the cosmos might exist through different causes, without there being a unitary cause of the cosmos itself. So it is gratuitous to suppose that Anselm, in accepting the above axiom, also accepted a proposition which is *not* entailed by the axiom. And it is apparent that the language of causation tends to transform Anselm's arguments into some fifth argument, which is not his — however Anselmian it may or may not appear to be.

So Anselm attempts to prove the existence of a Supreme Being precisely by proving (1) that there is a single Being through which everything exists and (2) that this Being is a Supreme Being. On Schmitt's view, the proof of oneness is separate from the proof of existence. Having insisted upon this separation, Schmitt must then insist upon the difference between *Wesensbestimmung* and *Existenzbeweis*. And this move reveals that he has failed to grasp how the proof of oneness is an integral part of the proof of existence. For (as was said) Anselm proves the existence of a Supreme Being by proving that the existence of various objects rationally requires the inference that these objects exist through one thing which exists through itself, etc.

What Schmitt seems to require for a proof to be a proof of

existence is that it be an "ontological" proof. First, he notices that the *Proslogion* proves the existence of that than which a greater cannot be thought, and does so *before* establishing that this Being is omnipotent, merciful, omnipresent, etc. Then he notices that in *Monologion* 1 and 2 there is not this same sharp division, that there is no proof of sheer existence. Finally, he concludes that the *Monologion*, unlike the *Proslogion*, does not purport to establish God's existence — except for the fact that in Chapters 3 and 4 there are initial, unessential premises that deal with existence. What Schmitt in fact attempts to do is to impose on *Monologion* 3 and 4 the *Proslogion's* division between *Existenzbeweis* and *Wesensbestimmung* and then to regard the *Existenzbeweis* as trivialized in the case of *Monologion* 3 and 4. But he ought rather to insist upon the difference between an ontological and a non-ontological proof of God's existence. For thereby he would be closer to realizing that although the *Monologion* does not aim at proving sheer existence *before* determining the divine attributes, it does nonetheless aim at proving existence.

Schmitt's third defense, we may remember, points to the fact (1) that each of the four chapters concludes with a statement about essence (viz., that the Being which is under discussion is a Supreme Being) and (2) that the chapter titles bear out this same emphasis. Now, this appeal seems to me to be the weakest of his three considerations. For the chapter titles of 1 and 3 can be read as statements about both essence and existence — as can also the conclusions of 1, 3, and 4. Interestingly, the conclusion of Chapter 3 virtually restates the title of Chapter 1. This fact could be (though need not be) construed as lending credence to the belief that if Chapter 3 is directed at proving existence, so also is Chapter 1.

In sum, Schmitt's earlier view seems to me the more tenable one: Anselm's marshaling of four proofs is an anticipation of the method of later Scholasticism as exemplified in Thomas' five ways. I cannot help wondering whether one factor underlying Schmitt's change of mind might have been his conviction that when construed as reflections upon the divine essence, the arguments of *Monologion* 1–4 somehow appear less implausible — and thus do more homage to the genius of St. Anselm. At any rate, the arguments are unsound (not to mention exasperating). Nevertheless, they do represent — in terms of sophistication — a considerable advance over the arguments of Augustine — including the argument begun in *De Libero Arbitrio* 2.12 and concluded in 2.15. Their historical — though not their philosophical — significance must be judged in the light of this advance.

3.2.2. In contrast to the extreme of Barth and Schmitt, Marilyn Adams goes to the extreme of identifying proofs of a sort which, in fact, are not present in Anselm:

> Anselm does not wish to conclude that the Platonic Ideas exist mind-independently. If he did, the arguments in cc. i and ii would not serve *his ultimate purpose, which is to prove the existence of God*. Instead, Anselm assumes that no Idea could exist independently of a mind. Given this assumption, proof of the existence of Goodness *per se* and Greatness *per se provide premisses for inferring the existence of a mind whose Ideas they are*. And, in cc. ix-xii, xxix-xxxvi, Anselm argues that all the Ideas exist in the mind of the supreme nature and, since this nature is simple, are identical with it.[71]

Now, there are both minor and major faults with this interpretation. On the minor side, Anselm does not use the word "*Idea*," but instead speaks in *Monologion* 9 of an *exemplum* or *forma* or *similitudo* or *regula*. Moreover, he uses these words in the singular, not in the plural; and in this respect he differs from Augustine. On the major side, we have already[72] noticed that *Monologion* 1 and 2 do not speak of the existence of Goodness (*bonitas*) *per se* and of Greatness (*magnitudo*) *per se* but instead of the existence of something which is good *per se* and great *per se*. How important this difference is is evidenced by how easily Adams concludes that for Anselm Goodness *per se* and Greatness *per se* are Ideas in the mind of God! But nowhere does Anselm teach that there is in the mind of God an Idea of Goodness or an Idea of Greatness. Indeed, Adams has misconceived the whole of the *Monologion's* beginning if she regards it as proving the existence of these Ideas — from which Anselm later infers the existence of God, in whose mind they are Ideas! For in *Monologion* 1 and 2 Anselm is proving that there exists a Being, which is supremely good and supremely great. And this Being is not envisioned as an Idea, to be accompanied by a mind. Adams has succumbed to the temptation to read too much of Plato's *Parmenides* into Anselm's *Monologion*. Excesses of a similar sort were what first provoked F. S. Schmitt to reexamine the issue of Anselm's alleged Platonism. For lines of thought similar to that sketched by Adams are indeed not Anselmian.

3.3. We come now to the final question, already dealt with preliminarily: viz., Does *Monologion* 1–4 imply that Anselm is an ultra realist? In particular, what are we told by the following statement?: "Whatever things are said to be something in such way that they are said to be it either in greater or lesser or equal degree in relation to one another, are said to be it through something which is understood to be identical in the different things (rather than through something different in the different things), whether it is observed in them in equal or in unequal degree." Someone might suppose that this statement somehow commits Anselm to the view that things of the same species have numerically one essence. (That is, someone might regard Anselm as adopting the position which Abelard allegedly[73] ascribed to William of Champeaux.) And yet, a close scrutiny of the quotation will reveal that ultra realism is not at all implied. To begin with, Anselm does not here call the one thing the essence of the many. Secondly, ultra realism is primarily a doctrine about the status of secondary substances; but the examples given by Anselm are examples of qualities (*good, great, just*). Accordingly, these examples do not serve to demarcate his position. Lastly, the one being with which Anselm's argument concludes is not a universal but is a particular.[74]

Those who view Anselm as an ultra realist usually do so on the basis of his doctrines of original sin and atonement — doctrines which, they feel, imply that human nature is numerically one thing. We shall have to face this issue in the next chapter. Let us presently agree, however, that if the sparse words of *Monologion* 1–4 tell us anything about universals, then what little they say counts against, rather than for, ultra realism. Yet, I am inclined to think that, taken by themselves, these chapters do not definitely exclude this alternative.

4. *Conclusion.* We have seen how elusive is the sense, and how perplexing the interpretation, of the opening chapters of the *Monologion*. Anselm's fellow-monks had requested "that in unembellished style and by uncomplicated arguments and with simplified discussion rational necessity would tersely prove, and truth's clarity would openly manifest, whatever the conclusion of the distinct inquiries declared." Ironically, the simplified discussion and the uncomplicated arguments make Anselm's reasoning

all the more ambiguous and, in places, even inscrutably vague. Thus, we do not glean from these chapters all that we seem at first to be gathering. Perhaps the chief lesson of *Monologion* 1–4 comes to be learned when one realizes how little this section tells us about Anselm's philosophical position. The main task of exegesis will thus be to ward off the overinterpretations which have been imposed upon these early chapters. If one can hold back the Platonizers and the Deplatonizers, can expose the gratuitous exegetical assumptions, can develop a more literal understanding, and can bracket out the global *Vorverständnis* that accompanies *Ideengeschichte*, then he may still have a slight chance of being able to rethink Anselm's thoughts in *Monologion* 1–4. Yet, the strain of this intellectual disinvestment may be so enormous, and the desire to find in Anselm a more tenable pattern of argumentation may be so intense, that one will continue to project into *Monologion* 1–4 more subtlety than is legitimate. The danger will be not that of oversimplifying but that of overly refining, overly disambiguating, overly expanding, comparing, and historicizing.

The significance of *Monologion* 1–4 resides not in what it accomplishes but in what it aspires to accomplish — i.e., not in its content but in its method. Setting out from putatively common-sensical truths, this section moves to the conclusion that there is one Being from which all other beings derive. Although it proposes to make as few metaphysical assumptions as possible, those few which it does make are not uncontroversial. To be sure, *sola ratione* is neither a presuppositionless nor a neutral methodology; and Anselm does not intend for it to be.[75] But since he presupposes only what he believes the educated man of his day would grant, he purports to be building upon common ground. In last analysis, we must not forget that the *Monologion* is a meditation, the record of someone who is thinking aloud and talking to himself. Its "arguments," therefore, are not fully elaborated but, instead, are only sketched. They are considerations and *Hinweise* — not rigorous proofs. If one wants to fill-in these sketches and to extend farther these considerations, then let him at least be clear about where his exegesis ends and his bolstering begins.

CHAPTER III

THE ANSELMIAN THEORY OF UNIVERSALS

I

Proverbially, the medieval controversy over the ontological status of universals defies clarification. The very labels used in focusing the issues seem themselves to foster much of the confusion. At various times Abelard, for example, has been called a nominalist, a conceptualist, and a moderate realist. Yet, these labels do not generally serve to demarcate three different views about Abelard's position. Indeed, some commentators regard nominalism and conceptualism as two different positions, whereas others identify a single position by the two different names. Moreover, in the case of Ockham, some interpreters attempt to distinguish *philosophical* nominalism from *theological* nominalism. To make matters still worse, the term "conceptualism" is sometimes used interchangeably with "moderate realism" rather than with "nominalism." Thus, Samuel E. Stumpf comes to identify Aquinas as a conceptualist *insofar as* he is a moderate realist.[1] By contrast, Ralph W. Clark attempts to show that Aquinas is a conceptualist by virtue of not being, exactly, a moderate realist.[2]

1.1. The same kind of mixed terminology pervades the literature on Anselm. Rémusat, agreeing with Cousin, declares that Anselm's realism is theological rather than scientific;[3] but it is not clear exactly what this distinction amounts to. Rousselot expresses doubts about whether Anselm's position deserves the name "realism,"[4] inasmuch as this name is reserved for a position like William of Champeaux's. And D. P. Henry states that Anselm is neither a realist nor a nominalist but something in-between, for which Henry offers no label.[5]

As Henry sees, the problem with the terms "realism" and "nominalism" is simply that there is no standard way in which they have come to be used. Accordingly, there exists the need for each interpreter to disambiguate these labels before attaching them to the thought of the writer he is discussing. For apart from such clarification there arises the danger that communication will fail. Similarly, the terms "Platonism" and "Aristotelianism," by themselves, connote something only vaguely. What is meant, we may legitimately wonder, when Grabmann[6] (or Fischer)[7] refers to Anselm as a moderate Platonist and when Schmitt[8] intimates that Anselm is more Aristotelian than Platonistic? After all, both Grabmann and Schmitt agree that, according to Anselm, particulars participate in a Form in the mind of God; and neither Grabmann nor Schmitt supposes that, according to Anselm, universals exist independently of particulars (except insofar as there is a Form of creation in the Divine Mind). So what exactly is involved in the claim — or in the denial of the claim — that Anselm is a moderate Platonist?

For my part, I would prefer to forego altogether the use of the terms "realism" and "nominalism," "Platonism" and "Aristotelianism." For if they are to be used, they will have to be defined. And no mere stipulative definition will suffice for expounding and comparing the various positions of historical figures. Likewise, it would be impossible to elicit a solitary nonstipulative definition which would be serviceable in all the different historical contexts. Furthermore, the procedure of distinguishing three or four different meanings of "realism" or of "nominalism" — and of then shifting back and forth among them when evaluating the accuracy with which Anselm's interpreters expound his theory — seems to me to be unduly complicated and needlessly cumbersome. Therefore, insofar as possible, I shall avoid these terms when speaking for myself. However, in alluding to what other writers on Anselm have said, I will not forbid myself the use of their own terminology; and I will assume, as do they, that the reader is already familiar with some of the ways in which realism and nominalism have typically been contrasted.

1.2. Roughly speaking, four different interpretations of Anselm's theory of universals have been advanced over the years.

Three of these center around Anselm's attack upon those heretics of dialectic "who think that universal substances are only vocal sounds [*flatus vocis*], and who cannot comprehend that a color is something distinct from the material object or that a man's wisdom is something distinct from his soul. . . ."

> Indeed, in the souls of these dialecticians, reason — which ought to be the ruler and judge of all that is in man — is so covered over by corporeal images that it cannot extricate itself from them and cannot distinguish from them those things which it ought to contemplate purely and in isolation. For example, how will someone who does not yet understand how several men are one man in species be able to comprehend how in that highest and most mysterious Nature several persons — each one of whom, distinctly, is perfect God — are one God? And how will someone whose mind is too darkened to distinguish between his horse and its color be able to distinguish between the one God and His several relations? Finally, someone who cannot understand a human being [*homo*] to be anything except an individual shall not at all understand a human being to be anything except a human person, for every individual man is a person. How, then, will he be able to understand that a humanity [*homo*], though not a person, was assumed by the Word? That is, another nature but not another person was assumed.[9]

I.2.1. According to the first interpretation of this passage, Roscelin and the dialecticians cannot plausibly be supposed to have denied that the human mind is capable of considering a quality apart from its subject. Instead, what they denied is that a quality thus abstracted from its subject has any extra-mental reality. So either Anselm's criticism of Roscelin is pointless or else its point was to affirm that colors do have extra-mental reality apart from the respective objects which are colored, just as the human species has reality independently of the individuals which compose it.

This interpretation of Anselm's position is, in fact, Victor Cousin's.[10] And Cousin criticizes Anselm for reifying abstractions and for teaching that these reified abstractions exist independently of particulars. B. Hauréau subscribes to the same interpretation (although he objects to some of Cousin's translations). Anselm, he thinks, believes that whatever human reason clearly distinguishes corresponds to a *substantial* reality. Thus, continues Hauréau, "Socrates is in a subject, and this subject is the species which sustains and supports, in addition to Socrates and Plato, all other men."[11] In calling humanity, wisdom, and color universal-substances, Anselm (insists Hauréau) is agreeing with Erigena and anticipating William of Champeaux. For he is teaching that "every vision of the subject reveals to him an object — an object which really exists and whose essence conforms perfectly to the image conceived or received by the intellect."[12]

1.2.2. According to the second interpretation Anselm is seen as the forerunner not of William of Champeaux but of Thomas Aquinas. Now, Thomas taught that human natures, for instance, have an extra-mental reality which itself is associated with the reality of the respective primary substances, viz., individual men. Thus, it is common to all men to have a human nature; yet, there is no human nature which is (numerically) common to all men. That is, each individual man has an individualized and numerically distinct nature. And this nature is something real. Moreover, the individualized nature of any given man resembles those respective individualized natures which other men possess. On the basis of this *objective* resemblance these natures are said to form a single kind. Accordingly, when individual men are grouped together and are said to constitute mankind, this grouping is not merely conventional. Furthermore, this single kind, as conceived, is a universal. For what is conceived is the similarity which every man bears to every other man. Hence, the concept of human nature is a concept which truly applies to every man because it corresponds both to the individualized nature which each man possesses and to the real resemblance which obtains between these individualized natures. Strictly speaking, then, human nature — on Thomas' view — is universal only as a concept in the mind. And although there is something objective which the concept represents, there is not a unique extra-mental universal entity which is thus represented. In this respect, Thomas' view differs from the view usually attributed to William of Champeaux: viz., that there exists independently of the human mind a numerically singular human nature which is common to all men. According to this latter theory — which coincides with the first interpretation presented above — it is not the case that each individual man has a numerically distinct human nature. For rather than there being many human natures, there is only one. And this one nature is universal in the sense that it is really shared (i.e., really participated-in) by all men.[13]

Now, both Thomas' theory and the theory ascribed to William of Champeaux are distinguishable independently of reference to the doctrine of exemplarism. Like Augustine and Anselm, Thomas himself subscribed to exemplarism. But when Martin Grabmann characterizes Anselm as a harbinger of Aquinas,[14] he is thinking not of Anselm's doctrine of creation in *Monologion* 9 but of his doctrine of secondary substances in *Monologion* 27 and in *De Incarnatione* 1. (Still, Grabmann is well-aware of the fact that Anselm's statements regarding universals are not as full as are Thomas'. For instance, in maintaining that species and genera are objective realities,[15] Anselm does not suggest that the concept alone is the true universal.) Yet, because of Anselm's doctrine of exemplarism Grabmann (and Fischer after him) gives to Anselm's theory the label "moderate Platonism."[16] For in *De Veritate* Anselm teaches — to quote Fischer — that "every being is true insofar as it is what it is in the Supreme Truth and insofar as it would not at all exist were it not (grounded, contained) in the Supreme Truth, and did it not participate in the Supreme Truth."[17] Thus, according to Fischer, Anselm teaches that everything true *participates* in God, who is the Supreme Truth. Yet, this particular claim by Fischer is not essential to the second interpretation; and, in fact, it could easily be accepted by advocates of the first interpretation. What is essential, however, is the claim that Anselm did not regard colors and other *qualities* as existing independently of colored objects.[18] That is, the first interpretation views *De Incarnatione* 1 as teaching that colors are universal *substances* — whereas the second interpretation rejects this reading, doing so on the basis of *De Veritate* 13 and the *De Grammatico* generally.

1.2.3. A third interpretation is that of D. P. Henry, who argues that the passage at the end of *De Incarnatione* 1 has been misconstrued by interpreters of the first and the second sort. "A closer inspection of the passage quoted," writes Henry, "shows that its general theme is the crudity of the ideas of the logicians who are false to logic, and it soon becomes evident that not just some more obvious facet of a discussion of universals, but something rather more subtle, is also in question."[19] Henry believes that insight into the proper exegesis of the passage may be gleaned from comparing it with the doctrine found in Section 14 of Anselm's earlier dialogue *De Grammatico*. For in this section Anselm also introduces the example of a horse and its color:

Teacher. Suppose that without your knowing about it a white horse has been shut up in a building. And suppose someone says to you: "In this building there is whiteness" (or "In this building there is white"). Would you thereby know that a horse is in that building?

Student. No. For whether he said "white" or "whiteness" or "that in which there is whiteness" I would not conceive of the being of any definite thing except of this color.

T. Even if you did conceive of something other than this color, it is certain that you would not — on the basis of the name "white" — conceive of the being of the thing in which this color is present.

S. This is certain. For even if [the thought of] a material object or [of] a surface came to mind (something which happens only because I have experience of the fact that whiteness is usually present in these things), still the name "white" would not itself signify any of these things (even as has been proven about "expert-in-grammar"). However, I am still waiting for you to show that it *does* signify [such things].

T. What if you saw a white horse and a black ox standing beside each other, and someone said to you with regard to the horse, "Poke it," but did not indicate by a gesture which one he was speaking of. Would you know that he was speaking of the horse?

S. No.

T. But if in reply to you — who do not know, and who have asked "Which one?" — he were to say "The white one," would you discern which one he was talking about?

S. On the basis of the name "white" I would understand that the horse was meant.

T. Therefore, the name "white" would signify to you the horse.

S. Yes, it certainly would.

T. Do you not see that [the name "white" would signify the horse] in a way other than does the name "horse"?

S. I see it. Surely, even before I would know that the horse is white, the name "horse" — of and by itself, and not on the basis of anything else — would signify to me the substance of the horse. But the name "white" would not of and by itself signify [to me] the substance of the horse, but would signify it on the basis of something else, viz., on the basis of the fact that I know the horse to be white. For since the name "white" would signify nothing other than does the phrase "having whiteness": just as by itself this phrase would signify to me whiteness but not the thing which has whiteness, so also the name "white" [would by itself signify to me whiteness but not the thing which has whiteness]. But I would know that whiteness is in the horse, and [I would know] this on some basis other than on the basis of the name "white" (viz., [I would know it] on the basis of sight). Therefore, having understood on the basis of the name "white" that whiteness is meant, I would — on the basis of the fact that I know the whiteness to be in the horse — understand that the horse was meant. That is, on some basis other than on the basis of the name "white," which is, however, appellative of the horse, [I would understand that the horse was meant].

Now, as Henry carefully explains, Anselm is here distinguishing between two different kinds of signification: viz., signification in the sense of *meaning* and signification in the sense of *reference*.[20] But certain difficulties arise for Henry when he attempts to make use of this distinction for his exegesis of *De Incarnatione* 1. "Given this doctrine," he declares, "it becomes plain that Anselm, in his fulmination[21] against the logical heretics, is accusing them of missing the distinction between meaning and reference, and of incorporating actual or anticipated reference (called 'imagination' in the passage from *Epistola de Incarnatione Verbi*) into meaning which, as the latter says, should be considered in isolation for logical purposes (*quae sola et pura contemplari debet*). At the same time Anselm's example [in *De Grammatico* 14] repels any suggestion that he believes the use of 'white' involves *reference* to a universal entity; Anselm does not here betray any sign of being a realist in this primitive sense which lies behind Quine's criterion."[22]

I find Henry's interpretation problematical for two sets of reasons. First, the passage in *De Incarnatione* 1 would have to be completely refocused in order to view it as accusing the logical heretics of missing the distinction between meaning and reference. For in *De Incarnatione* 1 Anselm is not discussing the relation between meaning and reference.[23] Nor is it the case that when (in *De Incarnatione* 1) he uses the expression "*imaginationibus corporalibus*" he is speaking of *actual or anticipated reference*. Furthermore, he is surely not accusing the logical heretics of incorporating reference into meaning. And he is not claiming — either explicitly or implicitly — that, for logical purposes, meaning should be considered in isolation. Indeed, "*quae*" in the expression "*ea quae sola et pura contemplari debet*" does not stand for "meanings" but for "things."[24] Anselm's point is that reason ought to distinguish the image (e.g., of an individual man) from the species (e.g., *man*), and the accident (e.g., a color) from the substance (e.g., the colored object). In short, Anselm is not here making a point about meanings — and so is not implying that they should be distinguished from references.

I find a second difficulty with Henry's interpretation: viz., I do not see, exactly, what the point is in saying: Anselm's example in *De Grammatico* 14 "repels any suggestion that he believes the use of 'white' involves *reference* to a universal entity." True, in Section 14 Anselm shows how the word "white" can be used to refer to a particular object such as a horse, even though the meaning of the word "horse" is not a part of the meaning of "white." And he maintains that "white" signifies having-whiteness. But he does not *exclude* the possibility that "white" can be used to refer to the quality whiteness as well as to something white. (The word "horse" — whatever its definition — can be used to refer to the *nature* horse as well as to an *individual* horse. Similarly, even though the word "*homo*" means "rational, mortal animal" it can be used to refer both to an individual human being and to rational, mortal animality, i.e., to human nature.) From Anselm's example in *De Grammatico* 14 we simply cannot tell whether or not he believed that whiteness is a universal entity. But if he did, nothing in his example would be inconsistent with the hypothesis that "white" can be used to refer to whiteness. Perhaps what Henry ought to have said is that Anselm's example repels any suggestion that he believes the use of "white" *necessarily* involves reference to a universal entity. But even so, a small difficulty would remain. For what Anselm's example teaches is that the word "white" may be used to refer even to such things as horses; and what his example repels is any suggestion that there is such a thing as *the use* of the word "white." For, on Anselm's view, it makes sense to talk about *the* definition of a word but not, *tout court*, about *the* use of that word.

Anselm states that the word "horse" signifies-*per-se* the substance (i.e., not an accident) of the horse;[25] and he maintains that "white" signifies-*per-se* the quality whiteness. Yet, signification-*per-se* cannot be taken as exclusively identical with *meaning* (as distinct from reference). For implicit in Anselm's example is the point that "horse" (because of its definition) can be used to signify-*per-se* (i.e., *to refer to*) the particular horse in question. Thus, in distinguishing between *significare per se* and *significare per aliud* Anselm is *not* clearly and systematically distinguishing between meaning and reference. Meaning and reference remain, for him, conflated in *significatio per se*. What

Anselm does is to distinguish between what a word signifies of and by itself (*per se*) and what it signifies on the basis of something else (*per aliud*). And although the latter corresponds to our contemporary notion of someone's using a word to refer to something, the former does not correspond exclusively to our contemporary notion of meaning. To be sure, Anselm does talk about meanings, in our contemporary sense, when he talks about definitions. Accordingly, he affirms[26] that the definition of "man" is "rational, mortal animal"; and he denies that "expert-in-grammar" has the same definition as does "man." But his theory of definitional meaning does not play an explicit role in his articulation of the difference between *per se* and *per aliud* signification.

Moreover, Anselm teaches that "expert-in-grammar" signifies-*per-se* having-expertise-in-grammar (i.e., signifies a quality and a having).[27] But this kind of signification is not reducible to *our* notion of meaning; for we would not say that "expert-in-grammar" *means* having-expertise-in-grammar. To make his point in terms closer to our notion, Anselm would have to say — though he does not — that "*being*-expert-in-grammar" signifies having-expertise-in-grammar. That it would not have been linguistically foreign to him to have said this is clear from his introduction of the verb "*esse*" in *De Grammatico* 5:

> *Being* (an) expert-in-grammar is not identical with being (a) man. (That is, there is not the same definition of each.)

Nonetheless, even had Anselm included "*esse*" in his discussion of what "expert-in-grammar" signifies, his notion of signification-*per-se* would still not be tantamount to our notion of meaning.

"But" — someone might interject — "in *De Grammatico* 14 and 15 Anselm *is* distinguishing meaning from reference, even though his notion of meaning is not exactly the same as our notion of meaning." With this ripost we may readily agree — provided three factors are acknowledged: (1) reference and meaning are conflated in Anselm's notion of *significatio per se*; (2) *De Grammatico* 14 distinguishes implicitly between two different ways of *referring* to a given object; (3) the basic aim of *De Grammatico* 14 is to distinguish signification-*per-se* from appellation.

Returning to Henry's analysis, we find a minor difficulty which remains. Henry states of Anselm that

> having decided that '*grammaticus*' signifies *habens grammaticam* or *grammatica* (*de voce* decisions), he is prepared to assert the correlated *de re* sentences '*grammaticus est habens grammaticam*' and '*grammaticus est grammatica*', the latter being a rank grammatical scandal, clean contrary to *usus loquendi*.[28]

And a little later, on the same page, Henry speaks of "Anselm's deliberate use of grammatical nonsense." Now, these two passages give the impression that Anselm is asserting and endorsing grammatical nonsense — thereby fostering a semiartificial language designed to express truths which involve semantical categories not distinguished by "ordinary" grammar.[29] But, in fact, both at *De Grammatico* 12 (S I, 157:7–8) and 16 (S I, 161:29–30) Anselm is disavowing the statement "*Grammaticus est grammatica*." And in doing so, he is in fact siding with ordinary language.

In last analysis, however, Henry's central point seems to me to be correct: viz., that statements such as "*Homo est species*" and "*Homo est substantia*" do not function, for Anselm, on the same level as do the statements "*Socrates est homo*" and "*Plato est homo*." Accordingly, they do not necessarily commit the user to the view that there is a unitary universal *homo* with a reality analogous to the reality of particular objects. Thus — as Henry recognizes — when Anselm indicates in *De Incarnatione* 1 that several men are one man in species, he is not *necessarily* endorsing (what Henry calls) crude realism. And Anselm's allusion to universal substances may perhaps best be understood, as Henry concludes, in the sense of Aristotelian secondary substances.

1.2.4. A fourth interpretation captures our attention because, unlike the foregoing ones, it suggests the possibility that Anselm's theory of universals may have changed. Now, most commentators have contented themselves with trying to articulate what they hoped was Anselm's single theory. And they have almost always conceded that at best this theory can be only surmised, given that Anselm does not directly and systematically deal with the topic of universals. Sometimes they have been willing to concede that not all the relevant passages in Anselm's texts can consistently be worked into this single theory. And so they would not be surprised to learn that Anselm really had two different theories. Still, a priori, they would expect that if there were a change it would be one which occurred over a sizable period of time. Hence, they *would* be surprised at being told that this change took place during the limited interval between Anselm's writing the *Monologion* and the *De Grammatico*. And it is precisely this initial evoking of surprise which makes intriguing Marilyn Adams' article "Was Anselm a Realist? The *Monologium*."[30] Adams does not quarrel[31] with Henry's claim that Anselm was not a realist at the time he wrote *De Grammatico*. But she does insist, against Henry, that Anselm was a realist at the time he wrote the *Monologion*; and she leaves open the question of what his views were when he wrote the *Proslogion*.

I have already given reasons for judging Adams' interpretation of *Monologion* 1–4 as mistaken; and I have argued that these chapters, by themselves, do not give any indication of Anselm's theory of universals.[32] Let it now suffice for me to point out another confusion which invalidates her argument, thereby rendering it harmless against Henry. In reconstructing the proof in *Monologion* 1, Adams states one of its premises as "It is better to be *F per se* than to be *F per aliud*."[33] Then — allegedly following Henry — she recasts this as: "What is *F per se* — i.e., the sense of the term '*F*' — is better than that which is *F per aliud* — i.e., the reference of the term '*F*'."[34] Now, this is a misformulation, because Anselm's use of the *per se/per aliud* distinction in *Monologion* 1 has nothing to do with the distinction in *De Grammatico* between *significatio per se/significatio per aliud*. (And Henry himself never thought that there was such a connection.) For *Monologion* 1 deals with *esse per se* vs. *esse per aliud*, not with *significare per se* vs. *significare per aliud*. This difference is extremely important — so much so that the proof in *Monologion* 1 is distorted by developing it in terms of the latter distinction instead of the former. Anselm himself clearly differentiates between these two sets of distinctions. And he recognizes four possibilities:

(1) What exists *per aliud* or is good *per aliud* can be signified *per se*. (E.g., in *De Grammatico* 14 Anselm states that the word "horse" signifies *per se* the substance of the horse. But, obviously, in terms of *Monologion* 1, the horse exists *per aliud* and is good *per aliud*.)

(2) What exists *per aliud* or is good *per aliud* can be signified *per aliud*. (E.g., a horse can be signified *per aliud* by the word "white.")

(3) What exists *per se* or is good *per se* can be signified *per aliud*. (E.g., in *Monologion* 65 Anselm states that we signify *per aliud* the attributes of the Supreme Nature. But, in terms of *Monologion* 1–4, the Supreme Nature exists *per se*.)

(4) What exists *per se* or is good *per se* can be signified *per se* (E.g., the Supreme Nature can be signified *per se* by the description "that than which a greater cannot be thought.")

Adams, however, is not clear about these distinctions, as we can see from still another of her examples. On p. 10 she takes the premise "The thing through which all *F*'s are *F* is *F per se*" and imagines that Henry (in accordance with his claim that Anselm has two types of "is" in *De Grammatico* — viz., a ground-level type and a higher-level type) would have to construe this premise as:

> The thing through which all *F*'s are (ground-level) *F*, is [higher-level] *F per se*.

"That is," — she adds by way of explication — "that through which all *F*'s are *F* is what is signified *per se* by the term '*F*'." But, again, Henry is not required to construe in this way this premise in *Monologion* 1. And, indeed to read the premise in this way violates the argument of *Monologion* 1. For a thing may be *F per se* without being signified *per se* by "*F*."[35]

In sum, Adams sees that Anselm's argument in *Monologion* 1 collapses if it is reformulated in terms of two types of "is." But she is wrong in letting the fact of this collapse become part of her reason for insisting that Henry, and with him everyone else, is required to concede that the proof in *Monologion* 1 either depends upon or entails realism. For in the process of her reformulation she falls into confusion over the *per se/per aliud* distinction. Henry's own recognition that there are (at least) two different such distinctions rightly kept him from applying his *De Grammatico* analysis to the *Monologion* (even though it did not keep him from wrongly applying it to *De Incarnatione* 1). For he sees that the distinction in *De Grammatico* 14 between two kinds of signification is *irrelevant* to the casual-type proof in *Monologion* 1. Thus Henry, and with him others of us, would never dream of supposing that this irrelevancy contributes to entailing the view that Anselm was a realist when he wrote the *Monologion*. Indeed, Anselm may have been a realist — but, if so, not for the reasons given by Adams. Still, her paper is interesting insofar as it cautions us against assuming, at the outset, that Anselm had a single, unified theory of universals.

II

The configuration of so many conflicting interpretations by so many reputable scholars casts a long shadow over any new proposal to illuminate Anselm's theory of universals. For must not any reexamination be itself hampered by the dimness of Anselm's unsystematic treatment? Or might something be gained, on the other hand, by exposing the various overzealous interpretations of those who have too quickly passed beyond surmise? Perhaps the best any reexamination can do is to make clear what Anselm's position is not — without professing to know exactly what it is, or even whether Anselm had decided upon one. And perhaps the best procedure will be to inspect each of the relevant treatises, so as not to jump to conclusions and not to beg any questions about consistency or change-of-mind.

2.1. *Monologion*, *De Grammatico*, *De Veritate*. In this group of philosophical works there are three striking topics which bear upon the theory of universals: viz., the "substance/accident" terminology, the use of the word "participation," and the doctrine of exemplarism.

2.1.1. The "substance/accident" terminology has its focal point in *Monologion* 25–27 and, additionally, in *Monologion* 79. Chapter 25 states that *all* colors and *some* relations are accidents. Chapter 26 denies that the Supreme Being is a substance in the ordinary sense of the word, because the Supreme Being does not have accidents and does not in any respect change. And Chapter 27 maintains that "every substance is classified either as a universal, which is essentially common to many substances (as to-be-a-man is common to individual men), or else as a particular (*individua*), which has a universal essence in common with other particulars (as individual men have in common the fact that they are men)." This terminology corresponds to that which is found both in Augustine's *De Trinitate* and in Boethius' commentaries.

A natural interpretation, therefore, would be to construe "universal substance" and "universal essence" as indicating the species (or genus) to which particular substances belong. Thus, all men belong to the same species by virtue of their being individual men.

Anselm does not appear to be suggesting that a universal essence is a numerically singular real-entity in which individual men participate (i.e., which they share). What is common to individual men is *to-be-a-man* (*hominem esse*), or *the-fact-that-they-are-men* (*ut homines sint*). But neither to-be-a-man nor the-fact-of-being-a-man is an entity. However, someone might claim that Anselm's words "*universalem essentiam*"[36] ("universal essence," or "universal being") do indeed refer to a universal entity. And he might allege that Anselm's example should be construed as follows: "Individual men have in common the fact-that-they-are-men because they have in common (i.e., participate in) a universal entity, viz., *hominem*, or human nature; and this human nature is numerically one thing and, indeed, a real thing." Now, to anyone who makes this exegetical move, two responses are due. First, the interpretation appears strained because it has recourse to the notion of participation, which is not explicitly present in *Monologion* 25–27 and which does not seem to be there implicitly either. And, secondly, it requires making an additional inference which is not required by the first interpretation; and so it appears more contrived than does the first rendering. Yet, it does not altogether lack initial plausibility and therefore ought not to be dismissed peremptorily. Rather, as we go along, we should look to see whether other passages support this interpretation more than they do the former one.

In Chapter 79 Anselm's use of "substance/accident" terminology does not contribute directly to determining his theory of universals. But it does illustrate how he draws upon Augustine's *De Trinitate* when he calls the three persons of the Trinity *three substances*.[37] And it does evidence the nontechnical nature of his vocabulary. For in this one chapter the word "substance" is put to three different uses. First, it is used to signify individual things which support accidents. A sub-stance is, therefore, what stands beneath these accidents and constitutes a substratum in which accidental changes occur. Secondly, "substance" is used of the Supreme Being, though not in the sense of "sub-stance";

for the Supreme Being is subject to no accidents. Instead, "substance" is here being used as a substitute for "being" — just as "nature" may also be interchanged with "being." (Accordingly, in *Monologion* 31 Anselm uses "living natures" and "living substances" interchangeably. And throughout the *Monologion* he uses "Supreme Being," "Supreme Nature," and "Supreme Substance" indifferently.)[38] Thirdly, "substance" is used with respect to each member of the Trinity, as was already mentioned. This third use created difficulties for Anselm because it conduced to confusion in the minds of his readers, who were accustomed to the credal formula "*una substantia, tres personae*," and who consequently found objectionable the phrase "*una essentia, tres substantiae*."

Moreover, the justification which Anselm gives for his use of "*tres substantiae*" is unclear:

> *Haec duo nomina* [*id est, persona et substantia*] *aptius eliguntur ad significandam pluralitatem in summa essentia, quia persona non dicitur nisi de individua rationali natura, et substantia principaliter dicitur de individuis quae maxime in pluralitate consistunt. Individua namque maxime substant id est subiacent accidentibus, et ideo magis proprie substantiae nomen suscipiunt* (S I, 86:5–10).

Now, there are several different ways of reading this text — depending upon (1) whether the "*quae*" clause is taken to be restrictive or nonrestrictive, (2) whether "*consistunt*" is construed as "consist" or "exist," and (3) whether the "*namque*" sentence explains the "*quae*" clause or what precedes the "*quae*" clause. For example, one might construe the text as saying:

> These two words [viz., "person" and "substance"] are quite fittingly selected for signifying a plurality in the Supreme Being, since the word "person" is predicated only of an individual rational nature and since the word "substance" is predicated mainly of individual things, which, most of all, consist of a plurality. For individuals, especially, support accidents — i.e., are subject to accidents; and so individuals are quite properly called sub-stances.

In accordance with this reading Anselm is saying, in effect: "The word 'substance' is appropriate for signifying a plurality in the Supreme Being because 'substance' principally signifies what is individual; and what is individual consists of a plurality; and the reason what is individual consists of a plurality is that it supports accidents." But this reasoning does not make sense. For the fact that a substance consists of a plurality might be relevant to explaining why the Supreme Being — which "consists of" the plurality Father, Son, and Holy Spirit — could fittingly be called the Supreme Substance. But it is *irrelevant* to explaining why the members of the Trinity can appropriately be spoken of as three substances; for in no member of the Trinity is there any plurality. This irrelevancy suggests a dichotomy: either Anselm is reasoning incoherently or else we have misapprehended his reasoning. Well, let us revise our apprehension. Perhaps, what Anselm means by "*consistunt*" is not "consist" but "exist"; and perhaps the "*namque*" sentence explains what precedes the "*quae*" clause:

> These two words are quite fittingly selected for signifying the plurality in the Supreme Being, since the word "person" is predicated only of an individual rational nature and since the word "substance" is predicated mainly of individual things (and these mostly exist in plurality). For individuals, especially, support accidents — i.e., are subject to accidents; and so individuals are quite properly called sub-stances.

According to this reading Anselm is maintaining that for two reasons the plurality of "individuals" in the Supreme Being is rightly spoken of as three *substances*: (1) "substance" is predicated principally[39] of individual things and (2) individual things are usually found in plurality (e.g., there is more than one man, more than one horse, more than one tree, etc.). On this reading, the sentence beginning with "For" gives the reason why individual things are called sub-stances; it does not give the reason why individual things exist in plurality.

To belabor this construal or to enumerate the further alternative construals of Anselm's Latin text would, I fear, be more tedious than profitable. And so with regard to the two interpretations presented, let me say simply that, for the time being, the second seems to me to be the more nearly correct. For it ascribes to Anselm's thought more intelligibility, while at the same time giving a semantically admissible construal of "*consistere*" — a construal which, in addition, corresponds to a previous use in *Monologion* 67 (S I, 78:4).[40]

In sum, the "substance/accident" terminology in the *Monologion* shows that Anselm aligns himself with the Aristotelian view of primary substance, which both Augustine and Boethius also accepted. Like Aristotle, too, he considers colors to be accidents.

And he shows little trace of subscribing to any other view of secondary substance than did his three predecessors. Finally, the fact that, like Augustine, he also predicates "substance" of the persons of the Trinity does not detract from the fact that, on the surface at least, the distinction in *Monologion* 27 between particular and universal substance corresponds to Aristotle's distinction between primary and secondary substance. This correspondence is reinforced, in *De Grammatico* 10, by the direct reference to Aristotle, by the explicit use of the phrases "primary substance" and "secondary substance," and by the overt Aristotelian-Boethian construal of these phrases.

2.2. In *Monologion* 16 and 25 Anselm has recourse to the word "participation." In the former he alludes to participating in a quality, viz., justice; in the latter he speaks of a subject's participating in its accidents. Interestingly, these uses of "participation" coincide with the same tradition as does Anselm's use of "substance/accident": viz., the so-called Aristotelian tradition which is common to Augustine and Boethius. According to this tradition a substance participates in its qualities, which are accidents; and to say that it participates in these qualities is tantamount to saying that it has these qualities, that it is subject to them. Accordingly, what participates in something cannot be identical with that thing in which it participates — just as what is something through itself cannot participate in that thing with which it is identical. Thus, according to Boethius, a strong man is a man who has strength, i.e., who participates in strength; and a white thing is a thing which participates in whiteness.[41] (In addition, when Boethius discusses paronymy he states that a paronymous term (e.g., "*grammaticus*") participates in the *name* from which it is derived ("*grammatica*").[42] And he thinks of individual human beings as participating in the definition of "humanity."[43]

In *Monologion* 16 Anselm singles out as examples the quality justice and the quantity greatness; but he clearly states that what holds true in these respective cases also holds true for other similar predicates — i.e., for other terms which signify a quality or a quantity. So we may legitimately take what he says about justice and apply it to goodness. To begin with, then, Anselm considers it self-evident that whatever is good is good through goodness (*bonitas*). Now, assuming that goodness is a quality, whatever is good is good through a quality. And if it is good through a quality, it is good through something which is other than what it itself is. It is thus good through something which it has, i.e., through something in which it participates; in short, it is good *per aliud*. Now, since the Supreme Nature is good, it seems to follow that the Supreme Nature is good by having (i.e., by participating in) goodness. But *Monologion* 1–4, continues Anselm, has already proven that the Supreme Nature is good through itself. Therefore, since the Supreme Nature is good through itself and since whatever is good is good through goodness, it follows that the Supreme Nature is goodness itself — is substantially (i.e., essentially) goodness.

The foregoing line of reasoning — to bracket-off the question of its intrinsic importance — lends itself to comparison with *Monologion* 1 by giving rise to two questions: (1) How can goodness and justice be qualities if they are identical with the Supreme Nature? (2) Does *Monologion* 16 implicitly teach that for a thing to be good *per aliud* is for it to be good by participation? In the following paragraphs these questions will be dealt with, though *en passant*.

Although *Monologion* 16 teaches that the Supreme Being is justice itself, it does not affirm that for a thing to participate in justice is for it to participate in the Supreme Being.[44] If a thing is just, it may be said to participate in justice — i.e., if it is *just* in such way that it is not identical with the quality of justice. By contrast, the quality of justice does not participate; rather, it is just through itself — i.e., it is justice itself. Now, precisely because justice is a quality, it does not *exist by itself* (*esse per se*), even though it is *just* in and of itself (*iusta per se*). Rather, the quality of justice exists "in" primary substances, even as does the quality whiteness. But unlike whiteness, Anselm teaches, justice and goodness and wisdom exist even independently of primary substances.[45] Yet, they do not exist-apart *as qualities*, or as abstract Platonic Forms; they exist-apart as identical with the Supreme Being, which, though an individual being, is not properly called a (primary) substance.[46] Thus, Anselm's statements function on two different levels. On the first level, goodness (for example) is a quality; on the second level, Supreme Goodness is the Supreme Being (i.e., is God). On the first level whatever is good either participates in the quality of goodness or else is identical with the quality of goodness; on the second level the Supreme Being alone is, substantially, the Supreme Goodness without either participating in any quality or being participated-in by anything qualified. Furthermore, Anselm nowhere at all refers to the relationship between level one and level two as a relationship of participation; rather, in *De Veritate* 13 he declares that right things *accord with* rightness (*secundum illam sunt*) and that true things *accord with* the Supreme Truth.[47]

In fact, in *De Veritate* 13 Anselm speaks of rightness and truth as being *in* statements, actions, the will, the senses, etc. But he makes clear that this is simply a manner-of-speaking.[48] Properly speaking, notes Anselm, rightness and truth are *present to* things which are as they ought to be; and these things accord with rightness and truth.[49] For instance, when a human will wills what God wills for it to will,[50] it wills rightly, and so rightness is present to it; and it, in turn, conforms to the Supreme Truth in conforming to the will of God, who is the Supreme Truth. But there is a second sense in which, simply by willing anything at all (including what is evil), a human will functions as it ought, inasmuch as it wills in accordance with its God-given and God-permitted power. In this sense too, then, it also conforms to the Supreme Truth and has rightness present to it. We need not here rehearse Anselm's familiar doctrine of "double truth." Let it suffice to notice that in *De Veritate* Anselm steers away from the language of participation, except for the Student's comment in Chapter 2:

> . . . nothing is true except by participating in truth; and so the truth of something true is in that true thing. But the thing stated is not in the true statement, and thus must not be called its truth; rather, it must be called the *cause* of the statement's truth. Therefore, it seems to me that the truth of the statement must be sought only in the statement itself.

But there is no reason to suppose that the Teacher endorses the Student's view. In fact, the rest of the dialogue *explicitly* rejects a part of the Student's claim: viz., that the truth of a statement is to be found only in the statement itself. On the other hand, suppose that the Teacher *does* accept the language of participation here. Then in the light of the *Monologion* and its use of "participation," we would seem to be on safer ground were we to construe "participating in truth" in the Boethian[51] sense rather than in some more ontologically ornate sense.

In *De Grammatico* 16 Anselm puts into the mouth of the Student: "If no one/nothing is (an) expert-in-grammar except by participating in expertise-in-grammar, then it follows that (a) man is not (an) expert-in-grammar except together with expertise-in-grammar." As with *De Veritate* 2, the Teacher here also does not repudiate the allusion to participation. But since here the use of "participation" coincides with the use in *Monologion* 16 and 25 (for expertise-in-grammar is a quality, and thus an accident), I see no reason to believe that Anselm would not endorse it. Yet, in no way would there follow from this endorsement that he subscribes to the theory of participation in God.

To return to the *Monologion*, then, Anselm's reasoning is very much different from Augustine's in one respect: it never moves immediately[52] from the statement that good things participate in the quality of goodness to the statement that good things participate in the Supreme Good, viz., God. Unlike Augustine, Anselm does not blend these levels. Nowhere does he say, as Augustine does in *Eighty-Three Different Questions*,[53] that the good in which all other goods participate is supremely good. Nowhere does he state, as Augustine does in *De Trinitate* 8.3, that God is the good of every good. Instead, in *Proslogion* 25, he is careful to speak of "the one Good in which are all goods" and of "the simple Good which itself is every good."

Thus, F. S. Schmitt is right, in one respect, about Anselm's deplatonizing Augustine. But Schmitt wrongly locates this deplatonization and sees it as more far-reaching than in fact it is.[54] For, first of all, Schmitt thinks that one crucial difference between *Monologion* 1 and *De Trinitate* 8.3 is the fact that Anselm's reflection does not move immediately from considering the many good things to *seeing* the Good itself, whereas Augustine's does. But the significance Schmitt should point to is that Augustine's reflection moves immediately from the fact that the many good things *participate* in goodness to the fact that they *participate* in God, whereas Anselm's does not. Secondly, Schmitt asserts that deplatonization occurs in *Monologion* 1. But what he ought to assert is that the argument of *Monologion* 1 is neutral with respect to (Neo-)Platonism and that what deplatonizing there is can only be detected by comparing the whole of *De Trinitate* with the whole of the *Monologion*, *De Grammatico*, and *De Veritate*. For in *Monologion* 1 Anselm's "failure" to mention participating in God is inconsequential, given the irrelevancy of such participation to his argument there. By contrast, his never mentioning such participation anywhere at all in these three works does become crucial. Thirdly, Schmitt makes much of the fact that *Monologion* 1 does not use the word "participation." But he ought rather to *emphasize* that in *De Veritate* Anselm's language of *according with* — i.e., *conforming to* — cannot be consistently translated into the language of participation, and that in *Monologion* 1 "*esse per aliud*" cannot be consistently reduced to the sense of "*participare*." By not emphasizing this point, Schmitt leaves room for the (mistaken) rejoinder that although in *Monologion* 1 Anselm does not use the *word* "participation" he does present the *doctrine* of participation, clothed (allegedly) in the language of "*per aliud*."[55]

2.1.3. We may turn now to the doctrine of exemplarism as found in *Monologion* 9–12 and 29–36. We have already[56] noticed one difference between Anselm and Augustine: viz., that whereas Augustine speaks in the plural of Forms in the mind of God, Anselm uses in the singular the words "*exemplum*," "*forma*," "*similitudo*," "*regula*":

> By no means can anything reasonably be made by anyone unless beforehand there is in the thought (*ratione*) of the maker a certain pattern, as it were, of the thing to be made — or more suitably put, a form or likeness or rule. Thus, it is evident that before all things were made there was in the thought of the Supreme Nature what they were going to be or what kind they were going to be or how they were going to be.[57]

Anselm's choice of singular nouns is not without significance. He is obliged to use the singular because he goes on explicitly to identify the *forma rerum* (in the Maker's thought)[58] with the *locutio* of the Maker. This *locutio* is then taken to be the *verbum* of the Supreme Being and is finally said to be *identical with* the Supreme Being. Thus, an important difference between Anselm and Augustine comes to light. For it is not the case that Augustine identifies the Form*s* in the mind of God with the Word of God; they are not the second member of the Trinity, consubstantial with the Father and the Holy Spirit. Indeed, Augustine teaches that God created all things through His Word, Wisdom, or Understanding, in which are present certain eternal Forms, or Ideas.[59] But Anselm teaches that the Word of God *is* the unitary Form of creation through which God made all things. Because

Anselm does not want to say that created things *participate* in God Himself, he does not use the term "participation" in conjunction with his doctrine of creation. Accordingly, F. S. Schmitt should not concede (as he does) that *Monologion* 9 tacitly contains a doctrine of participation, though in a reduced sense.[60]

However, Anselm does maintain[61] that created things, in greater and lesser degrees, resemble the Word through which they are created. Yet, this doctrine of resemblance does not really have anything to do with Plato's *Parmenides* or with any sense of "participation" found in the *Parmenides*. For, first of all, the *Parmenides* is not presenting a doctrine of creation. Secondly, the *Parmenides* does not teach that there is only one single Form — e.g., the Form of the Good — which all (created) things resemble. Thirdly, the *Parmenides* regards the Forms as universals, whereas Anselm explicitly denies (in *Monologion* 27) that the Supreme Spirit (which the Word is) is a universal. And, finally, the reason Anselm is able to maintain that created things bear degrees of similarity to the Supreme Being insofar as they exist, live, perceive, and reason is that the Supreme Being exists, lives, perceives, and reasons. But in the *Parmenides* there cannot be this kind of resemblance between particular things and Forms, because the Forms do not live, perceive, or reason. In short, any significant comparison between Anselm's *Monologion* and Plato's *Parmenides* cannot escape being disjointed, given that the two *problématiques* are so vastly different.

Additionally, any attempt to detect in Anselm's doctrine of exemplarism a significant correspondence with the Neo-Platonic tradition cannot escape the same disjointedness. For in the tradition of Neo-Platonism the doctrine of participation is inextricably linked to the doctrine of emanations. And this latter doctrine is at odds with the Christian dogma of creation *ex nihilo*, which Anselm defends. So in avoiding the language of participation, Anselm is primarily disassociating himself from the theory of emanations. And in maintaining that the whole of creation is (in varying degrees) similar to the Supreme Being, he is safeguarding the reliability of our knowledge of God's nature and is anticipating[62] what was later called the doctrine of *analogia entis*. Finally, in affirming that some beings *exist* more than do others, he is assenting to Augustine's view that God is *verum esse*.

Whereas *De Veritate* considers created things as *according with* the Supreme Truth, *Monologion* 31 and 66 regard them as *resembling* the Supreme Truth.[63] But in these two treatises neither the notion *esse secundum veritatem summam* nor the notion *esse similis veritati summae* plays the same role as the doctrine of participation, in its various versions, plays in the writings of Plato and Plotinus. Moreover, even the assertion in *De Veritate* 7 that "there is truth in the being of all that exists, because all things are what they are in the Supreme Truth" must be understood as primarily expressing the view that (in one sense) all created things are as they ought to be. At the same time, this passage is reminiscent of Anselm's statement in *Monologion* 34:

> Before [created things] were made and once they have been made and after they have perished or have changed in some manner, they always *are* in this Spirit what this Spirit is, rather than what they are in themselves. For in themselves they are a mutable being created *according to* immutable Reason. But in this Spirit they are the primary Being and the primary true Existence (*prima existendi veritas*); and the more created things [in themselves] are in any way like this true Existence, the more truly and excellently they exist. And so in this way one can, not unreasonably, maintain that when the Supreme Spirit speaks itself, it also speaks by one and the same Word whatever has been created.[64]

So the reason why all created things are what they are in the Supreme Truth (i.e., in God) is that they are spoken by the same Word by which God speaks Himself. They therefore cannot fail to *accord with* their Maker's thought (*ratio*), even though they in no way partake of — i.e., participate in — the Divine Being. For in no way do they possess a portion of the Divine Nature, even though in their respective degrees they resemble it and at every moment are sustained by it. Like Anselm, Augustine himself does not confuse the created and the uncreated orders. But when he moves, in reflection, from a man's being wise and participating in wisdom to his participating in God Himself,[65] who is Supreme Wisdom, he gives occasion for misunderstanding. Anselm prefers to forestall such misunderstanding by avoiding the expression which occasions it.

In last analysis, neither the *Monologion*, *De Grammatico*, nor *De Veritate* seems to present — either directly or by implication — a theory which regards particulars of a given kind as participating in that kind of which they are said to be. That is, a given universal substance does not seem to be regarded as a unique *entity* which is *numerically* common to all those particulars in which it is really present. On the other hand, this view is not clearly and definitely excluded — not even in *De Grammatico*. For in *De Grammatico* Anselm teaches that "white" signifies having-whiteness and that "expert-in-grammar" signifies having-expertise-in-grammar. But he says nothing which definitely excludes the possibility that whiteness and expertise-in-grammar, though qualities, are universals in the above sense and are named, respectively, by the words "whiteness" and "expertise-in-grammar." However, since the medieval dispute over the ontological status of universals was fundamentally a dispute over the status of secondary substances, Anselm's meager remarks in *De Grammatico* do not serve, by themselves, to determine his position. For this reason interpreters of his thought have usually sought to elicit his position from his more theological works, where the status of human nature becomes central to the doctrines of incarnation, original sin, and redemption.

2.2. *De Incarnatione Verbi*. Returning to the controversial passage[66] in *De Incarnatione* 1, let us scrutinize Anselm's statements in the light of what we have already noticed. And in doing so, let us be aware that Anselm's attack upon the heretics of dialectic need not on all counts be construed as an attack upon Roscelin. In fact, Anselm seems not actually to have had first-hand contact with Roscelin's views but seems, rather, to have been relying upon written and verbal reports. At the end of *De Incarnatione* 11 he acknowledges his limited acquaintance. And in Chapter 4 he writes: "*If* [my opponent] is one of those modern dialecticians who believe that nothing exists except what they can imagine. . . ." The word "if" shows again how uncertain Anselm is about Roscelin's actual beliefs. So in *De Incarnatione* 1 the opening attack against the dialecticians seems to be a general invective which Anselm regards as propaedeutic to dealing with the position of Roscelin. And when he turns to examine Roscelin's view, he confines himself — for lack of more information about Roscelin's teachings — to analyzing the formula "If the three persons are only one thing — and are not three things, each one [existing] separately in itself (as do three angels or three souls) and yet [existing] in such way that they are wholly the same in will and in power — then the Father and the Holy Spirit were incarnate with the Son." And he is not even sure that in this formula the words "as do three angels or three souls" are really Roscelin's (*De Incarnatione* 4). So when Cousin and others[67] give the impression that the celebrated passage in *De Incarnatione* 1 is directed primarily at Roscelin, they do so misleadingly.

Let us now turn our attention to a number of specific points in this text.

First of all, it is certain that Anselm rejects the view that "universal substances are merely vocal sounds." *Monologion* 27 has already informed us that by "universal substance" Anselm means to indicate what "is essentially common to many substances (as to-be-a-man is common to individual men)." And we have seen how there is good reason to infer — by reference to *De Grammatico* — that these universal substances are what Aristotle called secondary substances (viz., species and genera). Indeed, in *De Incarnatione* 1 Anselm makes the point that several men are one man in species. And in *De Incarnatione* 11 he alludes to *homo communis* (the common human nature) which, in the case of each person, becomes individuated by a collection of distinguishing properties. So what the above statement seems to deny is that the various species, such as human nature, are mere vocal sounds. And in the light of *De Grammatico* 18 (S I, 163:26–27) this denial can be restated as: Vocal sounds such as "human nature" are not mere vocal sounds but are names; for they name species, and species are not a mere nothing.

Secondly, even though Anselm, *in the same sentence* in which he speaks of universal substances, implies that colors are distinct from their corresponding material objects: he is not asserting that colors are universal substances.[68] Indeed, in the light of our earlier observations, we have no reason not to believe that he here continues to regard colors as accidents (*Monologion* 25) which do not exist independently of some physical object or other (*De Veritate* 13). In fact, *De Grammatico* teaches plainly that colors are qualities. And since qualities are accidents of substances, they do not exist independently of substances. In *De Incarnatione* 1 Anselm does not say that a color exists in isolation: he says that it ought to be *contemplated* in isolation. Similarly, he does not claim that the species *man* exists in the absence of individual men: he claims only that the species is distinguishable from an individual man. Presumably, the species accompanies the individual. For in *De Grammatico* 20 Anselm speaks of Plato as being composed of a species and a collection of distinguishing properties. And *De Incarnatione* 11 makes clear that this species is human nature.

Thirdly, although Anselm is arguing against those who assert that only individuals are real, he is also attacking those who fail to distinguish a concept from an image. He himself had already made this distinction in *Monologion* 10, where he wrote: "In a third way [I speak of a man] when my mind beholds him either by means of an image of his body or by means of his definition — by means of an image of his body, for instance, when [my mind] imagines his visible shape; but by means of his definition, for instance, when [my mind] conceives his universal being, viz., *rational, mortal animal*." Similarly, in *De Incarnatione* 1 and 4 he inveighs against the dialecticians because their minds, darkened by images, cannot distinguish what ought to be contemplated (i.e., conceived) purely and in isolation. What he is driving at is that a species is conceived, not imagined. Moreover, although a color can be *conceived* apart from conceiving of a material object,[69] it is not obvious that it can be *imagined* without imagining a material object. At any rate, Anselm is certain that anyone who overemphasizes imagining, at the expense of minimizing conceiving, will not advance toward comprehending the doctrine of the Trinity.

Fourthly, Anselm tacitly accuses the dialecticians of not distinguishing what is essential from what is inessential. That is, these dialecticians do not pay enough attention to the difference between substance and accident (even as they also trivialize the difference between universal substance and particular substance). In *De Incarnatione* 7 this distinction is invoked in order to refute Roscelin, who, Anselm contends, will have to concede that God's power is essential to Him (rather than accidental). For every subject can exist or be conceived apart from its accidents; but God can neither exist nor be conceived apart from His power. By comparison, Anselm mentions in *De Incarnatione* 1 three theological topics where the heretics err by virtue of conflating, in each case, a requisite distinction:

(a) If the "modern dialecticians" cannot even properly distinguish between primary and secondary substances, then they cannot hope to discern how the plurality of divine persons is one God.[70]

(b) If the dialecticians cannot even properly distinguish between a primary substance and its quality, then they cannot hope to discern how in the one God there are several relations.

(c) If the dialecticians cannot even properly distinguish between a person and his nature, then they cannot hope to discern how the Son of God assumed a human nature without assuming a human person.

So Anselm is worried by the conviction that the inadequate philosophical approach of the dialecticians prevents them from grasping the truth of theological doctrines. Accordingly, at the outset, he warns against sophistry.

Fifthly, and finally, we come back to Cousin's intriguing argument, reformulated as follows:

(1) It is implausible to suppose that Roscelin — or any of the other nominalists — denied that the mind has the capability of distinguishing a quality from its subject.

So: (2) Either Anselm's reproach is pointless or else Anselm is reproaching Roscelin and the others for not realizing that color has reality independently of the colored object.

(3) Anselm's reproach is not pointless.

So: (4) Anselm is reproaching Roscelin and the others for not realizing that the color has reality independently of the colored object.

So: (5) Since Anselm denies Roscelin's view by reproaching it, he affirms the view that colors do exist independently of colored objects.[71]

But we are now in a position to see that Cousin misidentifies the character of Anselm's reproach. For Anselm, as we have noticed, reproaches the dialecticians *not* for not realizing that colors have an independent reality but for not realizing that colors are to be *contemplated* independently — i.e., for not distinguishing adequately between concept and image. Yet, what about the remark "someone whose mind is too darkened to distinguish between his horse and its color"? Does this utterance not lend credence to Cousin's inference? — inasmuch as, surely, no one could fail to make the distinction in question. Well, the remark appears to be hyperbolic: It is a vivid way of insisting that the dialecticians are neglecting the distinction between essential and nonessential features, as well as a striking way of calling attention to their philosophical inability to think abstractly.

So Cousin is wrong in inferring from *De Incarnatione* 1 that Anselm believed that the color white or the color red, etc., exists apart from every material object. Perhaps, in the back of his mind, Cousin is dimly remembering Anselm's statement in *De Grammatico* 9: "A man can exist without (*sine*) the color white, and the color white can exist without the man." But if so, he is equally wrong in construing this statement analogously to his construal of the color-statements in *De Incarnatione* 1. For Anselm means that even in the absence of *this* man, there will still be whiteness, since there will still be other (white) objects in which there is whiteness. But *this* man's whiteness will have perished. (Cf. *De Veritate* 13.) He does not mean that the color white is numerically one entity — whether this one entity exist uninstantiated, or whether it exist only as common to the objects which have it. Unfortunately, Anselm's unclear language gives rise to confusion. One could wish that Anselm had distinguished explicitly between *type* and *token* — just as elsewhere in his writings (e.g., the *Proslogion* and the *Debate with Gaunilo*) one painfully misses a clear distinction between *use* and *mention*. Likewise, his frequent omission of personal pronouns, together with the Latin language's lack of a definite and an indefinite article, militates against the exact determination of his position. The resultant problem is nowhere more patent than in the *Cur Deus Homo* and in *De Conceptu Virginali*.

2.3. *Cur Deus Homo* and *De Conceptu Virginali*. In these two works Anselm speaks repeatedly as if human nature were an unindividuated universal. For instance, in Book I, Chapter 18 of the *Cur Deus Homo*, he writes (from a viewpoint before the Fall): "But even if human nature were to fall, it would much more greatly vindicate God against itself and the Devil, since — though created mortal and much weaker — it would (in the elect) ascend from such weakness to a place higher than that from which the Devil had fallen."[72] Although such expressions are not confined to the *Cur Deus Homo* and *De Conceptu Virginali*,[73] they are nonetheless concentrated in these two works. And they do foster the impression that human nature — as Anselm understands it — is a numerically singular universal entity which is present at once in all human beings who exist simultaneously, and which is present consecutively in human beings who exist at successive times. For unless there were this numerical identity, how could human nature, which fell in Adam, be said to ascend in the elect? And what sense would it make to assert that human nature could not keep justice for itself in Adam's posterity?

2.3.1. Two passages in *De Conceptu* become crucial for those who, like Joseph Colleran,[74] label Anselm's position ultra realism: viz.,

> (1) *Fecit igitur persona peccatricem naturam, quia cum Adam peccavit, homo peccavit.*[75]
> (2) *Sicut persona propter naturam peccatrix nascitur, ita natura per personam magis peccatrix redditur, quia cum peccat persona quaelibet, peccat homo.*[76]

Colleran translates these as:

> (1) The person, then, made the nature sinful, because when Adam sinned, man sinned.
> (2) Just as a person is born sinful on account of his nature, so the nature is rendered more sinful by the person, because when any person at all commits sin, man commits sin.

And, of course, the translations "When Adam sinned, man sinned" and "When any person at all commits sin, man commits sin" do make Anselm appear to be an ultra realist. But are these translations acceptable? Well, as far as literal translation of Anselm's Latin words goes, the translations are flawless. But as regards capturing Anselm's meaning, they seem to me to be defective.

In *De Conceptu* 23 much depends upon the sentence which precedes the one in question, so that the two must be read together:

> *Persona enim erat quod dicebatur Adam; natura, quod homo. Fecit igitur persona peccatricem naturam, quia cum Adam peccavit, homo peccavit.*

And I take the sense of these sentences to be:

> For the person was what was called Adam; and the nature was what was called man. Therefore, the person made the nature sinful, because when Adam sinned, the man [i.e., the nature] sinned.

So when Adam, the person, sinned: his nature sinned. And Anselm goes on to explain why this nature can reproduce itself only with the corruption which resulted from Adam's sin. Earlier Anselm had explained that all of Adam's descendants are in him in the way that what comes from a seed is in the seed. And he had indicated that infants are born with original sin in the sense that an infant, because of his nature, is unable altogether to keep from willing evil when he attains to understanding the difference between right and wrong.

Likewise, taken together with its preceding sentence,[77] the second passage seems to me best translated as:

> Indeed, whatever sin accrues to a man over and above original sin is personal sin. And just as the person is born sinful because of the nature, so the nature is made more sinful because of the person, since when any person sins, his human nature sins.

Now, someone will ask: "What justification can there be for inserting the word 'his' into the last line of the translation — given that '*sua*' does not appear in the Latin text?" And, of course, the presence of the word "his" makes this translation and Colleran's totally different. For Colleran interprets Anselm to mean that when any person whatsoever sins, man sins. And it is an easy step from this reading to the claim that the *homo* which sins is a universal entity which, though numerically one, is present in all men. By contrast, the second translation interprets Anselm to mean that a person's sin affects his nature, though there is no human nature, as such, which it affects.

In deciding which of these two conflicting translations more accurately displays Anselm's meaning, we must take a sophisticated look at the complete treatises. For the present conflict presents us with a case where we cannot decide about the correct rendering without concomitantly deciding about Anselm's theory of human nature and redemption. Were the above Latin text unequivocally clear, we would be able to determine Anselm's theory on the basis of the text's meaning; but precisely because the text is not unequivocally clear, we must decide its meaning on the basis of the theory. And the theory must be elicited, if possible, from other texts. The reason the text is not definitive is that Anselm, like other medieval authors, does not always bother to include the possessives "*suus*" and "*eius*" where he intends for them to be understood.[78] For instance, at the end of *Cur Deus Homo* II, 18 (S II, 129:19) he writes that the Son offered His humanity to His divinity (*humanitatem suam divinitati suae* [*obtulit*]). But toward the beginning of *Cur Deus Homo* I, 9 (S II, 61:18–19), where he means "Therefore, *that* man [viz., Jesus] owed this obedience to God the Father; and His humanity owed it to His divinity . . ." he writes only "*Hanc igitur oboedientiam debebat homo ille deo patri, et humanitas divinitati. . . .*" The possessive adjectives are understood rather than used. Similarly, in *De Incarnatione* 10 (S II, 26:9) he uses the phrase "*suae humanitati*," even though when making a different point a few lines later he reverts to the abbreviated "*ab humanitate ad divinitatem*."[79] Had Anselm in all other contexts been consistent in his use of personal and reflexive pronouns and of possessive and reflexive adjectives, then we would have good reason to regard the omission of "*sua*," in the disputed passage in *De Conceptu* 27, as decisive for determining his meaning. And then we could perhaps go on to maintain — depending upon the other texts in *De Conceptu* — that Anselm was or was not an ultra realist when he wrote this treatise. And we could profitably debate whether or not he was also an ultra realist when he wrote his other treatises. But since the omission is not decisive, we must beware of leaping to conclusions by dignifying the disputed text as a "proof-text." Instead, we must interpret the unclear in the light of the clear. Accordingly, we must judge the passages in *De Conceptu* 23 and 27 in the light of *De Incarnatione* 11 — being careful, however, not to beg the question of whether Anselm's view changed during the interval between these two treatises.

Now, plainly, in *De Incarnatione* 11 Anselm teaches that the common human nature is individuated, and marked off from other individuated human natures, by the collection of distinguishing properties which a person has. And this plain instruction licenses our speaking of a person's individuated nature as *his* nature. (And, in fact, even Colleran feels free to supply the word "his" upon occasions where it is not present in the Latin text.)[80] So the "his" reading of the disputed passage in *De Conceptu* 27 is consistent both with the doctrine expressed in *De Incarnatione* 11 and with Anselm's Latin style. Furthermore, there is evidence in *De Conceptu* which clearly excludes Colleran's interpretation. For in Chapter 24 (S II, 166:19–22) Anselm remarks:

> Although in Adam human nature retained some justice, so that it kept an upright will in some respects, nonetheless it was so deprived of the gift of being able to keep justice for itself in Adam's posterity that it is not able to propagate itself with any justice in any of them.

Now, if in Adam human nature was to some extent *just* at the same time that it was born in Abel as altogether lacking justice: Adam's nature and Abel's nature cannot be exactly and numerically identical. And this consideration seems to dispose of the ultra-realism interpretation of Anselm.

But perhaps Colleran — who does not explain what he means by "ultra realism" — will protest that we have not done justice to articulating the position. And I can think of at least three forms which this protest might take.

2.3.2. "Human nature," it might be argued, "has both essential and nonessential properties. Accordingly, in *Cur Deus Homo* II, 11 Anselm teaches that mortality and immortality do not belong to the essence of human nature. Similarly, the condition of being corrupt (fallen) or incorrupt (unfallen) is inessential to human nature. By contrast, freedom and rationality belong to human nature essentially. For without either of these human nature would not be human nature. Now, what possesses a nature need not possess anything inessential to that nature. And so, since justice is an accident of human nature, one and the same human nature might have been present in Abel as totally unjust at the same time it was present in Adam as only partially unjust."

But this argument is incoherent, as Anselm himself would have seen. Let us grant that justice and injustice are only inessential features of human nature. (For surely Abel, who was born without justice, was not essentially different from Adam, his father.) Still, the human nature could not at one and the same time be both in some respect just and in no respect just. For a thing cannot at one and the same time both in some respect and in no respect have some given characteristic — even an inessential characteristic. However, since the characteristic is not essential, it may at one time belong to the thing and at another time not belong to the thing. Or it may in different respects both belong and not belong to the thing at the same time. Yet, the argument in question is claiming that human nature both is and is not totally unjust at the same time and in the same sense of "unjust."

Moreover, the argument does not conform to what it itself admits to be the theological data. For *Cur Deus Homo* II, 11 shows that — according to Anselm — the body is a component part of human nature;[81] for *Cur Deus Homo* II, 11 is discussing *bodily* immortality. Similarly, the corresponding passage in *De Conceptu* 2 shows that — according to Anselm — the soul is a component part of human nature. Thus, when Anselm affirms that the whole of human nature existed in Adam and Eve,[82] he means that there were existing at the time no other human beings (each consisting of a body and a soul). And when he says that human nature as a whole was weakened and corrupted, he means that both the body and the soul became marred as a result of Adam's and of Eve's sinning. Now, even as Anselm does not suppose, absurdly, that Adam and Eve had numerically the same body or numerically the same soul, so he does not believe that they had numerically the same human nature. Instead, the phrases "(the) body," "(the) soul," and "human nature" are collective ways of speaking.[83]

2.3.3. In the light of these considerations, Colleran and others who agree with him might move to a second version of ultra realism. "Admittedly," they might recommence, "Adam and Eve and Mary and Jesus (and, in fact, every single human being) has (according to Anselm) *his own* human nature — just as surely as he has his own body and his own soul, each of which are components of his human nature. But Human Nature is something 'over and above' these individualized natures. Indeed, it is commonly present in them, rather than existing in the absence of them all. Anselm expresses this doctrine by remarking that when any person whatsoever sins, man (i.e., Human Nature) sins."

But this new formulation squares no more with the textual and the theological data than does the previous version. Indeed, virtually the same theological problem recurs. For if Human Nature sins whenever any person sins, then Human Nature is always sinful; for, presumably, at any given time some person or other is sinning. Now, Anselm teaches that, upon conversion, a sinner has uprightness restored to his will by the grace of God — even though the convert may subsequently forsake this uprightness by sinning again. Yet, how could the sinner, immediately after conversion and baptism, have uprightness of will and be free of personal sin, as well as of original sin (which is the inherited absence-of-uprightness-from-the-will), if the universal Human Nature in him were still sinful? In other words, what would be the relationship between the individualized nature and the universal

Nature such that the one could be free of sin while the other was contaminated?

Fortunately, in our capacity as exegetes, we do not have to worry about this question, because Anselm nowhere either introduces or alludes to a distinction between Human Nature and human natures. Such a distinction plays no role in his analyses of original sin, the Virgin Birth, baptism, and redemption. But had he subscribed to the view that Human Nature is present in each human being as something over and above the individualized nature, then he would surely have mentioned this distinction explicitly in one of these analyses.

2.3.4. At this juncture advocates of the ultra-realism interpretation of *De Conceptu* might opt for a still more refined version of this position. "Let us agree," they might concede, "that '*cum peccat persona quaelibet, peccat homo*' is to be translated as 'When any person sins, his human nature sins.' Nonetheless, Anselm believed that an individualized human nature is an instance of Human Nature. And this is his reason for saying such things as that in Jesus 'Human Nature freely and out of no obligation gave to God something its own, so that it might redeem itself in others in whom it did not have what it, as a result of indebtedness, was required to pay.'[84] So Human Nature is something real and is really common to every individualized human nature."

But this version is grasping at straws. For (to put an end to the matter) there is absolutely no basis in Anselm's writings for any systematic distinction between human nature and Human Nature — where the latter is thought of as a unitary universal entity which is common to all instances of the former. To be sure, we can conjure up all kinds of things that Anselm might hypothetically have said. For instance, to the question "Does Humanity exist in all individualized human natures?" we can imagine the reply "If it did not, then these natures would not be *human* natures," as well as the reply "If it did, then it would be superfluous." But imaginings unsupported by data are of no historical importance.

2.3.5. To me it seems clear enough that many of Anselm's statements about human nature are *modi loquendi*. At the beginning of *De Conceptu* 10, for example Anselm states that every descendant of Adam is Adam by virtue of being propagated from

Adam. But this statement actually amounts to a vivid way of reminding us that we all belong to the same race. And there remains a sense in which we are not, and cannot be, Adam himself. Similarly, in Chapter 16 Anselm remarks that in the case of the miraculous birth of John the Baptist "there is not something new given to Adam's nature, as there is in the case of the Son of the Virgin." Yet, the sense in which John had *Adam's* nature is (for Anselm) the sense in which he had *Adamic* nature. For had he really had *Adam's* nature, he would have been born with *Adam's* sin. But Chapter 26 denies that an infant is born with *Adam's* sin.[85]

A further example of how Anselm employs a *modus loquendi* is evident in his very statement that infants are born with original sin. For concomitantly with *saying* this, he affirms that no human being can be either sinful or just before he understands justice — i.e., before he understands the difference between right and wrong.[86] So the saying is a manner-of-speaking. And this fact is nowhere more evident than in the following text: "Therefore, it is clear both how there is no sin in infants from the moment of their conception and how those statements which I adduce from Divine Scripture are true. Indeed, there is no sin in those infants, for they do not have a will, which is a necessary condition for the presence of sin. Nevertheless, sin *is said to be* in them, since in the seed they contract the necessity of sinning at the time when they will become human beings."[87]

Likewise, it seems to me, Anselm is adopting a *modus loquendi* when he repeatedly refers to human nature in the singular number. For by using the singular he emphasizes the universal condition of fallenness which characterizes all of Adam's natural descendants. And he creates a context in which one man's performance of a service-of-merit on behalf of others can be expressed as human nature's paying to God what it owes. And this expression more readily "displays," as it were, the rationale for God's having become incarnate.

So in the *Cur Deus Homo* and in *De Conceptu Virginali* Anselm is adopting a certain style of presentation. And this style is reminiscent of his discussion in *De Casu Diaboli* 2, where the Student says: "Therefore, it is evident that just as the angel (*ille angelus*) who stood in the truth persevered because he had perseverance, so he had perseverance because he received it, and he received it because God gave it."[88] But in fact, "*ille angelus*" is a literary device for articulating a truth which obtains for all the good angels. And, indeed, throughout *De Casu Diaboli* the case of Satan exemplifies the cases of all the other evil angels who fell simultaneously with him. Of course, there is a difference between (1) singling-out Satan as a focal point for explaining the fall of all the evil angels and (2) singling-out Adam in order to explain the fall of all men (except the God-man). For the fall of any one angel is independent of the fall of any other; whereas the fall of Adam results in the fall of his descendants. Nonetheless, even as Anselm uses a literary device in the case of his discussion of the angels, so he uses a manner-of-speaking in the course of dealing with the topic of human nature. But from this manner-of-speaking it does not follow that he was an ultra realist — any more than from his use of the phrases "our will,"[89] "our body"[90] it follows that, according to him, all human beings have one will or one body. So, then, his use of "*humanitas nostra*"[91] does not commit him to the belief that we all share in a universal *entity*. Precisely here "we ought not to cling to the verbal impropriety concealing the truth as much as we ought to attend to the true propriety hidden beneath the many types of expression."[92]

III

3. *Conclusion*. Lamentably, Anselm does not develop a vocabulary of technical philosophical Latin. Thus, his use of such terms as "*homo*," "*ratio*," "*oratio*," "*species*," and "*essentia*" leaves us at times confused. What, for instance, is meant in *De Grammatico* 20 by his intimating that an individual human being, such as Plato, is composed of a species and a collection of distinguishing properties? By "species" does Anselm here mean "human nature" — and, if so, in what sense? Is to have a human nature to have a species — or is it to belong to a species? Since *De Grammatico* mentions Aristotle's *Categories* and alludes to his definitions of "primary substance" and of "secondary substance," we may surmise that by "species" Anselm signifies the secondary substance which we label "man." (And this surmise seems corroborated by the fact that in *De Incarnatione* 11 he states that a person is composed of a *nature* and a collection of distinguishing properties.) But we are still left wondering what he

believed the ontological status of secondary substances to be. And we are eager for a systematic presentation which moves as coherently and directly as does Boethius' in his *Commentary on Porphyry's Isagoge*.[93] Whether or not Anselm had access to this commentary, he certainly did not interact with it. And thus, in his writings, the debate over universals not only makes no advance over Boethius but even lags behind the advance already made by Boethius.

A final example will illustrate the difficulty of understanding Anselm's simplified language. In *Cur Deus Homo* II, 21 he writes: "Moreover, even as man ought not to have been lifted up through another man who would not be of the same race (even though he would be of the same nature), so no angel ought to be saved through another angel (even though all angels are of one nature), since angels are not — as men are — of the same race." Now, although there are a number of ways of construing this passage, let us examine only two of them. According to the first construal, Anselm is using "of the same nature" and "of one nature" interchangeably.[94] (Yet, he nowhere clarifies either of these expressions — unlike Boethius, who distinguishes three different senses of "same"[95] and who distinguishes the species *man* from the individual humanity in, say, Socrates.[96]) When he states that even a non-Adamic man would be "of the same nature" as Adam, he means that a non-Adamic man would be no less human than was Adam. Similarly, when he states that angels are "of one nature," he means that angels are alike in being *angels*. He does not mean, for instance, that individual angels are accidents of a universal angelic nature. For he is speaking loosely, not technically.

According to the second construal, Anselm is speaking technically, not loosely: When he uses the phrases "of the same nature" and "of one nature," he means that all angels and all men share, respectively, a numerically common nature. On this view — which is slightly different from the three formulations in the previous section — individual men are *accidents* of the common human nature, even as individual angels are accidents of the common angelic nature.

These two conflicting interpretations do not turn upon the question of translation. For the translation is not in dispute. Rather, they turn upon how to interpret the translated phrases "of the same nature'' and ''of one nature.'' And in the light of *De Incarnatione* 1 (where Anselm indicates that several men are one man in species) and of the remarks already made, I think that the first interpretation must be favored. Anselm is speaking as does the ordinary monk rather than as do the philosophers. He is not — even in passing — making a point about universals. How could angels — for Anselm — not all be of one nature, since all are essentially alike? And how could human beings not all be of one nature, since they too are essentially alike?

Anselm's nontechnical use of language is more likely to mislead those who approach it literalistically than those who approach it commonsensically. A good example of this point occurs in *De Conceptu* 3, which states: ''*Rationalis . . . natura non est nisi deus et angelus et anima hominis, per quam homo dicitur rationalis et sine qua non est homo*.'' Now, theologically educated common sense tells us that the correct English translation of ''*rationalis natura*'' will be in terms of a plural expression: ''Only God, angels, and the human soul (by virtue of which a man is called rational, and without which he is not a man) are *rational natures*.'' And only someone who did not know Christian theology would dare to think of Anselm as believing that God, an angel, and a man's soul share exactly the same rational nature. Yet, the more-literalistically-minded-person will construe the text in a way resulting in metaphysical aberrations. Similarly, in *De Libertate Arbitrii* 3, where the discussion centers on both Satan and Adam, Anselm remarks: ''Freedom of choice was given to rational nature in order to keep the uprightness-of-will which it had received.'' And, again, only someone perversely literal-minded would dream of inferring that, according to Anselm, Satan and Adam share exactly the same rational nature. But Anselm talks about *human* nature in the same singular way that he talks about *rational* nature. And there is no more reason to take the former set of expressions literalistically than to do so in the case of the latter.

So, as we noticed at the end of the previous chapter, there lurks the danger of overinterpreting Anselm's texts — of allegedly finding, beneath the surface, much more than initially meets the eye. To this persistent temptation toward overdetermination, the secondary literature on Anselm's theory of universals bears striking witness. In the end, the terms ''realism,'' ''moderate realism,'' ''ultra realism,'' and ''nominalism'' become labels empty of clear significance. And Anselm's position becomes debated in terms of *Ideengeschichte*. (''It is more Aristotelian than Platonistic''; ''It is more Augustinian than Boethian''; ''It is the harbinger of Aquinas' position'' — and so on.) Yet, in last analysis, even to speak of ''Anselm's position'' may be question-begging. For we cannot be sure that he had worked out a view extensive enough to be called a position. Perhaps, like Boethius, he was not ready to commit himself. At any rate, a general direction in his thinking can be glimpsed from what he clearly denied:

(1) That universal substances are mere vocal sounds.
(2) That individual things participate[97] in God Himself.
(3) That colors exist independently of material objects.
(4) That the Son of God assumed an individual man.

But if secondary substances are not mere vocal sounds, what exactly are they? Anselm does not inform us; and so we are left with our surmises about what he might have thought. I would venture to conjecture that of the four interpretations with which this chapter began, Anselm's thought is closer to being captured by the second. In other words — to pull out all the stops — I tend to agree with Henry that Anselm is no ''crude realist,'' while at the same time agreeing with Grabmann that Anselm is dimly aligned with Boethius and Aquinas. Finally, if in Anselm's texts there is not much evidence establishing his position, then *a fortiori* there is little evidence establishing that his position changed. At least, there is no sign of such a change.

Although this chapter ends aporetically, it has perhaps served to focus a continuing debate among Anselm scholars. In the process, it has illustrated Anselm's recourse to *modi loquendi*; and it has displayed how his simplified, nontechnical expressions can conduce to confusion. These modest results can best be appreciated, if at all, when measured against the staggering claims made by others: e.g., that the soundness of the argument in *Proslogion* 2 depends upon the presupposition of an uncritical conceptual realism;[98] that Anselm's arguments in *Monologion* 1–4 commit him to primitive realism;[99] that for Anselm the universal is the real, whereas the individual is an appearance;[100] that Anselm teaches that there are Forms in the mind of God;[101] that ''the Platonic-Neoplatonic doctrine of participation finds, through Anselm, its entrance into medieval Scholasticism'';[102] that Anselm's theory is virtually the same as Erigena's;[103] that when any person sins, man sins;[104] that Anselm believes colors to exist independently of material objects;[105] that Anselm teaches that created objects *participate* in an exemplar in the Divine Mind;[106] that Anselm accuses the nominalists of not distinguishing meaning from reference;[107] that (for Anselm) the world of sensible things is not the true world but is a sort of participation in intelligibles;[108] that (according to Anselm) a thing exists only because it participates in universal existence;[109] and so forth.

I have tried to bridle some of these headstrong and free-ranging interpretations. For they venture farther than the data warrant. In so doing, they betray one or another principle of hermeneutics.

What we look for in Anselm's texts, but fail to find regarding his theory of universals, is an *argument* — one whose premises will direct us step-by-step toward a conclusion. Accordingly, as we prepare to turn our attention toward the ontological argument, we do so with a mixed sense of relief and expectancy.

CHAPTER IV

ANSELM'S DEBATE WITH GAUNILO*

Gaunilo, monk of Marmoutier, is known almost exclusively for his attempted refutation of Anselm's ontological argument around 1079. Indeed, both his counter-example about the alleged island which is more excellent than all others and Anselm's rebuttal thereof have nowadays become standard items for courses in medieval philosophy. Over the past decade or so, which has witnessed a revival of interest in the ontological argument, Gaunilo has been either lauded for his brilliancy or disparaged for his mediocrity. Thus, R. W. Southern judges that, "in words which are as trenchant as, and in some details strikingly similar to, those of Kant," Gaunilo pointed out the main difficulty in accepting Anselm's argument.[1] By contrast, the most Charles Hartshorne can say on Gaunilo's behalf is that he is "a clever, but essentially commonplace mind."[2] Those who praise Gaunilo tend to do so because he "wisely" discerned the illegitimacy of inferring a factual statement from an a priori description. Those who speak derogatorily of his achievement tend to side with Anselm's two criticisms: (1) that he misunderstood the phrase "*aliquid quo nihil maius cogitari potest*" — replacing it by "*maius omnibus*" — and (2) that his definition of "understanding" is inconsistent with his having maintained that what is unreal can be understood.[3] Now, if Gaunilo did commit himself to two blatantly inconsistent statements within a few lines of each other, as the second criticism maintains, then to call him a *clever* mind would itself be an overstatement.

In this chapter, I want to clear up several misinterpretations both within and about the debate between Anselm and Gaunilo. At the same time, I want to articulate the reformulations of the ontological argument as they occur in *Reply to Gaunilo* 1. I shall not take up the issue of whether or not any of these reformulations present a sound argument for the existence of God, though in my judgment none of them do. Nor shall I worry about the respective degrees of brilliancy attributable to our two opponents, though on the present interpretation Gaunilo will fare better than Hartshorne supposes but not as well as Southern fancies.

1.1. *Problem of interpreting Gaunilo*. The Anselm-Gaunilo controversy has usually been approached with the preconception that Anselm's interpretation of Gaunilo's text is reliable. Anselm may or may not have successfully rebutted all of Gaunilo's objections, it is assumed, but he certainly was not mistaken about the nature of these objections. Now, it is strange that commentators find no apparent difficulty in allowing that Gaunilo misunderstood Anselm's argument while disallowing the reverse — i.e., disallowing that this "great mind [viz., Anselm] beside whom Gaunilo was not an intellectual giant"[4] should have misread *On Behalf of the Fool*. Thus, in a recent article[5] F. S. Schmitt deals section by section with Anselm's *Reply to Gaunilo*. But he deals with Gaunilo's text itself only through the eyes of Anselm's *Reply*, which he assumes to be exegetically definitive. Yet, when we look closely at Gaunilo's text and then at Anselm's interpretation of it, we will find that Anselm's charge of inconsistency is based upon a misreading.

1.2. *Gaunilo's misinterpretation of Anselm*. However, before taking up the issue of whether or not Anselm fully understood the logical structure of Gaunilo's work, let us admit outright that Gaunilo did not fully comprehend that of Anselm's. Most flagrantly of all, he failed to appreciate how uniquely the expression "*aliquid quo nihil maius cogitari potest*" fits into the structure of the argument in *Proslogion* 2. Thus, in Section 1 of *On Behalf of the Fool* he sees no harm in slipping from the expression "*aliqua . . . natura, qua nihil maius cogitari possit*" (S I, 125:3–4) to the shorter phrase "*maius omnibus*" (S I, 125:9). Now, as the beginning and end of Section 4 reveal, Gaunilo is using "*maius omnibus*" ("that which is greater than all others") as an abbreviation of "*illud maius omnibus quae cogitari possunt*" ("that which is greater than all others that can be thought").[6] But Anselm reads "*maius omnibus*" as a shorthand for "*maius omnibus quae sunt*": "that which is greater than all other existing beings."[7] He therefore reproaches Gaunilo for distorting his description of God. To be sure, Gaunilo *does* once use the expression "*maior natura omnium quae sunt*" in Section 7 (S I, 129:8–9). But there he is not confusing it with Anselm's formula. He is merely objecting to Anselm's inference from the a priori description of God as that than which nothing greater can be thought (or, in Gaunilo's formulation, the being which is greater than all others (that can be thought)) to the conclusion that God is *actually* the greatest of all beings. Only if *Proslogion* 2 had presented — as Gaunilo deems it not to have done — a sound argument for the conclusion that God exists, and therefore is actually the greatest being, would Anselm have had a legitimate basis for contending in *Proslogion* 3 that God exists so really that He is not able to be thought not to exist. In contesting the soundness of Anselm's proof, Gaunilo calls for a new argument to demonstrate the real existence of something which is greater than all others (that can be thought) and which thus is greater than all other existing natures (i.e., beings).

If Gaunilo's "*maius omnibus*" is really a shorthand for "*illud maius omnibus quae cogitari possunt*" — as I think it is — then he does not distort Anselm's formula by abridging it. Gaunilo's failure is rather a failure to comprehend how, within Anselm's *reductio ad impossibile* argument, the contradiction is arrived at. He does not understand the function of the contradiction nor the exact statement of the contradiction. Indeed, had he discerned exactly where the contradiction resided and what role it played within the structure of the Anselmian proof, he would not have used the abbreviation "*maius omnibus*" lest it should diminish the appearance of contradiction! Gaunilo's misapprehension is obvious when we compare Anselm's *Proslogion* 2 premise "If N[8] were only in the understanding, N could be thought to exist also in reality — which is greater [than existing only in the understanding]"[9] with Gaunilo's recapitulation: "Now, if this thing existed solely in the understanding, then whatever existed also in reality would be greater than it."[10] Obviously, the recapitulation does not capture Anselm's point. For Anselm is *not* arguing that if N existed merely in the understanding, then a really existing stone, say, would be greater than N. Rather he is reasoning that if N existed merely in the understanding, then N could be thought to exist in reality; and since for N to exist both in the understanding and in reality would be greater than for N to exist merely in the understanding, N could be thought to be greater than it is.

The next step of Gaunilo's recapitulation continues the misapprehension: "Thus," he writes, "that which is greater than all others would be less than some other and would not be greater than all others — surely a contradiction." Yet, in *Proslogion* 2 Anselm's next move had generated a contradiction *without comparing* N with any other actual or conceivable being: "Thus, if N existed only in the understanding, then N would be not-N."

Gaunilo's failure to grasp the *reductio* technique was not the *result* but the *cause* of his simplifying the longer expression to "*maius omnibus*." For, given this failure, nothing except prolixity would be gained by his having written: "Thus, that which is greater than all others *that can be thought* would be less than some other and would not be greater than all others *that can be thought* — surely a contradiction." For he had already missed the point in formulating his previous premise, where the misconception would also not have been corrected by his having written: "Now, if this thing *than which nothing greater can be thought* existed solely in the understanding, then whatever existed also in reality would be greater than it." Though Gaunilo does not include the italicized words, he intends for the reader to supply them. Consequently, he *does* regard Anselm's formula even though he does not see exactly how the formula functions in Anselm's argument.

1.3. *Anselm's additional misreading of Gaunilo*. So Gaunilo's abbreviation "*maius omnibus*" is not, as such, unfair to Anselm, though it is misleading. Indeed, it misled Anselm; and Anselm in turn has misled almost everyone else. Unfortunately, this is not the only respect in which Anselm has misinterpreted Gaunilo; for if he had not misread another passage, he would never have charged Gaunilo with a flagrant self-contradiction.

In particular, Anselm misconstrues Gaunilo's definition of "*intelligere*" as it occurs in *On Behalf of the Fool* 2. This can only happen because Anselm does not detect the rationale of Gaunilo's objections, just as Gaunilo did not discern the logic of Anselm's argument. In Section 2 Gaunilo is pointing out that *Proslogion* 2 presupposes the following principle: x is in A's understanding[11] whenever A understands the words of someone who purports to be talking about x. But surely, to paraphrase Gaunilo, I sometimes understand people who speak falsely and people who speak about unreal things. So if the criterion for something's being in my understanding is simply that I understand someone's words, then I can have in my understanding that to which no real object corresponds. So N too — whose description I understand when I hear it — might be in my understanding in just this way. Or are you, Anselm, going to tell me that N cannot be in my understanding in this way but must be there in the way that something is there when I understand someone who is speaking about real objects? Are you prepared to say that I can think this being only by way of understanding (i.e., only by way of apprehending with certainty) that it really exists?[12]

Gaunilo goes on to maintain that if this is Anselm's view, then three problems arise for it:

1. "There would no longer be a difference here between first having this thing in the understanding and subsequently understanding [judging] this thing to exist — as happens in the case of a painting, which first is in the artist's mind and then later is an actual product."
2. "Secondly, it could scarcely be plausible that when this thing is spoken of or heard of it could not be thought not to exist, in the way even God can [be thought] not to exist."
3. "The claim 'This being is such that as soon as it is thought of it must be indubitably understood to exist in reality' would have to be proved to me by an indubitable argument"[13] — not by the argument that you, Anselm, have used.

This third consequence, as Gaunilo sees it, requires Anselm to give an additional and independent argument to show that N must be *understood to exist* and cannot be understood in the way that some falsehoods are understood.

Now, Anselm fails to follow Gaunilo's reasoning; and thus in *Reply to Gaunilo* 6 he construes Gaunilo's phrase "*non* [*posse*] *hoc aliter cogitare, nisi intelligendo id est scientia comprehendendo re ipsa illud existere*" as if Gaunilo were defining "*intelligere*" as "*scientia comprehendere re ipsa illud existere.*" Yet, what Gaunilo did was to construe "*intelligere*" as "*scientia comprehendere*"; he thus identified *intelligere re ipsa illud existere* with *scientia comprehendere re ipsa illud existere*. Gaunilo's meaning would stand out better with the use of parentheses: *non* [*posse*] *hoc aliter cogitare, nisi intelligendo (id est scientia com-*

prehendendo) re ipsa illud existere. In other words, Anselm supposes that Gaunilo is defining "understanding x" as "apprehending with certainty *that x really exists*" — whereas all he is doing is defining "understanding" as "apprehending with certainty." This confusion on Anselm's part leads him to say that Gaunilo's position is inconsistent, inasmuch as the definition is incompatible with stating, as Gaunilo did a few lines earlier, that sometimes (discourse about) unreal things can be *understood*. Furthermore, Anselm fails to realize that Gaunilo at this stage is not *advocating* the definition but is simply hypothesizing about a move Anselm might want to make, and about the consequences thereof.

But how do we know that Anselm's reading is wrong? Surely, it may be contended, *he* better than *we* could make sense of Gaunilo's Latin; *he* better than *we* knew how to read the pericope beginning with "*Nisi forte*" (S I, 125:17). Nonetheless, that Anselm is mistaken is clear. In the first place, we may disqualify the a priori principle that Anselm must have interpreted the passage rightly simply because he understood the Latin of his day better than we do; for the correct interpretation of Gaunilo does not depend merely upon familiarity with ecclesiastical Latin of the eleventh century. It depends as well upon detecting the structure of an argument. And at this perhaps we today excel Anselm (as, for that matter, someone today might also surpass him in the knowledge of eleventh-century ecclesiastical Latin). Secondly, if there is any a priori principle involved, it is the a priori improbability that Gaunilo contradicted himself within the scope of a few lines. Any such apparent contradiction should lead us to question whether we are correctly interpreting his words. For such an apparent contradiction casts a *prima facie* doubt upon the interpretation and (in our case) the translation. All other things being equal, we are obliged to choose the interpretation which makes sense out of the passage since we recognize from the remainder of the treatise that Gaunilo was too clever to write so incoherently as Anselm's interpretation requires.

A further subtlety now arises. Given Anselm's construal of the definition of "*intelligere*" in *On Behalf of the Fool* 2, what does he take to be the relationship between this definition and Gaunilo's point in Section 7 to the effect that "properly speaking, unrealities cannot be understood?" At first it might be supposed that Anselm regarded this statement as just the obverse side of the inconsistency which he attributed to Section 2. For although, on his reading, the definition in Section 2 is *consistent* with the statement in Section 7, that statement itself is *inconsistent* with the assertion in Section 2 that sometimes unreal things *can* be understood. Nonetheless, since Anselm never mentions this additional inconsistency, we must be cautious about inferring that he believed there was one.[14] Indeed, had he held this view, it would have been easy for him to point out that in Section 7 Gaunilo need not have made an issue of our not being able to understand *God* not to exist; for nothing at all (let alone God) would be able to be understood not to exist, since the expression "understood not to exist" would be self-contradictory (given Anselm's construal of Gaunilo's definition of "understand").

Accordingly, it begins to appear more likely that Anselm realized something which present-day commentators seem to have overlooked, viz., that Gaunilo's point of view changes in the middle of Section 7,[15] where he begins speaking for himself, the believing monk, and stops speaking on behalf of the Fool, as he had been doing up to then. In Section 7 he writes: "I understand indubitably that that being which is supreme, viz., God, exists and cannot fail to exist." Obviously he is not speaking for the Fool. Rather, he is remarking: the Fool thinks a proposition which you and I, Anselm, regard as a falsehood, viz., that God does not exist; consequently, the Fool cannot *understand* this falsehood because, strictly speaking, only truths can be understood. So Gaunilo at this stage is identifying with Anselm's point of view and recommending a precision which he feels Anselm had neglected. Because of this shift in viewpoint Gaunilo's statement in Section 7 is not viciously inconsistent with the passage in Section 2 (i.e., there is no *self*-contradiction). Anselm probably realized this and thus did not accuse Gaunilo of a double inconsistency. Moreover, at the beginning of his *Reply* he refers to the writer of *On Behalf of the Fool* as a believing Christian even though he admits to not knowing who the author is. (Anselm did not so much as know Gaunilo's name.)[16] Thus, that Gaunilo was a believer Anselm could only have learned from Sections 7 and 8. Of course, someone might protest that Section 8 by itself is sufficient to reveal that Gaunilo was a Christian, and that therefore Anselm still might have overlooked the switch in viewpoint in Section 7. But such a protest would be gratuitous given the fact that Anselm does not charge Gaunilo with an inconsistency between Sections 2 and 7.

2. *Systematization of Anselm's text*. For all the fault that Anselm finds with Gaunilo, he nonetheless regards him as raising criticisms which others might also be prone to espouse. Therefore, he requests that Gaunilo's attack, together with his own rebuttal, be appended to future transcriptions of the *Proslogion*.[17] Moreover, his *Reply* parcels Gaunilo's criticisms into two groups: those which are regarded as having merit and those which are not.[18] This judgment about the merit, or force, of Gaunilo's objections determines the order of Anselm's *Reply* and is the reason for his not dealing with the objections in the order they were presented. Moreover, any attempt to rearrange the order of the *Reply*[19] will eclipse Anselm's weighting of both Gaunilo's objections and his own defenses. For instance, one reason for the brevity of the response (in Section 8) about the artist and the painting is Anselm's appraisal of the relative meritlessness of Gaunilo's criticism. This evaluation is readily evident from the fact that Anselm places it after Section 4; but this placing is lost sight of when the text of the *Reply* is broken up in order to map it over against *On Behalf of the Fool*.

One justification proffered for this truncation is that the *Reply* is but "a series of notes which Anselm put together without much attention to overall unity or development."[20] But this claim is especially weak for a number of reasons. First, it goes counter to Anselm's assertion that he did impose some order on this work, dealing with issues of two kinds — the more and the less weighty, as we said. Secondly, we know from Anselm's other works that he was not accustomed to let his imperfect writings be transcribed. He complains, for instance, about monks who had prematurely copied and set into circulation earlier drafts of *De Incarnatione* and the *Cur Deus Homo*.[21] Since his practice was to release a work only after he was satisfied with it, and since he requested that the *Reply* be copied together with the *Proslogion* and *On Behalf of the Fool*, we may conclude that it was neither something he threw together from notes nor simply a series of notes. Thirdly, he may have been careless about attending to Gaunilo's objections, but it does not follow that he was inattentive to the structure he gave the *Reply*. If anything, his oversights of Gaunilo's points occurred because he was "too preoccupied" with unfolding more fully his own viewpoint. On the whole, it seems to me, his reasoning in the *Reply* does not move haphazardly. Fourthly, extreme care must be exercised in dividing up Anselm's sequences, if this dividing is going to be done. For example, it *is* possible without obvious distortion to separate the first half of *Reply* 3 from the second half,[22] which begins right after Anselm's ironic comment about finding the lost island and making Gaunilo a present of it. Yet, in doing so, some continuity is lost. For at the end of *Reply* 2 Anselm is supporting his inference in *Proslogion* 2 that N must exist in reality as well as in the understanding. He turns aside for a moment to consider Gaunilo's counterargument with its suggestion that the reasoning of *Proslogion* 2 is faulty. Then, having dismissed the example by intimating that it is not analogous to the argument in *Proslogion* 2,[23] he goes on to show, as in *Proslogion* 3, that N exists *so* really that it cannot be thought not to exist. So although severing these passages may not be wrong, it is, to be sure, not obviously helpful.

Furthermore, what legitimate reason could there be for putting S I, 132: 10–21 immediately before 132: 3–9, as do J. Hick and A. McGill on p. 13 (*The Many-faced Argument*), thus reversing Anselm's order? This reversal would be acceptable only if thereby some clarity were gained — as it is not. Also, S I, 131: 6–11 is no more a reply to Gaunilo's 129:1–10 than to his 127:25–128:13. Worst of all, Hick and McGill fragment and restructure not only Anselm's *Reply*, which they deem but a series of notes; but they also do the same thing with Gaunilo's *On Behalf of the Fool*, even though they do not regard it as a collection of notes! Their procedure is utterly uncalled for; indeed, it even miscasts the entire debate with Anselm. For instance, they place next to last what Gaunilo placed first (viz., S I, 125:6–13). Thus, Gaunilo's initial misstatement and misapprehension of the logic of Anselm's argument — a misstatement which governs the rest of his short treatise — is lost sight of at the outset. This misstatement was so serious that it provoked Anselm's strong response at the beginning of his *Reply*. In fact, Anselm's three attempts in Section 1 (S I, 131:1–17) to reformulate the statement of his argument come in direct response to Gaunilo's misstatement in his, Gaunilo's, Section 1. Yet, Hick and McGill do not even bring these two sections together, let alone put them at the beginning!

Then too, Hick and McGill take Section 2 of Gaunilo's work and divide it in such way as to dissipate the strength of his reasoning. That is, we have noted previously how Gaunilo urges that three consequences would follow if Anselm were to conflate "understanding" with "understanding to exist" in the case of understanding N. Now, Hick and McGill simply *elide* the second consequence and move it elsewhere in order to mesh it conveniently with a section of Anselm's response[24] which, on their method, they have to do something with. This elision weakens the force of Gaunilo's reasoning and is editorially problematical. By their dubious method Hick and McGill betray that, like Anselm, they too have difficulty following Gaunilo's argument.

3. *Intelligere and intellectus*. It is necessary now to clarify Anselm's use of "*intelligere*" and "*intellectus*." According to McGill there is "little evidence that the word *intellectus* ever suggested to Anselm, as it does to us, an organ (such as the mind) or a faculty (such as the intellect). It was chiefly the noun form of the verb *intelligere* and signified the *act* of understanding."[25] Yet, it seems to me that in the present context Anselm has four different uses of "*intellectus*": to indicate (1) an act of understanding and (2) a capability, power, or faculty of the soul; and to indicate (3) intelligence and (4) a respect. The first two distinctions occur in *Reply to Gaunilo* 2 (S I, 132:19–20): "What is understood [*intelligitur*: act of understanding] is understood by the understanding [*in intellectu*: a capability of the soul] and is thereby in the understanding [*in intellectu*: a manner of speaking which generally but not necessarily indicates for Anselm the act of understanding]." Now, Anselm comments immediately beforehand: "What is thought is thought by thinking; and what is thought by thinking is thereby in our thinking." Is he here suggesting that *thought* is a faculty, and if not then why should his very next statement be construed as indicating that understanding is a faculty?, it might be asked. For Anselm, as for Augustine, man has a *rational* faculty which belongs to the soul. This rational faculty accounts for man's capacity to think rationally, to understand. So, in some contexts, whether Anselm

speaks of rationality (*rationalitas*) or understanding (*intellectus*) or thinking (*cogitatio*), he is regarding these as alternative designations for the same faculty of soul. Accordingly, in *Monologion* 23 he comments that "*intellectus* is there in the soul where *rationalitas* is" — although "there" and "where" are not being used as spatial locators (S I, 41:28–29).

A third meaning of "*intellectus*" occurs at S I, 132:12–13 (*Reply to Gaunilo* 2), where Anselm states that anyone who does not understand the description "N" has little or no *intellectus* — i.e., intelligence.[26] To borrow a terminology from *De Libertate* and *De Concordia*, such a person would have the instrument, or faculty, (*instrumentum*) of understanding but either would not be able to use (*uti*) this instrument adequately or else would have a defective instrument (as one might have defective vision). Anselm does not elaborate the point. Still, his view is clear: a fool might not have much intelligence (*intellectus*), but he must have the faculty of *intellectus*; otherwise he would not be a man, and therefore not a fool (nonrational animals are not fools).

The fourth meaning of "*intellectus*" has caused the most difficulty — especially to English translators of Anselm's Latin. In particular, the phrase "*in nullo intellectu*" has not made sense in English translations. For instance, at S I, 132:29–30 (*Reply to Gaunilo* 2) Anselm writes: "*Sed utique quo maius cogitari potest, in nullo intellectu est quo maius cogitari non possit.*" Charlesworth translates this as: "But surely 'that-than-which-a-greater-*can*-be-thought' is not for any mind [the same as] 'that-than-which-a-greater-*cannot*-be-thought'." McGill has: "But certainly that than which a greater *can* be conceived does not stand in relation to any understanding as 'that than which a greater *cannot* be conceived.' " And Wolter puts: "But surely in no intellect . . ." which is comparable to Deane's "in no understanding."[27] Yet a careful look at S I, 136:28–137:3 makes clear that "*intellectus*" in the phrase "*in nullo intellectu*" is sometimes an alternative for "*nullatenus intelligitur*" and "*nullo modo intelligitur*." So what Anselm means is best translated in S I, 132:29–30 as: "But surely that than which a greater cannot be thought is in no sense (or: in no respect) that than which a greater can be thought." And the line of reasoning continues: "Does it not follow, therefore, that if that than which a greater cannot be thought is at all in the understanding [i.e., is even partially understood], then it does not exist in the understanding alone?''

Since Anselm does not attempt to develop a vocabulary of technical Latin, we must be alert to his use of the one word ''*intellectus*'' in several different ways. In places he can interchange ''*intellectus*'' with ''*cogitatio*''[28] or ''*scire*''[29] or ''*sensus*,''[30] just as he interchanges ''*oratio*'' with ''*propositio*'' in *De Veritate* 2, and ''*essentia*'' with ''*existentia*'' in the *Philosophical Fragments*[31] or with ''*natura*'' in *Monologion* 4 (S I, 17:17–18) — though not supposing that these interchangeable terms have the same meanings in most contexts. Therefore, in translating Anselm's expressions we must avoid frozen renderings — i.e., avoid mechanically using the same English word to translate a given Latin word wherever it occurs. Thus, sometimes ''*intelligere*'' will come into English better as ''to know,'' ''to judge,'' ''to comprehend,'' ''to discern,'' or ''to think'' than as ''to understand.'' In *Proslogion* 2 Anselm means by ''*intelligere rem esse*'' to *judge* that the object exists. And at S I, 131:8 the expression ''*nec actu nec intellectu*'' is best rendered as ''neither actually nor *conceivably*.''[32] Failure to recognize the ''flexibility'' of Anselm's terminology will lead to confused and confusing translations. And there will be danger not only of translating the same Latin word by the same English word where this should not be done,[33] but also of translating two different Latin words by two different English words, where only one word is required.[34]

4. *Thinking secundum rem and thinking secundum vocem*. In *Proslogion* 4 Anselm distinguishes between two different ways of thinking an object: ''In one sense an object is thought when the word signifying it is thought, and in another when what the object is is understood.''[35]

> Thus, in the first sense but not at all in the second, God can be thought not to exist. Indeed, no one who understands what God is can think that God does not exist, even though he says these words [viz., ''God does not exist''] in his heart either meaninglessly or else bizarrely. For God is that than which a greater cannot be thought. Anyone who comprehends this [description], surely understands that this being [than which a greater cannot be thought] so exists that it cannot even conceivably not exist. Therefore, anyone who understands that God is such [a being] cannot think that He does not exist.

Now, Anselm never elucidates what, precisely, is involved in thinking an object by merely thinking the word which signifies it. Even at the end of *Reply to Gaunilo* 4 all he does is refer again to the above passage in *Proslogion* 4, calling it sufficient.[36] Apparently, in *Proslogion* 4 he meant that one can either conceive of God according to a correct description (e.g., the description "N" and the predicates licensed by "N"), or else one can think the word "God" either according to an incorrect signification or according to no signification (i.e., one thinks the word but does not know what the word signifies). In the latter case, one can think (and say) something inconsistent without realizing it to be inconsistent; for one has grasped a signification incorrectly.

For his part, Gaunilo is more explicit about thinking *secundum rem veram* and *secundum vocem*.[37]

> Although I can think of a non-existent man by reference to a real thing known to me, I cannot at all think of this thing [which is greater than all others] except only with respect to the verbal expression. And with respect only to a verbal expression a real thing can scarcely, if at all, be thought of. For when one thinks with respect to a mere verbal expression, he thinks not so much the verbal expression itself (i.e., not so much the sound of the letters or the syllables), which assuredly is a real thing, as he does the signification of the expression that is heard. Yet, [the signification is] not [thought] in the manner of one who knows what is usually signified by the expression — i.e., one who thinks in accordance with the thing, whether it is real or exists in thought alone. Rather, [the signification is thought] in the manner of one who does not know what is usually signified by the verbal expression but who (1) thinks only according to the movement of the mind brought about by hearing this expression and who (2) has difficulty in representing to himself the signification of what he has heard. (But it would be surprising if he could ever [in this manner discern] what the thing is.) So, then, it is still evident that this is the only way this thing is in my understanding when I hear and understand someone who says that there is something greater than all others that can be thought.

So Gaunilo, speaking for the Fool, supposes that what God is cannot be thought. And Anselm takes the trouble in *Reply* 8 to show him how God's nature can be thought without taking the trouble in *Reply* 4 to clarify how God's nonexistence can be thought.

Here we must notice two additional points. First, in *Reply* 8 Anselm's method of "analogically" conceiving God's nature is altogether different from the *via negativa* of John Scotus Erigena and Pseudo-Dionysius, who were willing to say only that God is more than goodness and is the cause of goodness.[38] Secondly, what Anselm means by his statement that the *Proslogion* develops *unum argumentum*[39] is that it proceeds to unfold a *single line of reasoning* — not that there is only one major argument, or argument-form. Of course, for him the major argument for God's existence is that of *Proslogion* 2.[40] He regards *Proslogion* 3 not as introducing a further such argument but rather as indicating (once *Proslogion* 2 has established the fact of God's existence) how really and certainly God exists. Nevertheless, the arguments of Chapters 2 and 3, together with the deductions he makes about God's attributes beginning with Chapter 5, are all aspects of the one line of reasoning. In last analysis, "*unum argumentum*" indicates all that is derivable from the formula "N." "For the significance of this utterance ["N"] contains so much force that what is spoken of is, by the very fact that it is understood or thought, necessarily proved really to exist and to be whatever ought to be believed about the Divine Substance."[41] Accordingly, even the reformulations presented in *Reply* 1 are variants of the single line of reasoning. Hence, the question of whether Anselm has one, two, three, four, or more different versions of the ontological argument in the *Proslogion* (and the *Reply*) is not settled by referring to the phrase "*unum argumentum*" and commenting that Anselm intended to be setting forth only one argument for God's existence. For even aside from the fact that a philosopher might *intend* to formulate only a single argument but in fact word his formulation in such way that there were really two (or more) distinct arguments, Anselm never claimed to have only *one* argument. He claimed only that the various arguments were derivable in accordance with a *single* unique description. Indeed, someone might even extend this single line of reasoning by observing that the description "N" entails the descriptions "*ens perfectissimum*," "*ens realissimum*," and "*ens necessarium*," and develop new ontological arguments à la Gottfried W. von Leibniz, Christian Wolff, and Immanuel Kant, whose formulations are different from Anselm's.[42]

5. *Three arguments from Reply 1*. Let us now look closely[43] at the three arguments in S I, 131:1–17.

5.1. The first of these, S I, 131:1–5, is formulable as:

(1) For any object x, if x can be thought to exist and yet x does not exist, then x can be thought to begin to exist. (premise)

So: (2) If N can be thought to exist and yet N does not exist, then N can be thought to begin to exist. (instance of (1))

But: (3) It is not the case that N can be thought to begin to exist.

(a) What exists without beginning is greater than what exists through a beginning. (presupposition)

Assume: (b) N can be thought to begin to exist.

Then: (c) N can be thought to be greater than it is. (impossible)

So: (d) It is not the case that N can be thought to begin to exist.

So: (4) It is not the case that N can be thought to exist and yet does not exist. (2) (3)

Thus: (5) If N can be thought to exist, it must be the case that N does exist. (4)

It is important to recognize that in the last step "*Si ergo cogitari potest esse*, *ex necessitate est*" is to be read as "Therefore, if it [N] can be thought to exist, it is necessary that it exist" instead of as "Therefore, if it [N] can be thought to exist, it exists necessarily." That is, the necessity applies to the inference not to the quality of existence (cf. S I, 135:30-31); hence, Anselm might equally have expressed the consequent as "Then, it must follow that N exists."[44] Now, this sentence, so construed and taken together with the one immediately preceding it, suggests that Anselm made use of the rule $\sim (p \cdot \sim q) \equiv (p \supset q)$, although he nowhere states this rule explicitly, and although what he actually says warrants only $\sim (p \cdot \sim q) \supset (p \supset q)$.

5.2. The next section in the Schmitt text (S I, 131:6–11) must be viewed, I think, as containing two interlinking arguments, some of whose premises are suppressed. As the argument is presented it is not in good logical form. For it is not clear how the stated premises could warrant the conclusion that N is *not able not to exist*. Yet, Anselm has told the reader enough to allow him to supply the missing premises and to combine them with the stated premises so that jointly they do entail the desired conclusion. This can be accomplished in two parts.

A. (1) If anything can be thought but does not exist, then if it were to exist, it would be able (either actually or conceivably) not to exist. (premise)

So: (2) If N can be thought but N does not exist, then if N were to exist, N would be able (either actually or conceivably) not to exist. (instance of (1))

But: (3) It is not the case that if N were to exist, N would be able (either actually or conceivably) not to exist.
- (a) What is not able (either actually or conceivably) not to exist is greater than what is able (either actually or conceivably) not to exist. (presupposition)
- (b) If if N were to exist N were able (either actually or conceivably) not to exist, then N could be thought to be greater than it is.

But: (c) It is not the case that N can be thought to be greater than it is.

Thus: (d) It is not the case that if N were to exist N would be able (either actually or conceivably) not to exist.

Thus: (4) It is not the case that N can be thought but N does not exist. (2) (3)

So: (5) If N can be thought, N exists. (4)

B. (1) If N can be thought, then N exists. (conclusion of A)

(2) If N exists, then N is not able not to exist.
- (a) What is not able not to exist is greater than what is able not to exist. (presupposition)
- (b) If N exists but N is able not to exist, then N can be thought to be greater than it is.

But: (c) It is not the case that N can be thought to be greater than it is.

Thus: (d) It is not the case that N exists and N is able not to exist.

Thus: (e) If N exists, N is not able not to exist.

So: (3) If N can be thought, then N is not able not to exist. (1) (2)

For Gaunilo's sake as well as for ours Anselm ought to have formulated his argument more explicitly. Still, he formulated it fully enough to allow the reader to detect its structure and validity.

5.3. A third argument begins at S I, 131:12 (and it would have been helpful had Schmitt placed a new paragraph at this point in the Latin text):

(1) If anything can be thought and does not exist, then if it were to exist it would not be N (because it would be able not to exist. Cf. Argument 2, steps A,1 and A,3.) (premise)

Thus: (2) If N can be thought and N does not exist, then if it were to exist it would not be N. (instance of (1))

Assume: (3) N can be thought and N does not exist.

Then: (4) If N were to exist N would not be N — an impossible hypothetical. (2) (3)

Hence: (5) It is not the case that N can be thought and N does not exist. (3) (4)

So: (6) If N can be thought, N exists. (5)

As just presented, these premises have a slightly different order from their order in the text;[45] yet this new order reveals the movement of the argument slightly better. What is stated above as the third premise is really Anselm's opening sentence, which says literally: "Let us suppose that it [N] does not exist if it can be even thought." Now, it would be *wrong* to construe the logical form of this proposition as $p \supset \sim q$. For the very next sentence (following the order of the text) states: "Whatever can be thought and yet does not exist would not, if it were to exist, be that than which a greater cannot be thought." Without doubt, Anselm regards the proposition expressed by the opening sentence as a substitution-instance of the proposition expressed by the second sentence. To make this clear to the reader, one is obliged to translate Anselm's meaning rather than his exact words. And the meaning of his opening sentence is $p \cdot \sim q$: "Let us suppose that N can be thought and yet does not exist."

6. *Cogitare and cogitare esse*. In looking back on Argument 1 and Argument 2, we notice a shift from "If N can be thought to exist" to "If N can be even thought."[46] What is the significance of this switch? Is Anselm making some important *epistemological* or *logical* point? I do not think so. Let it be acknowledged that he accepted a distinction between (1) thinking of something (i.e., conceiving or imagining it) and (2) thinking (i.e., believing, judging, understanding, or knowing) it to exist.[47] Indeed, if (à la *Proslogion* 2) one can understand something without understanding (judging) it to exist, then one can also *think* something without *thinking* it to exist — since understanding is a form of thinking, on Anselm's view as well as on ours. But here "thinking" is being used equivocally to mean that one can *conceive* something without *judging* it to exist. Yet, in the two arguments under discussion "thinking" is being used univocally to stand for "conceiving."

Anselm obviously regards "conceiving x" and "conceiving x to exist" as having different meanings. For were they synonymous the expression "conceiving x not to exist" would be, for every x, self-contradictory — a view foreign to Anselm. Yet, it seems that he did assume an extensional equivalence such that

x can be thought if and only if x can be thought to exist.

In *Proslogion* 2 this assumption allows him to infer "N can be thought to exist in reality" from "N is in the understanding."[48]

Now, although there is a semantical difference between "conceiving x" and "conceiving x to exist," still when Anselm switches from the one expression to the other in *Reply* 1, he is not leaning upon this semantical difference in order to make any epistemological or logical point. He is simply exhibiting two different arguments — each of which has a valid form irrespective of which expression is used. Moreover, the truth or falsity of the premises in which these phrases occur would remain unaffected by completely substituting the one expression for the other. So, then, in the process of exhibiting a second argument, Anselm indicates that, should we prefer, we can simplify "if N can be thought to exist" to "if N can be thought," for even the premise thus simplified will suffice for the logic of his argument.

7. *Relation between Proslogion 2 and the Reply*. There is, of course, a relationship between the argument of *Proslogion* 2 and the three arguments of *Reply* 1. But we must be careful about specifying this relationship. In *Proslogion* 2 Anselm's proof runs:[49]

(1) We properly conceive of God as N. (premise)
(2) We understand what the words "N" describe. (premise)
(3) Whatever is understood is in the understanding. (premise)
Hence: (4) N exists in the understanding. (2) (3)
(5) Either N exists in the understanding without existing in reality or else N exists both in the understanding and in reality. (premise)
Assume: (6) N exists in the understanding without existing in reality.
(a) N can be thought to exist in reality.
(b) For N, existing in the understanding and in reality is greater than existing only in the understanding.
Hence: (c) N can be thought to be greater than it is (and so N is that than which a greater *can* be thought). (impossible)
So: (7) N exists both in the understanding and in reality. (4) (5) (6) (c)

In this formulation *1* is an a priori description, *2* is a fact, and *6, b* is a presupposition. Now, both the main assumption in *6* and the steps *6,a&b* are elicited from Anselm's statement:

(S): For if it [N] were merely in the understanding, it could be thought to exist also in reality — which is greater.

The most natural interpretation of this sentence is to construe "which is greater" as indicating that N would be greater if it existed in reality as well as existing in the understanding. So what Anselm means by *S* can be restated:

> (S′): If N were only in the understanding, N could be thought to exist also in reality, and for N to exist in reality would be greater than for N to exist only in the understanding.

Accordingly, Anselm assumes that for N existence is a perfection. But does he assume that for conceivable objects other than N existence is also a perfection? We do not definitely know. Certainly in *On Behalf of the Fool* 1 Gaunilo attributes to Anselm this further assumption; and Anselm does not quarrel with the ascription. But this fact does not by itself prove (though it does warrant the presumption) that Gaunilo's construal was correct. For Anselm's argument to be valid no assumption stronger than *6,b* is required. Possibly, he might want to maintain that for something like an island existence is not a *perfection* (i.e., a great-making property), though it would be a *property* (*simpliciter*). For instance, in *Monologion* 15 he states that *being composed of gold* is a property which is a perfection for a metal but not for a man (e.g., not for King Midas' daughter). So some properties may be perfections for some kinds of things but not for other kinds of things. Still, it is hard to see what basis Anselm could have for allowing that existence is a perfection in the case of N but disallowing it in the case of other conceivable objects. For unlike the property of *being composed of gold*, the "property" of *existing* never detracts from any perfection which an object has. If, therefore, it is a perfection for any object, it must be a perfection for every object. My own sense of the matter is that Anselm recognized this implication[50] and in fact did accept the generalized premise

> (P): For any object x, if x exists in the understanding and in reality, then x is greater than if x exists only in the understanding.

I would imagine that he felt no more compunction about *P* than about the generalized premise.

> (Q): Being unable to be thought not to exist is greater than being able to be thought not to exist.

At any rate, whether Anselm presupposed *P* or *6,b* he has a valid argument in *Proslogion* 2.[51]

We are now in a position to notice the difference between *Proslogion* 2 and *Reply* 1. The former presupposes that existing in reality is greater than existing only in the understanding and not existing in reality. The latter presupposes that existing without a beginning is greater than existing with a beginning (Argument 1), and that not being able not to exist is greater than being able not to exist (Arguments 2 & 3). These differences have often been noted before and would not be worth repeating here were it not for the recent attempt to deny them. Thus, La Croix supposes that in *Proslogion* 2, *S* must be unpacked as:[52]

(a) If N exists only in the understanding, then N does not exist in reality.
(b) If N does not exist in reality, then N can fail to exist in reality.
(c) If N can fail to exist in reality, then N can be thought not to exist in reality.[53]
(d) If N can be thought not to exist in reality and N can be thought to exist in reality, then N can be thought to be greater.
(e) N can be thought to exist in reality.
(f) It is false that N can be thought to be greater than it is.

Now, *b* - *f*, La Croix claims, constitute Anselm's single argument-form (p. 124). But it seems to me that if there is such a form, it is better expressed as

(F): For any predicate x such that it is greater to be x than not to be x, if N were not x (e.g., existent, unable to be thought not to exist, omnipotent, etc.), then N would be not-N, for N could be thought to be greater than it is; but N cannot be thought to be greater than it is; therefore, N is x.[54]

This formula differs slightly from La Croix's. First, it recognizes explicitly that Anselm is committed to the presuppositions that

(i): to exist (in reality) is, in itself, better than not to exist (in reality)

and (ii): to be unable to be thought not to exist is, in itself, better than to be able to be thought not to exist

and recognizes that these enter into his reasoning. Secondly, the formula does not have to be unpacked by reference to *Reply* 5. Thirdly, it makes room for the presence of an independently valid argument in *Proslogion* 2. And finally, it allows that in *Reply* 1 Anselm develops new argument-forms — i.e., forms which do more than simply explicate *F*.

In one respect, then, Malcolm and Hartshorne are right about *Proslogion* 2 and its relation to the *Reply*. For they realize that *Proslogion* 2 constitutes for Anselm an "independent" argument for the existence of N, or God, and that in *Reply* 1 Anselm is opening up new arguments to prove the same conclusion (though he goes on in *Reply* 2 to reiterate the proof contained in *Proslogion* 2).

8. *Conclusion*. In *Anselm's Discovery* Hartshorne speaks disparagingly of the "Gaunilo tradition," or "Gaunilo legend"[55] — meaning the tradition of "mistaken" objections leveled by Gaunilo against Anselm. Hartshorne goes so far as to quote Koyré's verdict: "Gaunilo seems to have understood the corrections which Saint Anselm addressed to him; at least, he did not reply."[56]

Perhaps Hartshorne and Koyré are wrong. Perhaps there was simply too much mutual confusion for the debate to continue profitably. Now that some of these confusions have been cleared up, we ourselves will be in a better position to evaluate Anselm's response and to decide whether any substantive objections remain for the Gaunilo-tradition, or whether this tradition must succumb to the soundness of at least one reformulation of the ontological proof.

CHAPTER V

SOME ALLEGED METAPHYSICAL AND PSYCHOLOGICAL ASPECTS OF THE ONTOLOGICAL ARGUMENT

Among the many claims made regarding the ontological argument, two stand out as especially in need of analysis. The first is metaphysical: that God's greatness, not His excellence, is the basis of the argument in *Proslogion* 2.[1] The second is psychological: that individual guilt-preoccupation is an essential component in the consciousness which perceives the ontological argument as convincing.[2] In this chapter I shall examine these claims successively and shall comment upon the difference between exegesis and eisogesis.

I

1.1. In an article entitled " 'Greatness' in Anselm's Ontological Argument," R. Brecher writes:

> It is all too often assumed that Anselm used the words 'greater', 'better', and even 'more perfect' interchangeably in his *Proslogion*. I contend that this assumption is based on an insufficiently careful reading of the text, and on insufficient consideration of Anselm's metaphysical background.[3]

Brecher goes on to notice that in *Proslogion* 2–4 "*maius*" occurs fifteen times, whereas "*melius*" occurs only once, viz., in Chapter 3. "God's being *melius* follows from his being the supreme *bonum*," Brecher tells us. "His being the supreme good follows from the fact that every good exists through him, since he made everything else from nothing. And it is because he is the creator, the ground of all being, that he is 'that than whom nothing greater can be thought'. This distinction between God's ontological supremacy and his goodness is retained throughout the *Proslogion*."[4]

Brecher proceeds to make incidental comments about Chapters 9, 13, 15, 18, 22, and 23. These comments aim at reinforcing the claim that Anselm systematically distinguishes between "*maius*" and "*melius*" in the *Proslogion*. Thus, concludes Brecher, by "*maius*" — but not by "*melius*"[5] — Anselm means "ontologically greater."[6] And Brecher construes "ontologically greater" in terms of the notion of degrees of existence[7] — eliciting this construal from *Monologion* 31 in conjunction with the last few sentences of *Proslogion* 3.

Finally, Brecher views Anselm's language in the *Monologion* as so Platonic that "the Theory of Forms springs to mind again in the next paragraph, where Anselm tells us that 'every created being exists in so much the greater degree, or is so much the more excellent, the more like it is to what exists supremely, and is supremely great.''[8] The Theory of Forms — having sprung into Brecher's mind — suggests to him Gregory Vlastos' interpretation of Plato's doctrine of degrees of reality. For in a well-known article[9] Vlastos maintains that, for Plato, the Forms are in two respects more real than are particulars: They are cognitively more reliable, and they are more valuable. Brecher applies this interpretation to Anselm's notion of greatness and thereby "shows" the defect of Gaunilo's counter-example of the lost island. For "the phrase 'an island, than which *nothing* greater can be thought' is quite absurd, since there could not possibly be any such island. Something more cognitively reliable and valuable than any possible island can always be conceived."[10]

1.2. At first glance, Brecher's interpretation seems plausible. For, after all, Anselm uses two different words — "*maius*" and "*melius*." So should we not quite naturally expect that he "was generally careful to distinguish between them"?[11] And must we not chide Hartshorne and Malcolm, and a host of others, who so readily equate the notion of greatness with the notion of perfection? Have not Hartshorne and Malcolm failed to understand the meaning of the formula "that than which nothing *greater* can be thought"? And has not their failure been the result of an "insufficient consideration of Anselm's metaphysical background," as well as the result of "an insufficiently careful reading of the text"?

These are serious charges for Brecher to make. Indeed, if he is correct, then Hartshorne's exposition of a "logic of perfection" veers away from Anselm, at the very beginning, by conflating two notions which Anselm was generally careful to distinguish. On the other hand, perhaps Brecher moves too hastily to his conclusion. Perhaps he himself has not examined all the texts. As a matter of fact, a careful scrutiny of the texts will show, I submit, that Brecher is the one who is wrong and that interpreters such as Hartshorne and Malcolm can be vindicated.

1.2.1. To begin with, Brecher's survey of the *Proslogion* altogether fails to mention that in two different chapters (*Proslogion* 14 and 18) Anselm uses the phrase "*quo nihil melius cogitari potest*."[12] (And this phrase seems to be a straightforward substitution for "*quo nihil maius cogitari potest*.") Strangely, Brecher completely by-passes Chapter 14 in his rehearsal of Anselm's use of "*melius*." And when he mentions Chapter 18, he ignores mentioning the occurrence of the formula. Instead, he comments:

> In Ch. 18, Anselm says He [*sic*] is life, wisdom, truth, goodness, blessedness, eternity, and every true good — but not that he [*sic*] is greatness. God's greatness is in a different class from his virtues . . . .[13]

But the use of this quotation is misguided. For although Anselm does not in *Proslogion* 18 include greatness in the list of God's *perfections* — a better word than Brecher's word "virtues" — he does include it at the end of *Monologion* 16:

> But obviously the Supreme Nature is supremely whatever good thing it is. Therefore, the Supreme Nature is the Supreme Being, Supreme Life, Supreme Reason, Supreme Security, Supreme Justice, Supreme Wisdom, Supreme Truth, Supreme Goodness, Supreme Greatness, Supreme Beauty, Supreme Immortality, Supreme Incorruptibility, Supreme Immutability, Supreme Beatitude, Supreme Eternity, Supreme Power, Supreme Unity.

Moreover, at the beginning of *Monologion* 17 Anselm again refers to the items on this list as *goods*. Accordingly, when he writes in *Proslogion* 18 "Certainly You are life, wisdom, truth, goodness, blessedness, eternity — You are every true good," we may understand greatness to be among the true goods. So Anselm does *not* systematically classify greatness differently from eternity and truth and wisdom and goodness, etc. Indeed, the passage in *Monologion* 16, together with the fact that Anselm uses both the expression "*quo nihil melius cogitari potest*" and the expression "*quo nihil maius cogitari potest*," evidences that he regards greatness as a perfection, as a good. I would imagine that in *Proslogion* 5 and 18, and in *Reply to Gaunilo* 10, Anselm omits "greatness" from his list for the same reason that he omits "beauty," "immortality," "incorruptibility," etc.: viz., in order to abbreviate what would otherwise be a very long ennumeration.

1.2.2. But there is even more definitive evidence against Brecher's interpretation. For in *Proslogion* 18, where Anselm writes "*quo nihil melius cogitari potest*," the topic of discussion is the indivisibility of God:

> Whatever is composed of parts is not absolutely one but is in a way many and is different from itself and can be divided either actually or conceivably. But these consequences are foreign to You, than whom nothing *better* can be thought.

And this same topic recurs in *De Incarnatione* 4, where now Anselm uses "*maius*":

> If [my opponent] is one of those modern dialecticians who believe that nothing exists except what they can imagine, and if he does not think there to be anything in which there are no parts, at least he will not deny understanding that if there were something which could neither actually nor conceivably be divided, it would be *greater* than something which can be divided at least conceivably.

Similarly, in *Reply to Gaunilo* 1, Anselm uses the word "*maius*" in alluding to the doctrine that what exists as a whole everywhere and at once is greater than what has temporal or spatial parts.

So when we compare these three passages, we see that Anselm's use of "*melius*" in *Proslogion* 18 is no different from his use of "*maius*"[14] in *De Incarnatione* 4 and *Reply to Gaunilo* 1.

1.2.3. Furthermore, when Anselm comes to instruct Gaunilo on how he can conceive of that than which a *greater* cannot be thought, he does so in terms of conceiving of a hierarchy of *goods*.[15] What exists without end is *better* than what is limited by an end, and thus the former is *greater* than the latter. Brecher himself cites this passage as a counter-example to his own interpretation. But he remarks:

> Since this is the sole example of such a possible failure [to observe the distinction between goodness and greatness] throughout his *Reply*, and since there are grounds for holding that even here the confusion is more apparent than real, I do not think it seriously damaging to the argument. Moreover,

> Anselm's reply to the "Lost Island" counter-example does, as we shall see, tend to confirm it.[16]

Now, this response is bizarre. For this "sole example of a possible failure" is in fact a striking instance of an actual interchange of the notions of goodness and greatness. This example must be given much weight precisely because it is Anselm's *paradigm* of how to conceive of greater and lesser beings — i.e., of more and less perfect beings. Then too, Brecher never presents the alleged "grounds for holding that even here the confusion is more apparent than real." And we cannot help wondering what these might be. Finally, the case of the Lost Island will support Brecher's argument only if "greater" means "cognitively more reliable" or "more valuable." But, as we shall soon see, there is no reason to believe that Anselm's argument trades upon these meanings.

1.2.4. It begins to look as if Brecher's interpretation were tendentious. When he began his article with statistics about the frequency with which Anselm uses "*maius*" and "*melius*" in *Proslogion* 2–4, we received the impression that he had carefully surveyed the use of these words throughout the *Proslogion*. We were therefore surprised to notice both his subsequent failure to mention the phrase "*quo nihil melius cogitari potest*" and his hasty dismissal of the passage in *Reply to Gaunilo* 8. Yet, the culmination of his line of reasoning now forces him to contend that in *Proslogion* 3 Anselm *mistakenly* used "*melius*" instead of "*maius*":

> What, however, of the single occurrence of 'melius' in Ch. 3? . . . In view of the mass of evidence from the rest of the *Proslogion*, I think it reasonable to conclude that Anselm allowed the notion of *judging* to mislead him into writing *melius* instead of *maius*; this argument as to why God cannot be thought not to exist gains such force as it has, of course, from the notion of the supposed absurdity of creature's *judging* creator, which notion in turn makes clearer sense if applied to the idea of the creature's thinking of something (morally) better, as opposed to something greater, than God, something morally better which the creature could use as a yardstick whereby to judge God.[17]

But, indeed, Anselm has not made a mistake; for in the *Monologion*, the *Proslogion*, and the *Reply to Gaunilo* he is not systematically and generally distinguishing his use of "*maius*" from his use of "*melius*." Instead, he frequently — though not always — uses them interchangeably. And Brecher, who refuses to see this point, must — to save his argument — claim that Anselm made a linguistic error. One reason behind Brecher's misapprehension is his persistent glossing of "goodness" as "moral goodness." Now, sometimes when Anselm uses "*bonus*" and "*bonitas*" and "*melius*," he does so in a moral sense. In *Proslogion* 9 (S I, 107:10), for instance, "*melior*" means "morally better." By contrast, in *Monologion* 4 (S I, 17:1–2) "*melior*" does *not* mean "morally better." Now, when Anselm alludes to God as "whatever it is better to be than not to be,"[18] he is supposing that all compatible perfections ought to be ascribed to God. And whereas some of these perfections are moral perfections (e.g., truthfulness), some of them are not (e.g., indivisibility).

I do not deny that Brecher realizes that Anselm has a non-moral sense of "*melius*"; but I contend that he overemphasizes the moral notion of *bonitas* in his discussion of the *Proslogion*. And it is this moral notion which does, in certain respects, stand in contrast to the notion of greatness. However, when Anselm says that God is *quo nihil melius cogitari potest*, he does not limit himself to the notion of *morally better* — any more than when he says that God is *quo nihil maius cogitari potest*, he excludes from the scope of his phrase such moral attributes as truthfulness.

1.2.5. On the one hand, Brecher is certainly right when he indicates that, for Anselm, "*maius*" signifies "greater" in the sense of "existing in greater degree." For Anselm does indeed teach that what is sentient *exists* more than does what is non-sentient, that what is rational *exists* more than what is non-rational.[19] On the other hand, it is strange for Brecher to introduce Vlastos' interpretation of Plato's doctrine of degrees of reality and to apply this interpretation to Anselm's doctrine in the *Monologion* and the *Proslogion*. Let us remember that Vlastos formulates his interpretation of Plato in the course of denying that Plato believed the Forms to *exist more* than do particulars. Yet, as we have just noticed, Anselm does believe in degrees of *existence*. On the other hand, he does not clearly believe that the truth of God's existence or the truths about God's nature are more cognitively reliable — i.e., are knowable with more certainty — than are various other truths. For in *Reply to Gaunilo* 4 he remarks that "if any one of the things which *most assuredly exist* can be understood not to exist, then likewise other *certainly exist-*

ing things [e.g., God] can also be understood not to exist'' — implying that a number of things exist certainly. At any rate, there is no reason to suppose that either the *Proslogion* or the *Reply* makes use of or at all depends upon the doctrine that God's existence is cognitively more reliable than are various other objects.[20] And if it makes use of the notion that God is more valuable than all other objects, it does so in conjunction with the notion that He is more powerful, wise, just, blessed, real, etc., than all other things.

1.2.6. Thus, Brecher's basic claim is false: viz., that in the *Proslogion* Anselm does not use ``*maius*'' and ``*melius*'' interchangeably. But, contrary to Brecher's verdict, the reason that Anselm does not hesitate to use these terms interchangeably is that — true to Augustinian metaphysics — he employs a notion of ``better'' in which a horse can be said to be better than a tree, and what exists without parts can be said to be better than what exists through parts, and so on. Even before looking at the *Proslogion*, we should have been clear about Anselm's interchanging of ``*maius*,'' ``*melius*,'' and ``*dignius*.'' For we should have remembered his comment in *Monologion* 2:

> It follows necessarily that something is supremely great inasmuch as whatever things are great are great through some one thing which is great through itself. I do not mean great in size, as is a material object; but I mean great in the sense that the greater (*maius*) anything is the better (*melius*) or more excellent (*dignius*) it is — as in the case of wisdom.

And we should already have been aware from *Monologion* 4 that Anselm finds it easy to write:

> *Quare non sic sunt magnae, ut* illis nihil sit maius aliud. *Quod si nec per hoc quod sunt, nec per aliud possibile est tales esse plures naturas* quibus nihil sit praestantius, *nullo modo possunt esse naturae plures huiusmodi.*

Moreover, *Monologion* 4 gives clear witness to Anselm's tendency to say ``*naturae meliores*'' in place of ``*naturae maiores*'' — even though these very phrases do not occur there.

To say that Anselm sometimes interchanges ``*maius*'' and ``*melius*'' is not to say that he regards them as generally synonymous. Since greatness is a quantity and goodness a quality, it would be astounding if ``greater'' had the same definition as ``better,'' or if ``great'' had the same definition as ``good.'' Presumably, Anselm would agree with Augustine that ``not everything which is great is good, inasmuch as there are also great evils.''[21] Though ''*bonus*'' and ''*magnus*'' are not, *tout court*, synonymous, they can be used as substitutes for each other in specific contexts.[22] In the *Monologion* and the *Proslogion* Anselm permits himself this substitutability because of his metaphysical doctrine that every being is a good thing and that every good thing is a being.[23] This doctrine allows him to compare beings and to judge that some of them are better than others.[24] And if one thing is better than another, it is more excellent (*praestantius*) than that other.[25] And if it is more excellent, it is also (in one sense) greater.

Hartshorne and Malcolm are therefore right in interpreting Anselm's use of ''that than which nothing greater can be thought'' — in the context of the *Proslogion* — as encompassing ''that than which nothing more excellent can be thought,'' ''that than which nothing more real can be thought.''[26] At places, then, Anselm takes the contextual meaning of these phrases to be the same, even though the phrases are not synonymous. In a similar way, the verb ''*cogitare*'' is broader in signification than is the verb ''*intelligere*.'' And yet Anselm feels no more hesitancy over using ''*intelligere*'' in place of ''*cogitare*''[27] than he does over using ''*melius*'' in place of ''*maius*.''

Brecher has tried to insist that Anselm's use of terms is more systematic than in fact it is. As a result he has passed from exegesis into eisogesis. To ''find'' in Anselm's writings rigid meanings of terms turns out to be an illusory finding, except in those cases where Anselm gives explicit definitions (''truth,'' ''justice,'' ''freedom''). We have seen how Brecher, in his insistence upon rigidity, ends up insisting that in *Proslogion* 3 Anselm mistakenly wrote ''*melius*'' where he should have written ''*maius*.'' Only by this move can he make Anselm's terminology come out ''consistently.'' The problem, however, is that Brecher has misconceived the ideal of consistency in the domain of ordinary language. For consistent use is not the same as uniform use. Hence, the fact that Anselm uses ''*melius*'' in a moral sense in *Proslogion* 9 is not inconsistent with his using it in a nonmoral sense in *Proslogion* 18. And the fact that, in general, ''*maius*'' has more different uses than does ''*melius*'' does not prevent their uses from sometimes coinciding in a given context.

II

In "God, Guilt, and Logic: the Psychological Basis of the Ontological Argument" Lewis Feuer maintains that the ontological argument — in one form or another — appears convincing only to philosophers of a certain emotional temperament. And when he sets out to identify this temperament, he quite naturally does so by casting a glance at the lives[28] (or at least the comments) of some better-known defenders of the argument. Thus, after examining the writings of Anselm of Canterbury, Josiah Royce, Karl Barth, and Norman Malcolm, he finds that they "all shared a common concern with the experience of individual guilt. . . . This component of guilt-preoccupation is an essential one in the consciousness which perceives the ontological argument as convincing. It is the source of a mode of thinking which might be called 'logical masochism'. To assuage guilt, the ontologian is prepared in all humility to bow his logical powers submissively before an entity which is transcendentally exceptional to them."[29]

In the remainder of this chapter I shall analyze only one aspect of Feuer's article: viz., the claims made about the life and mind of St. Anselm.

2.1. Feuer alleges that Anselm "struggles to find a convincing proof of God's existence" in order "to overcome his own doubts." "In his own doubt, Anselm cried: 'Lord, if thou art not here, where shall I seek thee, being absent?' His own personal guilt tormented him: 'My iniquities have gone over my head, they overwhelm me; and, like a heavy load, they weigh me down. Free me from them; unburden me, that the pit of iniquities may not close over me.' "[30] Now, in maintaining that Anselm sought after his renowned proof of God's existence in order to overcome his doubts, Feuer goes against the textual evidence. For in the *Proslogion* Anselm presents himself as a believer who is seeking to understand. Indeed, this is the implication of the original title "*Fides quaerens intellectum*." Similarly, in *De Libertate Arbitrii* 3 Anselm puts into the mouth of the Student the words: "I believe, but I desire to understand." And in *Cur Deus Homo* I, 3 he has Boso remark that unlike those who seek a rational basis because they do not believe, we seek it because we do believe.[31]

Moreover, in *De Incarnatione* 1 he admonishes: "No Christian ought to question the truth of what the Catholic Church believes in its heart and confesses with its mouth. Rather, by holding constantly and unhesitatingly to this faith, by loving it and living according to it he ought humbly, and as best he is able, to seek to discover the reason why it is true." So Anselm's general program is to seek reasons not in order to overcome his doubts but in order to satisfy his understanding.

Of course, it is possible for even a believer to have doubts. So perhaps what Feuer would say is that while struggling to formulate the ontological proof, Anselm — though still a believer — was disquieted by doubts. "I believe. O Lord, help Thou mine unbelief" might have been his prayer. Well, indeed, it *might* have been. But we have no evidence that in fact it was. In the preface to the *Proslogion* there is no sign of personal or of philosophical doubt. Nor does Anselm repudiate the arguments and the conclusions which he had already presented in the *Monologion*. These arguments were meant to be doubt-excluding. After finishing the *Monologion*, Anselm began to have doubts not about the existence of God but about finding a *single, simplified* line of reasoning which would establish both the existence and the attributes of God. For the arguments in the *Monologion* had been more complex and numerous than he had thought desirable.

Furthermore, none of the statements in *Proslogion* 1 *evidence* a state of psychological doubt in Anselm. The question "If You are not here, Lord, where shall I seek You in Your absence?" does not arise out of personal doubt, as Feuer supposes. It is rather preparatory to Anselm's later explanation (in *Proslogion* 15 and 16) of how God can be present everywhere even though remaining in inaccessible light. So too, the beseeching lament

> Having mounted above my head, my iniquities cover me over; and as a heavy burden they weigh me down

does not show that at this time Anselm was undergoing "an intense experience of guilt."[32] Anselm is here alluding to Psalms 37:5 (38:4); and, in fact, throughout *Proslogion* 1 he is writing in a stylized way. His style is similar to Augustine's elevated language in the *Confessions*. By making use of the contrasting motifs of darkness-light, sin-forgiveness, poverty-richness, hunger-fullness, turmoil-rest, burdened-unburdened, Anselm is adopting a literary form — not keeping a diary of his personal dispositions at a given moment. Feuer makes a genre-mistake. And this mistake invalidates his exegesis.

Not only does Feuer (1) misinterpret Anselm's doubt as being about the existence of God, and (2) misconstrue Anselm's lamentation as revealing intense guilt-preoccupation, but he also (3) misreads Anselm's acceptance of the ontological argument as "a capitulation of logical masochism."[33] For, in order to assuage guilt, thinks Feuer, Anselm humbly bowed his logical powers. But, indeed, what is the true significance of Anselm's autobiographical account?:

> At last, despairing, I wanted to give up my pursuit of an argument which I supposed could not be found. But when I wanted to shut out the very thought [of such an argument], lest by engaging my mind in vain, it would keep me from other projects in which I could make headway — just then this argument began more and more to force itself insistently upon me, unwilling and resisting as I was. Then one day when I was tired as a result of vigorously resisting its entreaties, what I had despaired of finding appeared in my strife-torn mind in such way that I eagerly embraced the reasoning I had been anxiously warding off.[34]

Is it not clear that this account does not indicate the presence of any so-called logical masochism? Anselm is not intimating that he abandoned his logical powers in order to embrace what he was weary of thinking about. Instead, his remarks show just the opposite. In the course of trying to formulate a new argument he kept finding flaws in his various formulations. After a time he supposed that there was no way to formulate a valid version of the argument — whose invalid or incomplete versions he had been resisting. Then one day he struck upon a formulation — this is the meaning of "what I had despaired of finding appeared in my strife-torn mind" — whose logic seemed to him so cogent that he could no longer rationally resist it. He, therefore, eagerly embraced it.

In the foregoing passage Anselm is, once again, making use of a literary form: He is treating an argument as something transcendent to its different formulations; and he is depicting it in the guise of an importunate idea which seeks a domicile in his mind. But Feuer, who does not discern the literary form, believes that

Anselm is referring to a single argument-version, or a single set of thoughts, which kept haunting him — so that finally, being weary of it, he simply surrendered to it. And having once accepted it, he never again questioned it — even though later he was no longer weary.

2.2. Feuer's three misrepresentations of Anselm's texts illustrate how careful an interpreter must be in examining not only what Anselm has said but also the form in which he has said it. For a mistake about the genre may well result in a mistake about the meaning. Ironically, when we become aware of some of Feuer's other claims about Anselm, we begin to be more concerned about Feuer's *idée fixe* than about Anselm's alleged *masochisme logique*. "No philosophical system," Feuer contends, "has made guilt so central in its notion of the universe as did Anselm's."[35] What in the world — we are led immediately to wonder — warrants this startling assertion? After all, Anselm does not pay any special attention to guilt in his philosophical works the *Monologion, De Grammatico, De Veritate,* and *De Libertate*. Moreover, even in *De Casu Diaboli* and *De Concordia*, where the theme of the Fall and the theme of grace are (respectively) more prominent, there is no distinctive preoccupation with guilt. Were it the case that by "Anselm's philosophical system," Feuer meant to distinguish Anselm's philosophical from his theological system, then his claim would be patently false. But he means, instead, both the philosophical and the theological aspects of Anselm's thought, taken as a whole. Yet, even from a theological viewpoint, Anselm's thought is not distinctive in making guilt central to the notion of the universe. For, in a sense, the whole movement of Christian orthodox theology emphasizes the centrality of this notion. And surely Augustine and Jonathan Edwards are candidates more deserving of Feuer's label than is Anselm. Indeed, some of Anselm's own opponents surpassed him in emphasizing human depravity. For they taught — and Anselm denied — that original sin in infants is aggravated by the sins of their more recent ancestors, and thus is greater than Adam's first sin.[36] So what is the *textual* basis underlying Feuer's claim? It is, Feuer implies, the entire *Cur Deus Homo:*

> For man's guilt is the cardinal metaphysical fact, according to Anselm, from which the details of the Universal Drama necessarily follow. Anselm indeed

> professed to prove with deductive logic the necessity of the Incarnation and Atonement of Jesus. The logical steps, to his mind, were simple and rigorous. Man, in his disobedience, had committed a sin which was infinite; to atone for an infinite guilt, no finite sacrifice could be adequate; therefore God Himself had to become Man, so that an Infinite Atonement of Infinite Guilt could be achieved; therefore Jesus had become Man and was crucified. We may omit some of the intervening corollaries in the deduction; such in its essentials was Anselm's theology of guilt which became known in the history of theology as the 'satisfaction doctrine'. In its time, it represented a new departure in the theory of Man's Redemption. For us, it is remarkable for its projection on a cosmic scale of its central metaphysical notion of man's guilt. This is the mythology, above all, of guilt-consciousness.[37]

There are four troublesome features about this interpretation. First of all, the satisfaction-theory is no more cosmic in scope than is the Devil-ransom theory it replaced. Secondly, as already noted, the doctrine of original sin and original guilt is scarcely distinctive to Anselm. Thirdly, Anselm does not teach that God (in an unrestricted sense) became Man (in an unrestricted sense); he teaches that God in the person of the Son became a man, viz., the man Jesus. Finally, the notions of infinite sin and infinite guilt need more precision. For in one important sense Anselm does *not* maintain that Adam's sin and guilt were infinite. Indeed, the *Cur Deus Homo* has two different senses of "infinite sin"; and we are obliged not to conflate them. In *Cur Deus Homo* I, 21 Boso admits: "Even for the sake of preserving the whole of creation, it is not the case that I ought to do something which is contrary to the will of God." And in his very next speech he says: "If there were an infinitely multiple number of worlds and they too were exhibited to me, I would still give the same answer." Anselm then reasons that the satisfaction must be in proportion to the extent of the sin, and that therefore the sinner is required to pay "something greater than is that for whose sake you ought not to have sinned." That is, the sinner must pay something which is greater than everything other than God.[38]

Now, in *Cur Deus Homo* II, 14 Boso does refer to the above-mentioned sin as infinite: "I ask you now to teach me how His death outweighs the number and the magnitude of *all* sins — seeing that you have shown *one* sin which we regard as trifling to be so *infinite* that if an infinite number of worlds were exhibited, each as full of creatures as is our world, and if these worlds could be kept from being reduced to nothing only on the condition that someone would take a single look contrary to the will of God, this look ought, nonetheless, not to be taken.'' But this sin is *not infinite in magnitude*. It is ''infinite'' only in the sense that it ought not to be done even in order to save an infinite *multitude* of finite worlds from perishing. In other words, it is so grave that its evil outweighs the good of an infinity of worlds, each like our own.

By contrast, there is a sin which Anselm regards as, in principle, infinite in magnitude: viz., an injury knowingly done to the physical life of the God-man. For it would be a sin immediately against the person of God. Now, if this sin were done knowingly — something Anselm says could not happen — it would surpass immeasurably the collective gravity of all other conceivable sins. Thus, this sin would be the greatest conceivable sin. In II, 15 Anselm calls it *illud infinitum peccatum*.[39] And in II, 14 he reasons that ''if every good is as good as its destruction is evil, then [His life] is a good incomparably greater than the evil of those sins which His being-put-to-death immeasurably surpasses.'' Therefore, His life (which is so great a good) can pay for infinitely more sins than the sins of the entire world.

So Anselm holds that some sins are greater or lesser than others. Thus, Adam's personal sin was greater than is an infant's original sin, of which Adam's sin is the cause.[40] And Adam's sin is less than Satan's sin; for Adam sinned being tempted by another, whereas Satan sinned unabetted.[41] But Adam's sin is not *illud infinitum peccatum*. For no one's sin can actually be as great as is conceivable. And since after Adam sinned, his will retained some measure of justice,[42] his sin was not, strictly speaking, infinite in magnitude. It was infinite — to repeat — only in the sense that it ought not to have been committed even in order to save an infinite multitude of worlds. Similarly, Adam's *guilt* both is and is not infinite, depending upon the sense of ''infinite.''

Feuer does not make these distinctions. Thus, he gives the impression that the merit of Christ's death is infinite in the same sense as the merit of Adam's sin, except that the former is positive merit, whereas the latter is negative merit (= demerit). But in fact, the infinity of Christ's merit infinitely surpasses the *finitude* of Adam's demerit — even though Adam's demerit ought not to have occurred even for the sake of saving an infinite number of (finite) worlds. These distinctions are important, because without them Anselm's theory would immediately collapse. For were his theory saddled with only one sense of "infinity," Christ's infinite merit could not be thought to counterweigh more than the infinitude of Adam's sin alone.[43] Accordingly, it would not be sufficient to outweigh the sins of Adam's descendants as well. So in oversimplifying these distinctions Feuer does a disservice to Anselm's theology, without ever thereby proving that Anselm's theology is more guilt-oriented than is Augustine's or Jonathan Edwards' — without ever proving that "no philosophical system has made guilt so central in its notion of the universe as did Anselm's."

2.3. Besides not doing justice to Anselm's texts, Feuer's analysis in other respects betrays special pleading. For example, Feuer attempts to accentuate Anselm's personal sense of guilt by insinuating that he had "a strong maternal fixation,"[44] which conduced to guilt-feelings. Among the evidence offered for fixation is one of Anselm's prayers in which Christ is represented as a mother: " 'And Thou, Jesus, dear Lord, art Thou not a mother too? . . . Indeed, Thou art, and the mother of all mothers, who didst taste death in Thy longing to bring forth children unto life.' "[45] Perhaps if there were extensive evidence (from Anselm's biographer or from Anselm's own writings) of mother-fixation, the citing of the prayer might contribute to a total pattern of evidence, and hence might be given some credence. But in the absence of supplementary support, the prayer by itself carries not even circumstantial weight. Of course, Feuer has not produced the supplementary evidence. The few other data that he alludes to are — both singularly and collectively — flimsy. Strangely, he does not at all entertain the hypothesis that Anselm, in his prayer, is using a theologically legitimated locution. Even Augustine had said, in effect, that *Deus mater est, quia fovet et nutrit et lactat et continet*.[46] The usual expression was to speak of the Church as our mother, as Anselm does at the end of *De Conceptu Virginali*. But there was nothing theologically bizarre about referring to God as mother. The Old Testament prophet had himself portrayed God as a mother bringing forth children and comforting.[47] And in the New Testament Jesus had likened himself unto a mother hen gathering her chickens under her wings.[48]

Feuer fails to mention that in *Monologion* 42 Anselm states explicitly that the Supreme Spirit is more suitably called father than mother. And this statement is repeated at the end of *De Incarnatione Verbi*. So in Anselm's works there is no obsession with the image of God or of Jesus as mother. Accordingly, the mere fact that in one prayer Anselm uses mother-imagery is of no consequence for establishing fixation. Feuer's inference is as non sequitur as would be the inference that the author of the book of Job was psychotic because he wrote: "I have said to rottenness: Thou art my father: to worms, My mother and my sister."[49] Once again, Feuer has taken no cognizance of the fact that prayers and meditations are stylized forms of writing. Moreover, within Christianity these literary forms are as much under the influence of a continuing tradition as they are products of the unconscious recesses of a single individual's psyche.

Last of all, Feuer is undiscerning in his use of secondary sources. For he blithely draws upon Martin Rule's biography of St. Anselm[50] without scrutinizing it carefully. Now, we must place Rule not among the "scientific" historians but among the romantics, among those who believe that historical narrative must read like a novel, those who in the name of historical imagination interject their purely personal fancy. This judgment about Rule's work will be readily apparent to anyone who takes the trouble to check the narrative against its sources. But this verdict will be obvious even more quickly to one who takes a minute to examine his footnotes. So let us take those few seconds for a closer look at three sample passages.

The first passage is found on pp. 104–105, where Rule is discussing a disputed sentence in Eadmer:

> And, if it be not hypercritical to interpret Eadmer's phrase, as meaning that Anselm's journey was not so much one journey as two, the second sudden in its beginning as the first had been sudden in its ending, the interpretation is *justified* by the obvious reflection that he can scarcely have reached the borders of Normandy before the terrible news of the interdict arrested him like a 'shadow of eclipse,' and Normandy was, for the present, forbidden ground.[51]

In his footnote Rule adds: "This is, of course, conjectural; for the precise date of the interdict is not known." So Rule envisions himself as "justifying" an interpretation by means of a *conjecture*. And this way of reasoning reveals that his notion of historical justification is anything but rigorous.

A second passage is equally revelatory:

> In those days the Seine at Rouen, taking its tortuous course further to the north than now, washed the very precinct of the metropolitan church; and it requires but little effort of imagination to see the Prior of Le Bec and his pupil putting off in a ferry on the morrow of their interview with the Archbishop from close under the sacred pile, and slowly making for the southern bank of the river.[52]

In the footnote we read: "I frankly own that on revising these pages for the press I cannot find an authority for the suggestion that there was no bridge across the Seine at Rouen in the spring of 1060. I have no proof either way. So, *quod scripsi scripsi*." This note evidences that Rule's imagination is roaming freely, rather than being determined by the data. In effect, his attitude seems to be: "Lanfranc and Anselm had to cross the river. It is of no historical significance whether they crossed by bridge or by ferry. So in the absence of any evidence one way or the other, the historian is free to construct his narrative along probabilistic lines. (It is not, for example, likely that they swam across.) If there was a bridge, then in all likelihood they would have used it; if there was no bridge, then there would have been a ferry, etc. The historian, in his narrative, must get Lanfranc and Anselm across the river. Yet, for the historian to write 'probably' or 'in all likelihood' or 'presumably' or 'I surmise that' before each of his interpolations would make the narrative read clumsily. Besides, the reader already understands that these qualifications obtain. The historian will, to be sure, sometimes caution his reader about the lacunae in the data, as I am now doing; but he cannot be expected to do so in every case."

Now, if this account — or something like it — summarizes Rule's attitude and corresponding practice, then he has veered from the conception of history as *Wissenschaft*. R. G. Collingwood, for instance, was later to discourse about the historical imagination and was himself to insist that the historian must interpolate between the data in order to weave a coherent narrative. (This interpolation helps to distinguish history from chronicle.) The record says that Caesar's army moved from city A to city B in C number of days. The historian, knowing the route and the physical capability of the men, will infer that the army moved by forced marches, that it therefore arrived weary, etc.[53] Collingwood's point is that the scientific historian will make the inference which the consistent use of the data *necessitates*. He will not interject into his narrative anything arbitrary. Yet, in Rule's biography we are struck by how often he says what there is neither evidence nor need for saying. Why are we told about the tortuous Seine washing the precincts of the metropolitan church and about the ferry moving slowly toward the southern bank? The main reason, I suggest, is Rule's commitment to writing *vivid* history, to creating a mood of romance with the past. This commitment leads him to overspecify; and in moments of self-reproach, he simply adds a footnote.

A third passage displays how inveterate is Rule's tendency to overspecify: "The monks of Le Bec, some hundred and twenty in number, were seated round about their chapter house."[54] Here the footnote reads: "Not more, I should say, than a hundred and twenty. A hundred and thirty-seven names had been inscribed since the establishment of the house; and by this time there had certainly been thirteen removals, whether by death, preferment, or emigration, and there may, of course, have been a few more." In short, Rule does not know exactly how many monks there were; but he cannot resist placing the number at one hundred and twenty — give or take a few.

Once we recognize how free Rule's narrative is, we will be cautious about relying upon it uncritically. Yet, Feuer, who does not seem to be aware of Rule's method, uses the narrative incautiously. "We know," asserts Feuer confidently, "that for Anselm, the inventor of the ontological argument, mortification was the chief joy almost all his life."[55] Feuer's authority for this confident assertion is Rule's biography. But as found in Rule, the corresponding remark is simply another instance of imaginative interpolation. "And hence," writes Rule, "when in old age he [viz., Anselm] reviewed his mortal career, it was not without regret that he pointed to one period of it in which the intensity of his desire for the religious profession was allowed to relax; to one short interval in which, *mortification not being his sole joy*, he suffered his heart's barque — to use his own phrase — to ride indolently at anchor and run risk of drifting out to the open sea."[56] Now, Rule's own source — viz., Eadmer's *De Vita et Conversatione Anselmi Canturariensis Archiepiscopi* — does not so much as intimate that Anselm's sole joy was mortification.[57] One danger, then, of Rule's method is that it can result in a narrative that misleads people like Feuer. (For in the present passage Rule does not include the occasional footnote which expresses his reservations.) Correspondingly, one shortcoming of Feuer's analysis is that it borrows uncritically from Rule's history.

So Feuer is not alert to the difference between historical romance and scientific history, just as also he is not attuned to the various differences of literary genre. Yet, not only does he make use of historical fiction, he even misuses it by misreading it. In particular, he misreads Rule's reproduction — embellished reproduction, to be sure — of Eadmer's report of Anselm's boyhood dream:

Eadmer's Account

. . . it happened one night that he saw a vision, in which he was bidden to climb to the top of the mountain and hasten to the court of the great king, God. But then, before he began to climb, he saw in the plain through which he was approaching the foot of the mountain, women — serfs of the king — who were reaping the corn, but doing so carelessly and idly. The boy was grieved and indignant at their laziness, and resolved to accuse them before their lord the king. Then he climbed the mountain and came to the royal court, where he found God alone with his steward. For, as he imagined, since it was autumn he had sent his household to collect the harvest. The boy entered and was summoned by the Lord. He approached and sat at his feet. The Lord asked him in a pleasant and friendly way who he was, where he came from and what he wanted. He replied to the question as best he could. Then, at God's command, the whitest of bread was brought him by the steward, and he refreshed himself with it in God's presence. The next day therefore, when he recalled to his mind's eye all that he had seen, like a simple and innocent boy he be-

Rule's Account

. . . one night as he slept the summons came. He must climb the mountain and hasten to the Court of God. He set forth, crossed the river, scaled the Gargantua, where, grieved at finding the King's maidens gathering in His harvest after too careless and too indolent a fashion, he chid their sloth and resolved to lay charge against them, but passed on forthwith; for he must not delay. So, leaving the region of corn and vineyard, he plunged into the forest, and, threading his way upwards through belts of pine and over lawns of turf and lavender, and scaling precipitous blank rocks, had already reached the summit, when lo! heaven opened. The Invisible, in fashion as a king, sat before him, throned in majesty, and with none near Him but His seneschal, for the rest of the household had been sent down into the world to reap His harvest. The child crossed the threshold; the Lord called him, and he obeyed; he approached, and sat down at the Lord's feet; was asked with royal grace and condescension who he was, whence he had come, what he wanted; answered the questions, and was not afraid. Whereupon the King gave command to the

lieved that he had been in heaven and that he had been fed with the bread of God, and he asserted as much to others in public.[58]	seneschal, who brought forth bread and set before him. It was bread of an exceeding whiteness; and he ate it in the Lord's presence. He ate it and was refreshed, and slept his sleep, and awoke next morning at Aosta, and, remembering his journey, or, rather, not so much remembering it, as retracing it step by step, and incident by incident, flew to his mother's knee, and told her all.[59]

Feuer, in the course of psychoanalyzing this dream, states: "The careless King, disporting with maidens, is the earthly harsh father,[60] so unkind to the mother. . . ."[61] Yet, it is clear from Eadmer's report, which is faithfully (though more fancifully) restated by Rule, that the King is not disporting with the maidens. Nor is anyone at all disporting with them. Nor is the King called careless. Feuer has simply misread the record. Once we correct his error, we see that his particular psychoanalytic interpretation loses even the tenuous basis it may previously have seemed to possess.

In sum, Feuer has produced no evidence for his psychological interpretation of Anselm's life and argument. He has not shown that Anselm's life is distinguished by excessive preoccupation with guilt. Therefore, *a fortiori*, he has not proved that Anselm's excessive feelings of guilt explain his having formulated and accepted the argument of *Proslogion* 2.

3. *Conclusion*. Both Feuer and Brecher become entangled in the same general mistake: They approach Anselm's texts literalistically instead of literarily. This latter approach respects the different literary forms — treating historical narrative as historical narrative, prayer as prayer, figure-of-speech as figure-of-speech. By contrast, the former procedure tries stubbornly to read-off a surface meaning, irrespective of the attending genre. Accordingly, as soon as Feuer grasps a surface meaning, he adorns it in the garb of psychoanalytic theory, and exhibits its titillating aspects. Brecher, on the other hand, assumes that because — literalistically viewed — "*melius*" and "*maius*" are not synonymous, Anselm does not at all use them interchangeably in the *Proslogion*. Thereby Brecher fails to detect that the inter-

changeability, which really occurs, serves not only a metaphysical end but also the literary end of relieving monotony.

Sometimes people have spoken as if Anselm — Abbot of Bec and Archbishop of Canterbury — had no concern for literary style. They ignore his attempts at humor in his dialogues, his puns in the *Monologion*, his personification of the members and the senses in *De Conceptu Virginali* 4, his overall care to avoid the inelegant repetition of a word, his acceptance of the natural "imprecisions" of ordinary language, his vivid imagery in his meditations, and the proper forms of deference and humility in his letters. Still, we must not exaggerate. For the fact remains that, on the whole, his style is plain and unembellished. And so one would not expect that his terminology could be mistaken for technical or that his quotation of the Psalms could be construed as autobiography. Yet, we have just witnessed with what apparent ease such errors come to be made.

Thus, it is true that in Brecher and in Feuer exegesis gives way to eisogesis. But, in last analysis, each of these philosophers is tacitly giving vent to a legitimate protest. Feuer is rightly upset with those who, like Nicholas Rescher, articulate a special sense of "follow" in which God's existence is then said to follow from the definition of the term "God."[62] And he is rightly resisting the interpretations of those[63] who, like Karl Barth and A. Stolz, view Anselm as emphasizing the religious significance — more than the logic — of his *Proslogion* argument. Similarly, Brecher is implicitly protesting against Anselm's failure to develop a sophisticated metaphysic, a more extensive set of conceptual distinctions, and a special philosophical nomenclature. In these respects he would be right to exalt Aquinas over Anselm. Moreover, he correctly senses the irony involved in Anselm's supposing that he had presented to the world a "simplified" line of reasoning in *Proslogion* 2. For the controversies about what Anselm may have meant — or, at least, ought to have meant — will continue into the centuries. Brecher keenly suspects that much of the futility of the controversy could have been prevented had Anselm distinguished, clarified, specified, and even metaphysicized, more than he did.

With these fundamental insights and protests I can only agree.

CHAPTER VI

WHAT IS A TRANSLATION?

1. People who do not speak or read a foreign language often entertain false beliefs about the nature of translating. Many tend to regard it as a more or less mechanical process which resembles decoding. They seem to think as if along the following lines:

> Translating is to a printed foreign-language text what paleography is to medieval Latin manuscripts. The paleographer learns how to interpret symbols. For example, "÷" stands for "*est*"; "*dr*" stands for "*dicitur.*" Although these abbreviations vary from one writer to the next, when a paleographer masters a scribe's shorthand, he can accurately *transcribe* the latter's manuscripts into longhand. Similarly, if a translator has mastered a list of correlated words (e.g., "*das Pferd*" = "the horse"; "*der Baum*" = "the tree"), he can accurately *translate* the text into his native language.

The problem with this view is that it regards words as points-of-meaning instead of as spheres-of-meanings. And thus, it fails to recognize how crucial is the context in which a word occurs. Moreover, it oversimplifies the process of translation; for it envisions a gigantic word-list (i.e., a dictionary) by reference to which someone can readily know which word to correlate with the foreign word — just as by reference to a memorized Morse-code chart one knows what letters to put in place of the combinations of dots and dashes. Then too, the models of decoding and of rule-governed transcription foster the impression that translation is a word-for-word phenomenon, instead of manifesting that it is mainly a phenomenon of expression-for-expression. Finally, these models altogether miss sight of the fact that one must *understand* the text before he can translate it. Indeed, we have already seen abundant examples of how in numerous instances the Latin texts of St. Anselm cannot be accurately translated without recourse to that special kind of understanding which we dignify as "interpretation." For where what-is-said is embedded in, or implies, or is conditioned by, a philosophical theory, and where what-is-said can be "naturally" understood in two or more different ways: to disambiguate the language, the hearer (or the reader) may have to appeal to other information concerning what the speaker's (or the writer's) theory is; or he may have to appeal to what the logic of his argument requires. In such cases, we usually speak of *interpreting* (rather than merely of understanding) the words. Here I will give a final example of this phenomenon.

In *Proslogion* 4 we read:

> *Nullus quippe intelligens id quod deus est, potest cogitare quia deus non est, licet haec verba dicat in corda, aut sine ulla aut cum aliqua extranea significatione. Deus enim est id quo maius cogitari non potest. Quod qui bene intelligit, utique intelligit id ipsum sic esse, ut nec cogitatione queat non esse. Qui ergo intelligit sic esse deum, nequit eum non esse cogitare.*

Two questions can immediately be raised. What is the referent of "*quod*" in "*Quod qui bene intelligit*"? And how is "*sic*" to be read in the last sentence? At one period of time in the past I took "*quod*" to refer to the entire preceding sentence, so that the "*quod*" sentence itself would read: "Anyone who comprehends this [viz., that God is that than which a greater cannot be thought] . . . ." (Yet, being uncertain, I did not supply the bracketed words, but settled for leaving vague the reference of "*quod*.") And I read "*sic*" in the last sentence in the same way as "*sic*" in the preceding sentence, viz., as an adverb: "Therefore, anyone who understands that this is the manner in which God exists cannot think that He does not exist." Of course, both of these translations are consistent with the Latin sentences. But I now realize, from the sense of the argument, that each of these translations was incorrect. "*Quod*" refers only to a part of the preceding sentence; and "*sic*" in the last sentence is being used adjectivally, even though in the preceding sentence its use is adverbial. Accordingly, a correct translation of the entire passage will be:

> Indeed, no one who understands what God is can think that God does not exist, even though he says these words [viz., "God does not exist"] in his heart either meaninglessly or else bizarrely. For God is that than which a greater cannot be thought. Anyone who comprehends this [description],

> surely understands that this being [than which a greater cannot be thought] so exists that it cannot even conceivably not exist. Therefore, anyone who understands that God is such [a being] cannot think that He does not exist.

The decoding-model fails, then, because it is inadequate to account for the phenomena of understanding and interpretation, which are inseparable from translation.[1] Given a code-book, one can decipher a text without understanding it; but, given a dictionary, one cannot translate a text except as one understands it. To be sure, this contrast is — in its purity — a sharper one than can be made in practice. A manuscript, we all know, is often illegible or unclearly written. Accordingly, the paleographer may have to be guided by his understanding of what is being said.[2] Moreover, a redactor will have to choose which of the conflicting manuscript-readings to follow. And often his choice will be guided more by which reading better fits the discussion than by which manuscript is in general more authoritative.[3]

2. There are at least three different notions of interpreting which we need to keep distinct. The ancient sense accords with one of the meanings of the Latin words "*interpretatio*" and "*interpretari*": to interpret is to translate, to give a translation. This sense has passed out of current English usage. The second and more usual sense has to do, loosely, with explaining the significance of something — whether it be the meaning of a literary text, the rationale for certain actions in the scene of a play, the intent underlying a physical gesture, etc. In this sense, we have agreed, one must sometimes *interpret* an author's position in the course of deciding which of several semantically legitimate translations to use.

A third sense of "interpreting" is standard in European and American institutes of foreign-language study. To interpret a foreign-language speaker's words is to give their gist in the native language without fretting about exact translation. When the diplomat says "*Es ist schon Mittag*," the interpreter may well report: "It's time for lunch." An interpreter will feel free to abbreviate, paraphrase, idiomatize in ways that are not permitted to the translator, who must give a more faithful rendering. Informal conversations thrive on the services of an interpreter; formal documents need the attention of a translator. And whatever falls into a middle category will need a bit more of the one than of the other. But if paraphrase is allowable to an interpreter, is it forbidden to a translator? Obviously, there are no set rules. Some translations of solemn materials do make use of paraphrase. In connection with the writings of St. Anselm, we have the examples of D. P. Henry and of Benedicta Ward. Now, the notion of *a translation* is a normative notion: What a translation is must be decided, not discovered. Some people would, and others would not, refuse to call "It's time for lunch" a translation of "*Es ist schon Mittag*." Some people would, and others would not, call various of D. P. Henry's paraphrases translations.

3. According to F. S. Schmitt, translations of Anselm's treatises ought ideally to be very literal. Thus, in prefacing his German translation of the *Monologion*, Schmitt cites the verdict of Igor Stravinsky: "*Die Sünde gegen den Geist eines Werkes beginnt immer mit der Sünde gegen den Buchstaben*." And in the introduction to his translation of the *Cur Deus Homo* he says (p. xi): "The German translation takes pains to render the meaning of the author as faithfully as possible. This [faithfulness] was not possible by means of a freer rendering, but only through a literal translation. Hereby, in particular, even the conjunctions (which are so important for literal translation) have as a rule been translated; and the sentence-structure (which in Anselm's case is often lengthy) has, as far as possible, been preserved." Schmitt's translations themselves are virtually word-for-word renderings — so much so that they sometimes even preserve the text's ambiguities. Thus, they do not regularly aim at disambiguating the reference of, say, "*hoc*" but simply put the corresponding German word "*dieses*." Thus, where Anselm's meanings are not immediately clear in the Latin text, Schmitt does not strive to make them immediately clear in the translation. His rationale is obvious: By not recasting Anselm's sentence-structure, by not being more explicit than Anselm is, by not worrying unduly about style, there results a very cautious translation which conveys on its face Anselm's Latin forms.

For my part, I have come a long way toward agreeing with Schmitt's conception — at least vis-à-vis Anselm's *Monologion* and *Proslogion*. These two texts are so condensed that a change in sentence-structure may well tend to change the emphasis and thereby, in subtle ways, the meaning. This fact was never more apparent to me than in *Monologion* 1-5, which I have retranslated more literally in the appendix of this present volume. However, unlike Schmitt, I see no virtue in giving the flavor of Anselm's lengthy sentences or of his sometimes inelegant Latin style. For in English these clumsy features would actually *detract* from the clarity of the argument. And this clarity I regard as the primary goal of the English translation. Where ambiguity is deliberate — as in the case of certain of Plato's dialogues — the translator is obliged to preserve it in the translation. Where it is not deliberate — as in the case of St. Anselm — the translator ought to eliminate it by giving an unambiguous rendering. It is better, I would judge, for a translation to be clearly wrong than for it to be so opaque or so amphibolous that the reader does not know what to make of it.

Thus, I do not agree completely with Schmitt's approach. For I do not view a translation as some uninterpreted edifice which is syntactically congruent with its original. (Nor do I regard it as part of a translator's task to indicate to the reader every place at which there occurs in the text a word-switch — marking it, that is, by a corresponding change of words in the translation.)[4] There is, of course, a danger in giving a clear and explicit translation: viz., that one will overinterpret a passage or will even misinterpret it. But there is a similar danger in giving an opaque translation: viz., that the point of the argument will be missed. Schmitt's method — for all its virtues — has limits to its application. For instance, a word-for-word translation of Gaunilo's text or even a translation which exactly preserves Gaunilo's sentence-structure, will more than likely be unintelligible. From time to time I have asked myself why Schmitt included with his translation of the *Proslogion* the Latin texts of the debate between Anselm and Gaunilo — without, however, translating these. And I cannot help wondering whether there is something about his *wortgetreue und periodenbauliche Methode* that prevented the kind of translation he would have desired.

At any rate, different translators have differing convictions about how literally Anselm's treatises should be translated. Some believe that the *dialogues* should be rendered more freely and spritely than, say, the *Monologion* or *De Concordia*. Others believe that the *ipsissima verba* should be "reproduced," as it were. Still others, such as Rudolf Allers, have no qualms about resorting to précis. Although I have come to believe that literal translations — and "literal" is not here synonymous with "word-for-word" — of Anselm's treatises are preferable, I would be the last person to object to a more free translation. (As Henry recognizes, some of Anselm's logical points are best understood when construed concisely and in the terminology of contemporary logic.) On the other hand, I would probably be among the first to voice reservations about *mot-à-mot*. For we have noticed how Anselm omits words like "*eius*," "*aliud*," and (in *Monologion* I) even "*bonum*."[5] And — to repeat — the *Debate with Gaunilo* testifies to the impossibility of producing, in every case, a coherent translation which does *not* "fill in" between the words.

4. I have not answered the question posed by the title of this chapter. For I do not think that there is any one thing which a translation either is or must be. Whatever it is, it is neither a decoding nor an exact facsimile uninfluenced by the translator's conceptual apparatus. In principle, there is no such thing as "the best possible translation" (although there might be such a thing as the best translation currently available). With respect even to a single sentence, there will be various words, word-orders, and sentence-structures which all adequately translate the sentence's meaning. It would be naive to suppose that a passive construction in Anselm's text will in every case be *better* rendered by the passive form in English, or that in some cases an infinitive construction cannot satisfactorily be rendered participially. And it would be folly to presume that a translation which preserves the very *punctuation* of the text will to this extent be better than one which does not.

I do not think, either, that there is any such thing as *definitive* translation. Or better, I am not sure what the phrase "the definitive translation" would mean. For I have never yet seen an extended translation which did not contain mistakes, could not in one way or another be improved upon, and was not *in some respect* inferior to those it replaced. Now, Joseph Colleran's translation of the *Cur Deus Homo* and *De Conceptu Virginali* bears on its cover the epithet "the definitive translation from the critical edition." Since Colleran's work is altogether worthy of admiration, our noting some of its shortcomings will be worth-while.

These are noted *not* in order to dispute the admirable quality of Colleran's version but in order to attest to the fact that every translation has shortcomings — even "the definitive" one.

(1) omissions: e.g., p. 114, between lines 24–25 (two speeches omitted); p. 146, line 5 ("*nec est aliquid quod huic obviet ratione*" omitted); p. 158, line 8 from bottom ("*ad honorem suum . . . sibi sicut*" omitted).

(2) mistakes: e.g., p. 98, line 7 (has "wicked angels" instead of "wretched angels"; p. 148, line 13 from bottom (has "Son of Man" instead of "Son of God").

(3) inconsistencies: e.g., cf. p. 67, line 5 ("until God in some way manifests it to me with greater clarity") with p. 100, lines 2–3 from bottom ("until God in some way makes known to me something better"); cf. p. 205, line 3 from bottom ("original sin is naturally equal in all infants conceived") with p. 208, lines 11–12 ("this is equal in all infants generated in the natural way").

(4) sentence fragments: e.g., p. 97, last line and the succeeding ones on p. 98.

(5) faulty punctuation which affects the meaning: e.g., p. 210, line 13 (Delete comma after "angels").

(6) unclear antecedent of a demonstrative pronoun: e.g., p. 80, line 11 ("this"); p. 122, line 19 from bottom ("this").

(7) wrong sequence of tenses: e.g., p. 129, lines 15–16 from bottom ("were" . . . "will").

I do not myself think that all such imperfections can be eliminated from a translation. Nor do I regard the presence of these and other imperfections as detracting from the overall excellence of Colleran's accomplishment. Only someone who did not understand the inescapable practical limits[6] of any translation would dream of measuring a translation against some illusory ideal of inerrancy. Perhaps the problem with the epithet "the definitive translation" is that, to the uninitiate, it suggests a kind of finality which translations simply do not have — as well as displaying an immodest degree of self-confidence. (Colleran is not even modest enough to write "the definitive *English* translation from the critical edition.") Furthermore, this epithet — by its very connotations — tends to minimize the credit due to all the previous translations, which in one way or another have given guidance to "the definitive" one.

If it is true that history must be written anew by each generation, it is equally true that each generation must make its own new translations. Therefore, the three volumes of translations just published by Professor Richardson and me cannot — even apart from any outright errors — be thought of as more than provisional. They reflect our present understanding of the thought of St. Anselm. Thus, they render the title "*Cur Deus Homo*" as "Why God became a man" rather than as "Why God became Man." They present Anselm as teaching that the Son of God assumed a human nature, rather than as teaching that He assumed Human Nature. They render "*grammatica*" by a phrase construed as one word. Moreover, in order to clarify the meaning of *Monologion* 32, they take the liberty of saying "Every word [or image] is a word [or image] of some thing. . . ." At places, they construe "*in nullo intellectu*" as "in no respect," or as "not at all"; and for "*nec actu nec intellectu*" they say "neither actually nor conceivably." In *Proslogion* 2 "*intelligit esse*" is construed as "judges to exist"; and at S I, 128:9 "*constare*" is taken as "to exist." It would be tedious to rehearse the dozens of other instances which testify that these translations are in no sense decodings, and which reveal how our (at least putative) comprehension of Anselm has become integral to the translations themselves. As our understanding progresses, we shall no doubt want to emend certain of these readings. And those who do not share with us our current understanding will, no doubt, not be able to accept the present readings. We invite them to help us to attain a better understanding, since we are willing to be led.

In last analysis, the utility and the viability of these translations of Anselm's Complete Treatises will have to be judged by the community of Anselm-scholars. If the translations serve in some measure to convey the thoughts behind the words of the Latin text, if they serve as a basis for someone's subsequently giving more elegant or more accurate renderings, if they serve to reawaken interest in Anselm's ideas — then even though they are not definitive, they will perhaps be of some intermediate value. Of course, the serious student of Anselm will follow the example of the seasoned scholar in taking as his motto: *Zu den Lateintexten selbst*! But he may find himself confronted by the inability to understand the author of these texts *as well as* this author understood himself.[7] And this outcome may affect his evaluation of Schleiermacher's claim that the goal of hermeneutics is to teach us how to understand an author *better than* this author understood himself.

Whittemore, Robert C. "Panentheistic Implications of the Ontological Argument," *Southern Journal of Philosophy*, 9 (Summer 1971), 157–162.

Wilbanks, Jan J. "Some (Logical) Trouble for St. Anselm," *New Scholasticism*, 47(Summer 1973), 361–365.

Wilks, Washington and Mark. *The Three Archbishops: Lanfranc-Anselm-A'Becket*. London: Alfred W. Bennett, n.d.

Williams, George H. "The Sacramental Presuppositions of Anselm's *Cur Deus Homo*," *Church History*, 26(September 1957), 245–274.

Yandell, Keith. "Richard R. La Croix, Proslogion II and III: A Third Interpretation of Anselm's Argument," *Journal of Value Inquiry*, 3(Summer 1974), 143–157.

Zimmermann, Albert. "Die Ratio Anselmi in einem anonymen Metaphysikkommentar des 14. Jahrhunderts," AA IV, 1, 195–201.

Zimmermann, Karl. "Anselm von Canterbury, der ontologische Gottesbeweis und das Problem der metaphysischen Erkenntnis" in *Die Metaphysik im Mittelalter. Ihr Ursprung und ihre Bedeutung*, pp. 184–191, (*Vorträge des II. internationalen Kongresses für mittelalterliche Philosophie, Köln, 31. August – 6. September 1961*), ed. Paul Wilpert. Berlin: W. de Gruyter, 1963.

INDEX OF PROPER NAMES

APPENDIX I

MONOLOGION CHAPTER TITLES AND A TRANSLATION OF CHAPTERS 1–5

1. There is something that is the best, the greatest, the highest of all existing things.
2. The same topic continued.
3. There is a Nature which exists through itself, which is the highest of all existing things, and through which exists whatever is.
4. The same topic continued.
5. Just as this Nature exists through itself (*per se*) and [all] other things exist through it, so it exists from itself (*ex se*) and [all] other things exist from it.
6. This Nature was not brought into existence through the assistance of any cause. Nevertheless, it does not exist through nothing or from nothing. How it can be understood to be through itself and from itself.
7. How all other things are through and from this Nature.
8. What is meant by "[This Nature] made all things from nothing."
9. Before their creation those things which have been made from nothing were not nothing with respect to the thought (*rationem*) of their Maker.
10. This thought (*ratio*) is an expression of things, just as a craftsman first tells himself what he is going to make.
11. Nevertheless, this comparison contains many differences.
12. The Expression of the Supreme Being is the Supreme Being.
13. As all things were created through the Supreme Being, so they are sustained through it.
14. The Supreme Being is in all things and through all things; and all things are from it, through it, and in it.
15. What can and cannot be predicated of the Supreme Being substantively.
16. For the Supreme Being to be just is the same as for it to be justice. The same type of identity holds for other predicates of a similar kind. None of these predicates indicates the quality or the quantity of this Being, but they indicate what it is.
17. [The Supreme Being] is so simple that anything which can be said of its essence is one and the same in it. And something can be predicated substantively of the Supreme Being only with respect to what it is.

18. [The Supreme Being] is without beginning and without end.
19. How nothing existed before or will exist after the Supreme Being.
20. The Supreme Being exists in every place and at all times.
21. [The Supreme Being] exists in no place at no time.
22. How [the Supreme Being] exists in every place at every time and in no place at no time.
23. How [the Supreme Being] can better be understood to be everywhere than in every place.
24. How [the Supreme Being] can better be understood to exist always than to exist at every time.
25. [The Supreme Being] is not mutable in virtue of any accidents.
26. In what sense [the Supreme Being] is to be called substance. It is beyond every substance. It is uniquely whatever it is.
27. Although [the Supreme Being] is not included in the usual classification of substances, it is a substance and an individual spirit.
28. This Spirit exists in an unqualified sense; compared to it created things do not exist.
29. This Spirit's Expression is the very same thing as this Spirit. Nevertheless, there are not two spirits but only one.
30. This Expression does not consist of many words, but is one word.
31. This Word is not the likeness of created things but is true Existence (*veritas essentiae*). Created things are a likeness of this true Existence. Which natures are greater and more excellent than others.
32. The Supreme Spirit speaks itself by means of a coeternal Word.
33. The Supreme Spirit speaks both itself and its creation by means of one word.
34. How [the Supreme Spirit] can be seen to speak creatures by its own Word.
35. Whatever was created exists as life and truth in the Word and knowledge of the Supreme Spirit.
36. In what an incomprehensible manner the Supreme Spirit speaks and knows the things made by it.
37. Whatever the Supreme Spirit is in relation to creatures this Spirit's Word also is. Nevertheless, both together are not more than one.
38. It cannot be said what two they are, although they must be two.
39. This Word exists from the Supreme Spirit by being begotten.
40. The Spirit is most truly parent, and the Word most truly offspring.
41. The Supreme Spirit most truly begets and the Word is most truly begotten.
42. It is the property of the one to be most truly begetter and father; and it is the property of the other to be most truly begotten and son.
43. Reconsideration of what is common to both and of what is proper to each.
44. How the one is the essence of the other.
45. The Son can more fittingly be called the essence of the Father than the Father [can be called the essence] of the Son. Similarly, the Son is the strength of the Father, the wisdom of the Father, and the like.
46. How various of the statements expressed above can also be understood in another way.
47. The Son is understanding of understanding, truth of truth, etc.
48. The Father is referred to as memory, just as the Son is referred to as

understanding. How the Son is the understanding (or wisdom) of memory, the memory of the Father, and memory of memory.

49. The Supreme Spirit loves itself.
50. This love proceeds equally from the Father and the Son.
51. The Father and the Son love themselves and each other in equal degree.
52. This Love is as great as the Supreme Spirit.
53. This Love is the same thing that the Supreme Spirit is; and yet, this Love is one spirit with the Father and the Son.
54. [This Love] proceeds as a whole from the Father and as a whole from the Son. Nevertheless, there is only one love.
55. [This Love] is not the son of the Father and of the Son.
56. Only the Father is begetter and unbegotten. Only the Son is begotten. Only their Love is neither begotten nor unbegotten.
57. This Love is uncreated and creator, even as are the Father and the Son. Nevertheless, they are together one uncreated creator, not three. This Love can be called the Spirit of the Father and the Son.
58. As the Son is the essence and wisdom of the Father in the sense that He has the same essence and wisdom as the Father, so their Spirit is the essence, wisdom, and the like, of the Father and the Son.
59. The Father and the Son and their Spirit exist equally in one another.
60. No one of them needs the other for remembering, understanding, or loving — because each singly is memory, understanding, love, and whatever else must be present in the Supreme Being.
61. Nevertheless, there are not three [fathers or three sons or three spirits] but one father, one son, and one spirit common to them.
62. How from these [viz., the Father, the Son, and their Spirit] many sons seem to be begotten.
63. How in the Supreme Spirit there is only one son and one who has a son.
64. Although inexplicable, this [teaching] must be believed.
65. How regarding this ineffable matter something true was stated.
66. Through the rational mind one comes nearest to knowing the Supreme Being.
67. The mind is the mirror and image of the Supreme Being.
68. The rational creature was created for loving the Supreme Being.
69. The soul which always loves the Supreme Being lives at some time in true happiness.
70. The Supreme Being gives itself as a reward to the soul which loves it.
71. The soul which despises the Supreme Being will be eternally wretched.
72. Every human soul is immortal.
73. The soul is either always wretched or else at some time truly happy.
74. No soul is unjustly deprived of the Supreme Good. The soul is supposed to seek the Supreme Good wholeheartedly.
75. We are to hope for the Supreme Being.
76. We are to believe in the Supreme Being.
77. We ought to believe equally in the Father, the Son, and their Spirit — in each distinctly and in all three together.
78. Which faith is alive and which is dead.
79. What three the Supreme Being can in some respect be said to be.

80. The Supreme Being exercises dominion over all things and rules all things and is the only God.

Chapter One: There is something that is the best, the greatest, the highest of all existing things.

There may be someone who, as a result of not hearing or not believing, is ignorant of the one Nature, highest of all existing things, alone sufficient unto itself in its eternal beatitude, through its own omnipotent goodness giving and causing all other things to be something and in some respect to fare well. And he may also be ignorant of the many other things which we necessarily believe about God and His creatures. If so, then I think that in great part he can persuade himself of these matters merely by reason alone (*sola ratione*) — if he is of even average intelligence. Although he can do this in many ways, I shall propose one way which I regard as the most accessible for him. For since all men seek to enjoy only those things which they consider good, at some time or other he can readily turn his mind's eye to investigating that thing from whence are derived these goods which he seeks only because he judges them to be good. Thus, with reason guiding and with him following,[2] he may then rationally advance to the matters of which he is unreasonably ignorant. Nevertheless, if in this investigation I say something that a greater authority does not mention: I want it to be accepted in such way that even if it is a necessary consequence of reasons which will seem [good] to me, it is not thereby said to be absolutely necessary, but is said only to be able to appear necessary for the time being.[3]

It is, then, easy for someone to ask himself the following question: Although the good things whose very great variety we perceive by the body's senses and distinguish by the mind's reason are so numerous, are we to believe that there is one thing through which all good things are good, or are we to believe that different goods are good through different things?[4] Indeed, the following is thoroughly certain and is evident to all who are willing to give heed: Whatever things are said to be something in such way that they are said to be it either in greater or lesser or equal degree in relation to one another, are said to be it through something which is understood to be identical in the different things (rather than through something different in the different things), whether it is observed in them in equal or in unequal degree. For example, whatever things are said to be *just* in relation to one another — whether they are said to be equally just or whether some are said to be more just and others less just — can be understood to be just only through justice, which is not something different in these different things. Therefore, since it is certain that if compared with one another all good things are either equally or unequally good, it is necessary that all [good] things are good through something which is understood to be identical in these various goods — although at times, ostensibly, some goods are said to be good though different things. For, ostensibly, a horse is said to be 'good through one thing because it is strong,' and is said to be 'good through another thing because it is swift.' Although, ostensibly, it is said to be good through strength and good through swiftness, nevertheless strength and swiftness are seen not to be the same thing. Now, if a horse is good because it is strong or swift, how is it that a strong and swift robber is evil? Rather, then, just as a strong and swift robber is evil because he is harmful, so a strong and swift horse is good because it is useful.[5] Indeed, ordinarily, nothing is thought to be good except because of a certain usefulness (e.g., health and whatever conduces to health are called good) or because of some kind of excellence (e.g., beauty and whatever conduces to beauty are considered good). But since the reasoning already seen can in no way be faulted, it is necessary that even every useful and every excellent thing — if they are truly goods — be good through that very thing (whatever it be) through which all [good] things must be good.

But who could doubt that that through which all [goods] are good is [itself] a great good? Therefore, it is good through itself since every [good] thing is good through it.[6] So it follows that all other [good] things are good through something other than what they are and that this other alone [is good] through itself. But no good which is good through something other [than itself] is equal to or greater than that good which is good through itself. Hence, only that which alone is good through itself is supremely good; for that is supreme which so excels others that it has neither an equal nor a superior. Now, what is supremely good is also supremely great. Therefore, there is one thing which is supremely good and supremely great — i.e., which is the highest of all existing things.

Chapter Two: The same topic continued.

Just as something has been found to be supremely good inasmuch as all good things are good through some one thing which is good through itself, so it follows necessarily that something is supremely great inasmuch as whatever things are great are great through some one thing which is great through itself. I do not mean great in size, as is a material object; but I mean great[7] in the sense that the greater anything is the better or more excellent it is — as in the case of wisdom. Now, since only what is supremely good can be supremely great, it is necessary that something be both supremely great and supremely good, i.e., the highest of all existing things.

Chapter Three: There is a Nature which exists through itself, which is the highest of all existing things, and through which exists whatever is.

In fact, not only are all good things good through the same thing, and all great things great through the same thing, but also whatever *is* is seen to exist through some one thing. For whatever is exists either through something or through nothing. But it is not the case that anything exists through nothing. For it cannot even be conceived that there is anything which exists other than through something. Thus, whatever is exists only through something. Accordingly, either there is one thing or there are many things through which all existing things exist. But if there are many things, then either (1) they are traced back to some one thing through which they exist, or (2) each of the many exists through itself, or (3) they exist mutually through one another. (1′) But if these many exist through one thing, then it is not, after all, the case that everything exists through a plurality, but is rather the case that everything exists through that one thing through which the many exist. (2′) But if each of the many exists through itself, then surely there is some one power (or nature)-of-existing-through-itself which they have in order to exist through themselves. And there is no doubt that they exist through this one thing through which they have the fact that they exist through themselves.[8] Thus, all things exist through this one thing more truly than through the many things which themselves are not able to exist without this one thing. (3′) But [sound] reasoning does not allow that the many exist mutually through one another, for the thought that a thing exists through that to which it gives existence is irrational. For not even relational things exist in this manner through one another. For example, when a master and a servant are referred to relatively to each other, the two men referred to do not at all exist through each other, nor do the relations by which they are referred to exist at all through each other (for these relations exist through their subjects).

Therefore, since the truth altogether excludes [the possibility] of there being a plurality through which all things exist, that through which all existing things exist must be one thing.

Since, then, all existing things exist through one thing, without doubt this one thing exists through itself. Thus, all existing things other [than this one] exist through something other [than themselves]; and this one alone exists through itself. But whatever exists through something other [than itself] exists less than that which alone exists through itself and through which all other things exist. Accordingly, that which exists through itself exists most greatly of all. Therefore, there is some one thing which alone exists most greatly and most highly of all. But what exists most greatly of all and is that through which exists whatever is good and great and whatever is anything at all — this must be supremely good, supremely great, the highest of all existing things. For this reason, there is something which —whether it is called a being, a substance, or a nature[9] — is the best and the greatest and the highest of all existing things.

Chapter Four: The same topic continued.

Moreover, if anyone considers the natures of things, he cannot help perceiving that they are not all of equal excellence but that some of them differ by an inequality of gradation.[10] For if anyone doubts that a horse is by nature better than a tree and that a man is more excellent than a horse, then surely this [person] ought not to be called a man. So although we cannot deny that some natures are better than others, nonetheless reason persuades us that one of them is so preeminent that no other nature is superior to it. For if such a division of gradation were so limitless that for each grade a higher grade could be found, then reason would be led to the conclusion that the number of these natures is boundless. But everyone holds such a view to be absurd, except someone who himself is utterly foolish. Therefore, necessarily, there is a nature which is so superior to some other or others that there is no nature to which it is ranked as inferior.

But this nature which is thus superior is singular — or else there is more than one nature of this kind, and they are equal. Assume that they are many and equal. Since they cannot be equal through different things but only through the same thing, this one thing through which they are equally so great either is the same thing which they are (i.e., is their essence) or else is something other than what they are. Now, if it is nothing other than their essence, then just as their essences are one rather than many, so too the natures are one rather than many. For here I am taking the nature to be identical with the essence. On the other hand, if that through which these many natures are equally great is something other than what they are, surely they are less than that through which they are great. For whatever is great through something other [than itself] is less than that other through which it is great. Therefore, they would not be so great that nothing else is greater than they. Now, if neither through what they are nor through something other [than what they are] it is possible for there to be many equal natures than which nothing else is more excellent, then there cannot at all be a plurality of such natures. Therefore, the alternative which remains is: There is only one Nature which is so superior to [all] others that it is inferior to none. Now, that which is such is the greatest and the best of all existing things. Thus, there is a Nature which is the highest of all existing things.

But it can be the highest only if through itself it is what it is and only if through *it* all [other] existing things are what they are. For since a few moments ago reason taught that that which exists through itself and through which all other things exist is the highest of all existing things: either, conversely,[11] that which is the highest of all exists through itself and all other things exist through it, or else there are many supreme beings. But it is evident that there are not many supreme beings. Hence, there is a Nature, or Substance, or Being (*essentia*)[12] which through itself is good and great, and through itself is what it is; and through this Nature exists whatever truly is good or great or something. And this Nature is the Supreme Good, the Supreme Greatness (*summum magnum*), the Supreme Being (*ens*), or Subsistence (*subsistens*) — in short, the highest of all existing things.

Chapter Five: Just as this Nature exists through itself (*per se*) and [all] other things exist through it, so it exists from itself (*ex se*) and [all] other things exist from it.

Since, then, our discoveries so far have been rewarding, it is agreeable to investigate whether this Nature and all that is something exist only *from* this Nature, even as they exist only *through* this Nature. Clearly, we can say that what exists from a thing exists also through it, and that what exists through a thing exists also from it. For example, what is from matter and through a craftsman can also be said to be through matter and from a craftsman. For through both and from both (i.e., by both) it has its existence, even though the way it exists through matter and from matter is not the same as the way it exists through a craftsman and from a craftsman. As a logical consequence, then: Just as through the Supreme Nature all existing things are what they are, and thus this Nature exists through itself, whereas [all] other things exist through an other [than themselves] — so all existing things exist from the Supreme Nature, and thus this Nature exists from itself, whereas [all] other things exist from something other [than themselves].

APPENDIX II

CORRIGENDA FOR VOLUME I

A. *First SCM Edition:*

p. 19, lines 16–17: Change to read: 'Each of these three kinds of speaking has its corresponding kind of word'.
p. 39, last line: Change 'limitedness' to 'unlimitedness'.
p. 48, line 22: Add to beginning: 'and understands'.
p. 108: Transpose lines 6 and 7.
p. 140, lines 10 and 30: Change 'repay' to 'pay'.

B. *First SCM Edition and Second North American Edition:*

p. 11, lines 17–19: Literally: 'what is said to exist through something is seen to exist either through something efficient or through matter or through some other *aid*, as through an *instrument*.'
p. 66, line 6: Change 'without qualification' to 'at all'.
p. 72, line 9 from bottom: Change 'Word alone' to 'sole Word'.
p. 82, last line: Change 'striving unto' to 'striving for'.

C. *First SCM Edition and Second North American Edition:*

The following improvements will make the translations in Volume I more literal:
p. 12, lines 14 and 19: Put brackets around 'have to'.
p. 12, line 33: Change 'such great good' to 'so great a good'.
p. 13, lines 5–7: Change to read: 'anything efficient or from anything material, and was not helped to begin existing by any [auxiliary] causes'.
p. 14, last line: Change to read: 'which is the Supreme Good itself, would not be a good'.
p. 16, line 14: Change 'the greatest' to 'most greatly'.
p. 25, lines 10–11: Change to read: 'Indeed, ostensibly, it is said to be any one of these through a quality or a quantity;'.
p. 25, lines 14–15: Change to read: 'Hence, the supremely good Substance, it seems, is being said to be *just* by participation in a quality, viz., justice.'
p. 25, lines 23 and 30: Change 'itself justice' to 'justice itself'.
p. 42, line 2 from bottom: Change 'cannot' to 'cannot at all'.
p. 43, line 9: Change 'what they were' and 'what they will be' to 'their past existence' and 'their future existence' respectively.
p. 47, line 8 from bottom: Put brackets around 'are we to think'.

p. 47, line 2 from bottom: Change 'not' to 'not at all'.
p. 55, line 2: Change 'the Word' to '[the Word] which is begotten'.
p. 58, lines 15–16: Change to read: 'Therefore, the complete Father exists through Himself and likewise the complete Son exists through'.
p. 60, line 9: Delete 'is not different'.
p. 74, line 5: Change 'stated' to 'stated about it'.
p. 75, line 13: Change 'For' to 'For example'.
p. 75, line 16: Change 'express' to 'express to me'.
p. 77, line 10: Change 'In the last analysis' to 'In fact'.
p. 79, line 5: Delete 'so'.
p. 85, lines 9–10: Change to read: 'individual things (and these mostly exist in plurality).'
p. 85, line 12: Change 'substances' to 'sub-stances'.
p. 92, last line: Change 'begun hungering' to 'in hunger begun'.
p. 94, line 3: Change 'For' to 'For example,'.
p. 94, line 22: Put brackets around 'God'.
p. 95, lines 20–21: Delete: '[i.e., its essence]'.
p. 95, line 9 from bottom: Change to read: 'Anyone who comprehends this [description], surely understands that this being [than which a greater cannot be thought] so exists that it cannot even conceivably not exist. Therefore, anyone who understands that God is such [a being] cannot think that He does not exist.'
p. 95, line 5 from bottom: Delete footnote 33.
p. 104, line 4: Change 'For since something of this kind can be thought' to 'For since there can be thought to be something of this kind'.
p. 110, line 2 from bottom: Change 'goodness' to 'a good'.
p. 116, line 9: Put a comma after 'exist'.
p. 119, line 10: Put comma after 'lands'.

Where '*per aliud*' is translated as 'through another,' the sense is usually 'through something other [than itself/themselves]'.

On Behalf of the Fool 4 reads more literally as follows: [4] To this may be added a point previously alluded to: viz., that upon hearing of that which is greater than all others that can be thought (which is said to be able to be no other than God Himself), I cannot think of this thing (or have it in the understanding) by reference to any object known to me through species or genus — just as in this way I also cannot think of God Himself (whom surely, for this reason, I can indeed think not to exist). For neither am I acquainted with this thing itself nor am I able to infer [what it is like] by reference to some other similar being, since, as even you maintain, it is such that there cannot be anything else similar [to it]. Now, suppose that I were to hear something being said about a man totally a stranger to me — a man whom I was not even sure existed. Still, I would be able to think of him by means of the specific or generic notion by which I know what a man is (or what men are) — i.e., by reference to the very thing a man is. However, it could happen that the one who told [me about this stranger] was lying and that the man whom I thought of does not exist. Nonetheless, I would still have conceived of him by reference to the reality which *any* man is, though not by reference to the reality which *that* man is. But when I hear someone speaking of God or of something greater than all others, I cannot have this thing in my thought and understanding in the way that I might have that unreal man in my thought and understanding. For although I can think of a nonexistent man by reference to a real thing known to me, I cannot at all think of this thing [which is greater than all others] except only with respect to the verbal expression. And with respect only to a verbal expression a real thing can scarcely, if at all, be thought of. For when one thinks with respect to a mere verbal expression, he thinks not so much the verbal expression itself (i.e., not so much the sound of the letters or the syllables), which assuredly is a real thing, as he does the signification of the expression that is heard. Yet, [the signification is] not [thought] in the manner of one who knows what is usually signified by the expression — i.e., one who thinks in accordance with the thing, whether it is real or exists in thought alone. Rather, [the signification is thought] in the manner of one who does not know what is usually signified by the verbal expression but who (1) thinks only according to the movement of the mind brought about by hearing this expression and who (2) has difficulty in representing to himself the signification of what he has heard. (But it would be surprising if he could ever [in this manner discern] what the thing is.) So, then, it is still evident that this is the only way this thing is in my understanding when I hear and understand someone who says that there is something greater than all others that can be thought.

All of this is my reply to the claim that that supreme nature already exists in my understanding.

APPENDIX III

ADDENDA AND CORRIGENDA FOR F. S. SCHMITT'S *SANCTI ANSELMI OPERA OMNIA*, VOLS. I AND II

Probably no critical edition of any medieval text is inerrant. Thus, it is to F. S. Schmitt's praise that his edition of Anselm's treatises contains so relatively few errors. At S II, 35 the note for line 7 has "unam substantiam *B*" instead of "unam essentiam *B*." S II, 264:18 has "salvator" instead of "salvatur." S II, 288:12 has "qui" instead of "quid." S II, 284:28 supplies "procedit" in brackets, while failing to indicate that "est" occurs in *B*. And at S II, 259 the note for line 15 mistakenly indicates that *B* adds the word "esse." Such discrepancies — recorded below, together with still others — pose no special threat to the overall reliability of the Schmitt edition. Given the difficulties of proofreading and the unwieldiness of working with more than one manuscript, it is remarkable that there are not far more such discrepancies. At any rate, what makes an edition a *critical* edition is not that it is totally error-free but that (like Schmitt's edition) it is judicious in its choice of the "best" reading. As examples of such judiciousness we may note S II, 40:15, where Schmitt selects "aliquantum" in preference to "aliquando," and S II, 129:3, where he favors "debere" over "debent." These choices assume importance because they represent deliberate deviations from Lambeth 59 and Bodley 271 respectively.

The main problem with Schmitt's edition is that the notes do not list all of the variant readings in the manuscripts which are being compared. Indeed, there appears to be arbitrariness with respect to which readings are signaled in the notes and which are not. For example, at S II, 66 the note for line 6 tells us that "voluisse" is the variant-reading given in *M*; yet, we are not told that this same reading occurs in *B*. At S II, 264:18 there is no note at all to indicate that for "quia gratia" *B* and *E* have "quia gratis." Or again, although Schmitt takes the trouble to let us know such minutia as that at S II, 89:12, *B* and *N* have "nil" instead of "nihil" (see also S II, 281:7 and II, 287:14), he does not bother to inform us that at S II, 133, *B* has "et" instead of "etiam." Similarly, although he indicates at S II, 245:5 that *S* has "dignatur" instead of "dignabitur," he does not mention that *B* and *E* also have "dignatur." And in editing *De Concordia* he cites only three-fourths of the variant-readings from *E*.

At the very beginning of Vol. I Schmitt cautions the reader by writing: "Quidquid non omnino ad emendatum textum conficiendum necessarium erat, restrinximus. Apparatus igitur qui varias praebet lectiones amplus non est, quoniam quantum fieri poterat codices nisi optimos et antiquissimos non adhibuimus. Historiam enim textus qui per saecula traditus est scribere in animo nobis non erat, cum hanc rem parum cuique cordi esse arbitremus.'' However, there is a difference between not making use of all the manuscript-versions and not signaling all the variant-readings in a manuscript of which one does make use. Because Schmitt neglects this signaling, his critical apparatus is defective. For, indeed, the reader should be pointed to such facts as that *B* and *E* have ''ut'' and not ''et'' at S II, 276:10.

The following list of addenda and corrigenda makes no attempt to be exhaustive.

1. S I, 17: add as note for line 25: 'nulli (*sicut a Schmitt correctum est*)] nullo *B*'.
2. S I, 22: add as note for line 13: 'Nam] *hic incipit c. VIII B*'.
3. S I, 25: add as note for line 27: 'factae (*sicut a Schmitt correctum est*)] facta *B*'.
4. S I, 56: add as note for line 13: 'significant (*sicut a Schmitt correctum est*)] significat *B*'.
5. S I, 67: add as note for line 25: 'proprie] propriae *B*'.
6. S I, 163: add as note for line 5: 'ipsae] ipse *B*'.
7. S I, 164: add as note for line 9: 'appellativae] appellative *B*'.
8. S I, 183: delete note for line 1.
9. S I, 186: add as note for line 24: 'malae] male *B*'.
10. S I, 205: add as note for line 16: 'peccans sit] peccans fit *B*'.
11. S I, 213: add as note for line 28: 'Quod] *c. IV incipit B*'.
12. S I, 232: add to note for line 21: 'etiamsi] si etiam *B*'.
13. S I, 243: add as note for line 14: 'Aliter] *c. VI incipit B*'.
14. S I, 251: add to note for line 17: *Dubium est ubi c. XII incipiat B*'.
15. S I, 268: add as note for line 24: 'non meruerat (*sicut a Schmitt correctum est)*] non *om. B*'.
16. Enclose in brackets the Roman-numeral divisions in DIV.
17. S II, 9: add as note for line 21: 'dialecticae] dialectice *B*'.
18. S II, 12: add as note for line 10: 'opposite] oppositae *B*'.
19. S II, 32: add as note for line 9: 'temporis] vel compositionis partium *add. B*'.
20. S II, 35:4: put 'esse cuius' for 'esse; cuius'.
21. S II, 35: change note for line 7 to read: 'unam personam] unam essentiam *B*'.
22. S II, 42:6: put 'congruo' for 'cungruo'.
23. S II, 55: add as note for line 2: 'posset] possit *B*'.
24. S II, 66: add to note for line 6: 'valuisse] voluisse *B*'.
25. S II, 76: note for lines 2–3: change to read: 'Cf. *De casu diaboli*, cc. II, III, XXV . . .'.
26. S II, 80: add as note for line 6: 'aeterne] aeternae *B*'.
27. S II, 86:26: put 'misericordiam' for 'miserico diam' (Frommann Verlag reprint only).
28. S II, 91: add as note for line 12: 'ut] Ut *B*'.
29. S II, 97: change note for lines 4–5 to read: 'c. IX, p. 61, 29–30'.
30. S II, 119: add as note for line 18: 'EVA] evam *B*'.
31. S II, 128: add as note for line 19: 'sed] sed et *B*'.

32. S II, 133: add as note for line 8: 'etiam] et *B*'.

33. S II, 133:14: put 'attribuere' for 'attribuire'.

34. S II, 144: change note for line 3 to read: 'Cf. *De concordia*, qu. III, n. XI'.

35. S II, 146:29: put 'breviter' for 'brevitur'.

36. S II, 166:16: change 'rectudinem' to 'rectitudinem'.

37. S II, 195:9: put 'intelligi' for 'intellig'.

38. S II, 195:10: put 'aereo' for 'aereoi'.

39. S II, 223: change note for line 3 to read: 'Annis 1091–1111'.

40. S II, 245: change note for line 5 to read: 'dignatur *BES* . . .'.

41. S II, 247: add to note for line 10: 'quoniam] quod *add. E*'.

42. S II, 249: note for lines 15 and 17: change 'Signum *E*' to 'Linum *E*'.

43. S II, 249: add as note for line 23: 'esse non] non esse *E*'.

44. S II, 250: add as note for line 31: 'praescientiam] praescientia *E*'.

45. S II, 253: add as note for line 10: 'attendimus] videbimus quod *add. E*'.

46. S II, 253: add as note for line 12: 'quod ipsum] ipsum *om. E*'.

47. S II, 257: change note for line 10 to read: 'voluntas . . . qua] voluntas aliud rectitudo voluntatis quae *E*'.

48. S II, 259: change note for line 7 to read: 'est a deo] a deo est *E*'.

49. S II, 259: add as note for line 8: 'recte . . . recte] rectum . . . rectum *E*'.

50. S II, 259: add as note for lines 9–10: 'recte . . . recte] rectum . . . rectum *E*'.

51. S II, 259: delete from note for line 15: 'quod est] esse *add. B*'.

52. S II, 259: add as note for line 28: 'imputando] imputanda *BE*'.

53. S II, 261: add as note for line 9: 'autem] *om. BE*'.

54. S II, 261: add as note for line 10: 'ut] sicut *E*'.

55. S II, 261: add as note for line 17: 'aperte] aperta *E*'.

56. S II, 262: add as note for line 4: 'Quamvis tamen] tamen *om. E*'.

57. S II, 263: add as note for line 9: 'illum] eum *E*'.

58. S II, 264: add as note for line 10: 'esse penitus] penitus *om. E*'.

59. S II, 264: add as note for line 10 'hac itaque] hac igitur *E*'.

60. S II, 264: add as note for line 18: 'salvator] salvatur *BE*'.

61. S II, 264: add as note for line 18: 'quia gratia] quia gratis *BE*'.

62. S II, 265: add as note for line 19: 'et] de *add. E*'.

63. S II, 266: add as note for line 1: 'quoniam] quia *E*'.

64. S II, 266: add as note for line 17: ''servari] salvari *E*'.

65. S II, 267: add as note for line 3: 'solo deo] deo solo *E*'.

66. S II, 268: add as note for line 16: 'perpetuam] aeternam *E*'.

67. S II, 268: add as note for line 23: 'illis] eis *E*'.

68. S II, 270: change note for line 1 to read: 'in iniquitate et in duritia sua *E*'.

69. S II, 270: add as note for lines 11–12: 'liberum arbitrium . . . invitare] liberum . . . invitare arbitrium *E*'.

70. S II, 270: add as note for line 12: 'invitat] invitet *E*'.

71. S II, 270: add as note for line 28: 'potest quod] potest aliquid quod *E*'.

72. S II, 274: add as note for line 2: 'nisi per mortem] nisi morte *BE*'.

73. S II, 274: add as note for line 7: 'irae] ire *B*'.

74. S II, 276: add as note for line 10: 'et] ut *BE*'.

75. S II, 277: add as note for line 10: 'promereremur] mereremur *BE*'.
76. S II, 277: add as note for line 18: 'intrusus] retrusus *E*'.
77. S II, 277: add as note for line 24: 'irrecuperabiliter] irreparabiliter *E*'.
78. S II, 278: add as note for line 9: 'promittant] promittunt *BE*'.
79. S II, 279: add as note for line 1: 'aptae] apte *B*'.
80. S II, 279: add as note for line 22: 'est] *om. E*'.
81. S II, 284: add as note for line 25: 'meriti boni] boni meriti *BE*'.
82. S II, 284: add as note for line 28: 'non] est *add. BE*'.
83. S II, 285: add as note for line 4: 'mala est (*sicut a Schmitt correctum est*)] est *om. BE*'.
84. S II, 286: add as note for line 2: 'haberi] habere *BE*'.
85. S II, 286: add as note for line 29: 'servandum] servandam *E*'.
86. S II, 287: add as note for line 2: change 'est: aliquid' to 'est aliquid:'.
87. S II, 287: add as note for line 8: 'illa] ipsa *E*'.
88. S II, 287: add as note for line 27: 'illi] *om. E*'.
89. S II, 288: add as note for line 12: 'qui] quid *BE*'.
90. S II, 288: add as note for line 15: 'fluctuabat] fluctabat *B*'.

Note also the addenda and corrigenda listed at the end of Vol. II of *Sancti Anselmi Opera Omnia* in the Frommann Verlag reprint.

ABBREVIATIONS

Anselm's Works

M	*Monologion* (A Soliloquy)
P	*Proslogion* (An Address)
DG	*De Grammatico*
DV	*De Veritate* (On Truth)
DL	*De Libertate Arbitrii* (Freedom of Choice)
DCD	*De Casu Diaboli* (The Fall of the Devil)
DIV	*Epistola de Incarnatione Verbi* (The Incarnation of the Word)
CDH	*Cur Deus Homo* (Why God Became a Man)
DCV	*De Conceptu Virginali et de Originali Peccato* (The Virgin Conception and Original Sin)
DP	*De Processione Spiritus Sancti* (The Procession of the Holy Spirit)
DC	*De Concordia Praescientiae et Praedestinationis et Gratiae Dei cum Libero Arbitrio* (The Harmony of the Foreknowledge, the Predestination, and the Grace of God with Free Choice)
PF	*Ein neues unvollendetes Werk des hl. Anselm von Canterbury* (Philosophical Fragments). Latin text ed. F. S. Schmitt and published in *Beiträge zur Geschichte der Philosophie und Theologie des Mittelalters*, 33/3. (Münster: Aschendorff Press, 1936)

Other Works

DT	Augustine's *De Trinitate* (On the Trinity) E.g., DT 7.4.7 indicates Book 7, Chapter 4, Section 7
PL	*Patrologia Latina* (ed. J. P. Migne)
AA	*Analecta Anselmiana* (Frankfurt/M.: Minerva GmbH). Vol. I (1969); Vol. II (1970); Vol. III (1972); Vol. IV (1975); Vol. V (1976). Vols. I–III ed. F. S. Schmitt; Vols. IV–V ed. Helmut Kohlenberger. A continuing series.
S	*Sancti Anselmi Opera Omnia*. Ed. F. S. Schmitt. (Edinburgh: Thomas Nelson and Sons). 6 Vols. (1946–1961). Vol. I first published in Seckau, 1938; Vol. II first published in Rome, 1940. All volumes reprinted by Friedrich Fromann Press (Stuttgart, 1968) with an intro. by Schmitt drawing together his articles on Anselm's text, and with corrigenda for the text.

NOTES

Preface

1. J. Hopkins, *A Companion to the Study of St. Anselm* (Minneapolis: University of Minnesota Press, 1972). With regard to the present book, even the advanced scholar may prefer to bypass Section II of Chapter II, which is much too detailed to be interesting.

2. Benedicta Ward in *Speculum*, 49 (October 1974), 742–743.

3. By "simple" the author seems to mean "uncomplicated." Words such as these two are notoriously vague.

4. See Appendix I of the present volume.

5. AA V (1976), 25–53.

6. N.B. *An Essay on Philosophical Method* (Oxford: Clarendon Press, 1933), p. 217: "Comprehension and criticism, or understanding what the writer means and asking whether it is true, are distinct attitudes, but not separable. The attempt to comprehend without criticizing is in the last resort a refusal to share in one essential particular the experience of the writer; for he has written no single sentence, if he is worth reading, without asking himself 'is that true?', and this critical attitude to his own work is an essential element in the experience which we as his readers are trying to share. If we refuse to criticize, therefore, we are making it impossible for ourselves to comprehend."

See also J. Hopkins, "Bultmann on Collingwood's Philosophy of History," *Harvard Theological Review*, 58 (April 1965), 227–233.

Chapter I: On Translating Anselm's Complete Treatises

1. Toronto and New York: The Edwin Mellen Press. Vol. I, 1974; Vols. II & III, 1976.

2. See DIV 4 (S II, 18:3–5).

3. Cf. *Meditatio Redemptionis Humanae* 88:109–110 with 88:113–114. See DV 12 (S I, 193:23–24).

4. P 2 (S I, 101:12).

5. CDH II, 11 (S II, 111:5).

6. DP 2 (S II, 188:23).

7. DC III, 13 (S II, 286:4).

8. DP 9 (Cf. S II, 201:17 with 202:1).

9. CDH I, 18 (S II, 81:13): "*cum intelligi possit quia*" ("since it is plausible that").

10. M 19 (S I, 34:21); DC I, 2 (S II, 248:5); DV 8 (S I, 186:6).

11. DC III, 5 (S II, 270:2).
12. DC III, 5 (S II, 270:7).
13. *Reply to Gaunilo* 2 (S I, 132:13).
14. DG 14 (S I, 160:31).
15. Cf. *Reply to Gaunilo* 2 (S I, 132:29); DV 10 (S I, 190:26); DC III, 5 (S II, 270:5).
16. DG 4 (S I, 149:11–13).
17. DC III, 13 (S II, 286:11). Sometimes Anselm says "*mens humana*" (DIV 10. S II, 26:12), sometimes "*humanus intellectus*" (CDH II, 16. S II, 117:16), and "*humanus sensus*" (DCV 7. S II, 148:5).
18. DCD 1 (S I, 233:11).
19. CDH II, 16 (S II, 119:10. Cf. 119:8); DCV 23 (S II, 165:20).
20. DP 6 (S II, 197:11).
21. M 79 (S I, 86:8).
22. P 2 (S I, 101:17).
23. Likewise, much confusion has arisen over *On Behalf of the Fool* 5. For translators have failed to recognize that at S I, 128:9 "*constare*" means "to exist" — even though in the previous line "*constet*" means "it is evident."
24. In DV 2.
25. DG 21 (S I, 167:18).
26. Cf. DG 21 (S I, 168:10–11) with DP 1 (S II, 177:16), where "*argumenta*" is used in the sense of arguments and of premises, respectively. Cf. S I, 93:6–8 with S I, 135:18–20, where in both cases the sense seems to be the same.
27. *Proslogion II and III: A Third Interpretation of Anselm's Argument* (Leiden: E. J. Brill, 1972).
28. Ithaca, New York: Cornell University Press, 1962, p. ix.
29. Cf. Michael Loux's statement: "Since Latin lacks the definite article, Ockham does not consider the case of definite descriptions." *Ockham's Theory of Terms: Part I of the Summa Logicae* (South Bend: University of Notre Dame Press, 1975), p. 46, n. 14.
30. P 2 (S I, 101:15–16). Note the last few speeches of *De Veritate* 12, where Anselm illustrates how in Latin the perfect passive participle may be used as a substitute for the present passive participle, which Latin lacks, and how the present active participle may be used as a substitute for the perfect active participle, which Latin also lacks.
31. Note CDH I, 1 (S II, 48:2–3); I, 8 (S II, 60:3–4); II, 16 (S II, 118:1–2); II, 16 (S II, 121:3, 9); II, 17 (S II, 124:7); II, 17 (S II, 125:25); II, 18 (S II, 126:25); II, 19 (S II, 130:29–30); II, 22 (S II, 133:6). See p. 200, n. 38 below.
32. Also cf. S II, 105:3–4 with 105:12–14 (in CDH II, 9). Note Augustine's expressions in *On the Trinity*: (1) "*Verbum Dei dico carnem factum, id est, hominem factum . . .*" (4.2.31. PL 42:910); (2) "*Christus . . . factus est homo*" (7.3.4. PL 42:937). Also note 8.5.7. (PL 42:952).
33. See CDH I, 21.
34. CDH II, 18 (S II, 127:2–5).
35. Quoted from E. D. Hirsch, *Validity in Interpretation* (New Haven: Yale University Press, 1967), fifth printing (1974), p. 248.
36. See Anselm of Canterbury. *Why God Became Man and The Virgin*

Conception and Original Sin. Trans. and intro. Joseph M. Colleran (Albany: Magi Books, 1969), p. 208.

37. E.g., cf. M 64 (S I, 75:7) with M 65 (S I, 76:3), and DCD 4 (S I, 241:31) with DCD 4 (S I, 242:1).

38. *On Behalf of the Fool* 4 (S I, 126:30).

39. Cf. S II, 102:25 with 102:26–27 (in CDH II, 8).

40. DG 4 (S I, 149:11–14).

41. See M 32, 33, and 48. In some cases there is a problem about how to capture in idiomatic English the sense of a single Latin word in its Anselmian context. The most striking example is the word "*grammaticus*."

42. See M 32 (S I, 50:20). Anselm's terminology comes from Augustine, who likewise calls an image of a thing *its word*: e.g., DT 8.6.9 (PL 42:955). See also 9.10.15 (PL 42:969).

Chapter II: Monologion 1–4: The Anatomy of an Interpretation and a Translation

1. Not many recent interpreters would agree with J. M. Rigg that "the substance of the argument of the *Monologion* is of undeniable force" — that the argument may be "pronounced essentially cogent as against all but the pure positivist." *St. Anselm of Canterbury: A Chapter in the History of Religion* (London: Methuen & Co., 1896), 65–66.

2. E.g., in J. Hopkins, *A Companion to the Study of St. Anselm* (Minneapolis: University of Minnesota Press, 1972), 68–69.

3. Anselm uses "*unde*," "*per*," "*propter*," and "*quia*" instead of "*causa*" and "*facere*."

4. Misleading, that is, in the absence of an explanatory note.

5. As an additional example, note the difference of opinion regarding the translation of "*sicut*" in the opening sentence of *Proslogion* 2: "Ergo, domine, qui das fidei intellectum, da mihi, ut quantum scis expedire intelligam, quia es *sicut* credimus, et hoc es quod credimus." Professor John Rist believes that "quia es sicut credimus" ought to be translated as "that You exist in the way that we believe You do." See "Notes on Anselm's Aims in the *Proslogion*," *Vivarium*, 11 (November, 1973), p. 110. He adopts this translation because he is in part influenced by A. Stolz's understanding of the *Proslogion*. (Jonathan Barnes also has this same construal of "*sicut*." See his book *The Ontological Argument* (New York: Macmillan, 1972), 3.) Since Professor Richardson and I have a different global understanding of the *Proslogion*, we have said: "that You exist, as we believe, . . ."

6. Note the similar problem of whether to take "*videtur*" as "seems" or as "seen."

7. S I, 14:25.

8. S I, 14:13.

9. S I, 14:14. See also 14:12 and 14:17.

10. S I, 14:27. Cf. 13:12.

11. Viz., "Whatever things are said to be something in such way that they are said to be it either in greater or lesser or equal degree in relation to one another, are said to be it through something which is understood to be identical in the different things. . . ."

12. S I, 30:16–17.

13. "Sive igitur dicatur veritas habere, sive intelligatur non habere principium vel finem. . . ."

14. As occurs in the Penguin Classics series' (1973) translation of *Meditatio Redemptionis Humanae* (*The Prayers and Meditations of Saint Anselm*, trans. and intro. Benedicta Ward). For example, the Penguin translation (pp. 232–233) has "Immutable truth and plain reason then demand that whoever sins should give something better to God in return for the honour of which he has deprived him, that is more than the supposed good for the sake of which he dishonoured him" instead of having (something like): "Therefore, without doubt, unchanging truth and clear reason demand that the sinner give to God, in place of the honor stolen, something greater than that for which he ought to have refused to dishonor God." And it has "for his death was more than all that can be thought outside the person of God. It is clear that such a life is more good than all sins are bad" instead of having (something like): "For if putting Him to death [is a sin which] surpasses the multitude and magnitude of all conceivable sins which are not against the person of God, clearly His life is a good greater than the evil of all those sins which are not against the person of God."

Similarly, for stylistic reasons the Penguin translation leaves out words such as "since" and "therefore," which are crucial to understanding the reasoning. (E.g., the translation of S III, 87:82–88 = Penguin p. 233 neglects the "causal" relationship between "Human nature alone could not do this . . ." and "the goodness of God came to help. . . .") Moreover, in this same edition, the same kind of problem occurs in the translation of the *Proslogion*. For instance, in the first paragraph of P 3 the translator twice omits the word "therefore" ("*quare*," "*ergo*"). Now, by failing to put "*Therefore*, if that than which nothing greater can be thought . . ." and "*Therefore*, something than which nothing greater can be thought . . ." the translator fails to display the movement of Anselm's argument. Or again in P 3: for the logical notion "*quod convenire non potest*" she puts the nonlogical expression "and that simply will not do." Obviously, she wants to play-down Anselm's logical terminology because she feels that it is "out of place" in a *meditation*. Yet, by her combined omitting and minimizing of the logical terms, she presents inaccurately the arguments contained in the two meditations under discussion.

15. There is, of course, a sense in which native speakers are also "translators" of one another's speech-acts.

16. One cannot avoid agreeing with Philip Levine that "a translation properly done is in fact an essential, and perhaps the most creative, part of a commentary on the text." See his preface to Books XII–XV of *The City of God* (The Loeb Classical Library, 1966).

17. See his list of corrigenda at the end of the *Opera Omnia Anselmi*, Vol I, published by Friedrich Frommann Press (Stuttgart, Germany), 1968.

18. Quoted from Harold W. Johnston, *Latin Manuscripts* (Chicago: Scott, Foresman and Co., 1897), 113.

19. At S I, 14:13 "*Nam*" should be read as "For example."

20. Cf. *De Grammatico*, where Anselm argues that expert-in-grammar (*grammaticus*) is both a substance and a quality.

21. And thus F. S. Schmitt ought not to cite these words as a basis for

disqualifying the view that Anselm is an extreme realist. See Schmitt, AA I, 51: "It is not said that justice is something existing for itself. On the contrary: justice is . . . *in* the just things, not outside them. Accordingly, an extreme realism is not called for." Instead of intimating that the words "*in diversis*" cast an aspersion upon the interpretation of Anselm as an extreme realist, Schmitt should point out that they are irrelevant to determining Anselm's position.

22. This feature is more noticeable when he subsequently repeats the gist of Proposition 3: "It is necessary that even every useful and every excellent thing — if they are truly goods — be good through that very thing (*whatever it be*) through which all [goods] must be good" (italics mine).

23. Only at the conclusion of M 16 does he first introduce the abstract noun "*bonitas*," employing it in the phrase "*summa bonitas*." This phrase occurs again in *Monologion* 70.

24. That Marilyn Adams misses this point invalidates much of her article "Was Anselm a Realist? The *Monologium*," *Franciscan Studies* 32 (Annual X, 1972), 5–14.

25. Although "proves" is usually a success-verb, I shall be using it and the corresponding noun ("proof") without necessarily implying that I regard the so-called proof as sound.

26. M 1.

27. M 16.

28. S I, 60:21: "Summa sapientia semper sapit per se. . . ." Anselm goes on to speak of a man's wisdom as wise: "If some wise man were to teach me his wisdom which previously I lacked, surely his wisdom would not improperly be said to do this [i.e., to cause my wisdom]. But although my wisdom would owe its existence and its being-wise to his wisdom, nevertheless once my wisdom existed it would exist only by its own being and would be wise by itself only."

29. Note also that in M 7 he says, by implication, that the Supreme Good is a good.

30. PL 42:935. Note also DT 5.10.11 (PL 42:918), where Augustine says that greatness is great.

31. The entire argument, as reformulated, is:

(1) Whatever things are either equally or unequally x in comparison with one another, are x through something which is identical in the different things.

(2) All good things are either equally or unequally good in comparison with one another.

So: (3) All [good] things are good through something which is identical in the different good things. (1) (2)

(4) That through which all [goods] are good is itself a great good.

So: (5) That through which all [good] things are good is good through itself. (3) (4)

So: (6) All other [good] things are good through something other than themselves, and this other alone [is good] through itself.

(7) No good which is good through something other than itself is equal to or greater than that good which is good through itself.

So: (8) Only that which alone is good through itself is supremely good.

(9) What is supremely good is also supremely great.
So: (10) There is one thing which is supremely good and supremely great and the highest of all existing things.

32. Step 9 of the first proof: "If it is supremely good, it is supremely great." Step 9 of the second proof: "If it is supremely great, it is supremely good."

33. Unfortunately, in *Fides quaerens intellectum* Barth scarcely deals with the *Monologion*; and in AA I Schmitt concentrates on M 1 and 2.

34. Having gathered experience by dealing with Argument I, let us venture to reformulate — where need be — the steps of Argument III without first writing out Anselm's "exact words."

35. This premise may be stated more simply as: "Since *c* is irrational, it is not the case."

36. Each of the many would *in some respect* exist through itself; but this one thing would *in every respect* exist through itself.

37. In Argument III Anselm needs no premise corresponding to Proposition 4 of Argument I. That is, he does not need to say "That through which all existing things exist is itself an existent thing." For he has already shown — cf., Propositions 3 and 11 — that this one thing is something (= something existent).

38. See n. 21 above.

39. Only in the first and the last chapters does Anselm use the word "God." That is, only after he has established the existence of a triune and supremely good, etc., Being does he identify this Being as God. The initial use of "God" precedes his actual argument and divulges the intent of the writing.

40. S I, 19:29–20:1.

41. "For if anyone doubts that a horse is by nature better than a tree and that a man is more excellent than a horse, then surely this [person] ought not to be called a man."

42. I.e., not every farm, not every house, not all food, is good.

43. Anselm is not this charitable with Gaunilo. See my Ch. IV: "Anselm's Debate with Gaunilo."

44. Everywhere else in M 1–4 Anselm uses "nature" to mean "a being," "an existent." It would be strange for the meaning to change suddenly in Argument IV, Proposition 12.

45. It renders Section B *plausible* without making the reasoning *appear sound*. That is, an argument may seem plausible without seeming sound. The argument of P 2, some people say, illustrates this distinction.

46. Also cf. S I, 14:7–8 with 14:12.

47. See Boethius, *De Trinitate* 1 (PL 64:1249D).

48. In fact, "*essentia*" is an appropriate translation for *οὐσία*. (Note Augustine, DT 5.2.3.) Οὐσίαι was one of Plato's words for the Forms, each of which he considered to be the "essence" of a plurality of particulars.

49. I.e., on the basis of the statement that all good things are good through one thing *in them*.

50. AA I, 48.

51. AA I, 49.

52. See the first few lines of DT 8.3.5, where the words "*percipere*" and

"*intelligis*" occur (PL 42:950). In DT 11.9.16 Augustine distinguishes perceptual from conceptual vision.

53. "For if the individual good things are enjoyable, reflect attentively upon how enjoyable is that Good which contains the joyfulness of all good things" (P 24). "O insignificant man, why then do you go from one good to another in quest of what is good for your soul and good for your body? Love the one Good in which are all goods, and it shall suffice you. Desire the simple Good which itself is every good, and it shall be enough for you" (P 25). In P 12 Anselm refers to God as Goodness itself (*bonitas ipsa*).

54. AA I, 41.

55. "Eine Teilhabe der geschaffenen Dinge kennt Anselm nur insofern, als sie an der Idee, die Gott von ihnen hat, teilnehmen (*Mon*. c. 9), aber nicht insofern sie reale Dinge sind, geschaffen aus dem Nichts. Im ersten Falle hat die Bezeichnung 'Teilhabe' kaum einen Sinn, jedenfalls ist die platonische Teilhabe eine solche der real existierenden Dinge am höchsten Guten." *Loc. cit.*

56. E.g., DT 14.8.11; 14.12.15; 15.3.5; and by implication in 8.3.5.

57. Anselm allows that just things participate in the quality of justice, that good things participate in the quality of goodness, that great things participate in the quantity of greatness. But he does not intimate that they participate in Supreme Justice, Supreme Goodness, and Supreme Greatness, respectively.

58. I.e., if we were to take it to mean that all just things are just through participation in the quality of justice.

59. This sense of "participation" corresponds, for example, to DT 7.1.2; 5.10.11; 6.5.7; and Boethius, *On Aristotle's Categories* (PL 64:168A, 239B).

60. Karl Barth. *Fides quaerens intellectum* (2nd edition, Zürich, 1958), p. 85. English translation I. W. Robertson. *Anselm: Fides Quaerens Intellectum*, London, 1960; reprinted Cleveland, 1962), pp. 89–90.

61. Anselm von Canterbury. *Monologion*, trans. F. S. Schmitt (Stuttgart: Friedrich Frommann Verlag, 1964), 19–20.

62. Anselm von Canterbury. *De Veritate: Über die Wahrheit*, trans. F. S. Schmitt (Stuttgart: Friedrich Frommann Verlag, 1966), 23: "[In M 1–4] Anselm proceeded from the empirical fact that there are many different goods. Now, he does not ask *whether* there is a cause for these really existing goods — something which he takes as self-evident — but asks whether there is *one* cause or are many causes. [And he asks this] in order — from the unity of the cause — to derive per-se-ity and therefrom to conclude with the essence of God as the highest of all that is. (Consequently, the 'proofs of God' in the *Monologion* are not proofs of God in the usual sense.)"

63. AA I, 45–46.

64. AA I, 45.

65. Schmitt's translation for "*essentia*" is "*Wesen*." That he means *Wesen* in the sense of "essence" is clear from the fact that he contrasts it with both "*Dasein*" and "*Existenz*" (pp. 45–46). Also note the word "*Wesenheit*" in his translation of the opening sentence of the *Monologion* Preface, *op. cit.*

66. Viz., a proof — different in the different chapters — that the cause of everything good and great is one; that this cause "is" through itself; that this cause is the best and the greatest and the highest of all.

67. AA I, 46.

68. Regarding Anselm's use of "*essentia*," see n. 12 of the *Monologion*-translation by Professor Richardson and me. N.B. There is no justification for Barth's equating of *essentia* and *potentia* (2nd German edition, p. 85; English trans., p. 90).

69. AA I, 45.

70. S I, 20:11–12.

71. Adams, *op. cit.*, p. 13. Italics mine.

72. See the earlier discussion of Step 3 of Argument I.

73. I say "allegedly" because of John Benton's attack on the authenticity of *Historia Calamitatum*. See his article "Fraud, Fiction and Borrowing in the Correspondence of Abelard and Heloïse," in *Pierre Abélard — Pierre le Vénérable: Les courants philosophiques, littéraires et artistiques en occident au milieu du XIIe siècle*, pp. 469–506. Paris: Editions du centre national de la recherche scientifique, 1975.

74. Cf. M 27, where Anselm maintains that the Supreme Being is not a universal but is an individual.

75. Schmitt overstates things in maintaining that the arguments of M 1–4 were intended to be absolutely presuppositionless (AA I, 60).

Chapter III: The Anselmian Theory of Universals

1. Samuel E. Stumpf, *Socrates to Sartre: A History of Philosophy* (New York: McGraw–Hill, 1975, second ed.), p. 171.

2. "Saint Thomas Aquinas's Theory of Universals," *Monist*, 58 (January 1974), 163–172.

3. C. de Rémusat, *Saint Anselme de Cantorbéry* (Paris, 1853), p. 496.

4. Xavier Rousselot, *Études sur la philosophie dans le moyen-âge (première partie)*, (Paris, 1840), p. 236.

5. *The Logic of Saint Anselm* (Oxford: Clarendon Press, 1967), pp. 97–98. To his credit, Henry is one of the very few writers who state explicitly what they mean by the terms "realism" and "nominalism."

6. Martin Grabmann, *Die Geschichte der scholastischen Methode* (Freiburg, 1909), Vol. I, p. 307.

7. Joseph Fischer, *Die Erkenntnislehre Anselms von Canterbury nach den Quellen dargestellt* (*Beiträge zur Geschichte der Philosophie des Mittelalters*, 10/3), (Münster, 1911), p. 78.

8. See Anselm von Canterbury, *Monologion*. Trans. and intro. F. S. Schmitt (Stuttgart: F. Frommann Verlag, 1964), p. 22.

9. DIV 1 (S II, 9:22–10:13).

10. Victor Cousin, *Ouvrages inédits d'Abélard* (Paris, 1836). The introduction is reprinted under the title *Fragments de philosophie du Moyen Age* (Paris, 1855). See p. 119 of the reprinted edition.

11. B. Hauréau, *Histoire de la philosophie scolastique. Première Partie*. (Paris, 1872), p. 281.

12. *Ibid.*, pp. 281–282.

13. We need not here worry whether or not the theory, as articulated above, was really William of Champeaux's. According to Abelard's *Historia*

Calamitatum William had two different theories: "Erat autem in ea sententia de communitate universalium, ut eamdem essentialiter rem totam simul singulis suis inesse astrueret individuis, quorum quidem nulla esset in essentia diversitas sed sola multitudine accidentium varietas. Sic autem istam tunc suam correxit sententiam, ut deinceps rem eamdem non essentialiter sed indifferenter diceret" (Critical text and intro. by J. Monfrin. Paris: J. Vrin, 1959. p. 65). Cousin's interpretation of William's view is: "The identity of the individuals of the same kind does not come from their essence itself, for this essence is different in each of them. Rather, it comes from certain elements which are found in all these individuals without any difference, *indifferenter*. This new theory differs from the first one in that universals are no longer [regarded as] the essence of the being, the very substance of the things. But it agrees with the first theory (1) in that universals really exist and (2) in that, existing in several individuals without difference, they form their identity and thereby their kind" (*Ouvrages inédits d'Abélard*. Paris, 1836, p. cxvii).

Rousselot rejects the reading "*indifferenter*," favoring "*individualiter*" (*Études*, *op. cit.*, Vol. I, p. 274).

John Benton has challenged the very authenticity of the authorship of *Historia Calamitatum* and, by implication, the reliability of the report of William of Champeaux's views. See n. 73 of Ch. II above.

14. *Die Geschichte der scholastischen Methode*, *op. cit.*, Vol. I, pp. 307–308.

15. See Grabmann, *ibid.*, p. 311.

16. *Ibid.*, p. 307. See Fischer, *op. cit.*, p. 78.

17. Fischer, p. 55.

18. See Fischer, p. 73.

19. D. P. Henry, "Was Saint Anselm Really a Realist?," *Ratio*, 5(1963), p. 182.

20. Henry elaborates this distinction in his impressive work *The De Grammatico of Saint Anselm* (South Bend, Ind.: University of Notre Dame Press, 1964).

21. I.e., in DIV 1.

22. "Was Saint Anselm Really a Realist?," p. 183. Ironically, according to Henry's criteria, Aquinas would also not be a realist. That is, Henry seems to have no use for the distinction between crude realism and moderate realism.

23. In a very restricted sense, Anselm's discussion does, however, imply something about signification. See p. 81 of the present chapter.

24. The notion of *things* could in principle, of course, include the notion of *meanings*. But (in fact) images, species, accidents, and substances — the objects of Anselm's discourse — are not meanings.

25. Cf. Boethius' statement: "White" does not signify the substance of anything (PL 64:195C).

26. In DG 8 and 5, respectively.

27. Cf. the last part of DG 12 with DG 19. N.B. In DG 9 and 18 Anselm indicates that names (putatively) signify things. As *Reply to Gaunilo* 8 makes clear, he does *not* assume that a word can be significative only if the "thing" signified really exists.

28. "Was Saint Anselm Really a Realist?," p. 184.

29. Note p. 188, *ibid.*, where Henry says: "Medieval philosophical and logical Latin is, as Anselm was already aware, a semi-artificial language designed to express truths which involve semantical categories not distinguished by ordinary grammar. . . ."

30. Marilyn Adams, "Was Anselm a Realist? The *Monologium*," *Franciscan Studies*, 32 (Annual X, 1972), 5–14. N. B. It is time for everyone to begin writing "*Monologion*" in place of "*Monologium*."

31. The tone of her article fosters the impression that she agrees with Henry's interpretation of DG, though she does not explicitly say so.

32. See pp. 54–55 of the previous chapter.

33. Adams, p. 8.

34. Adams, p. 10.

35. Cf. M 16 with M 65.

36. This phrase occurs also in M 10 (S I, 25:9).

37. See Augustine, DT 8 (preface).

38. Cf. DIV 8.

39. I.e., "substance" is predicated primarily of individual things and only secondarily of universal things. Cf. Anselm's reference, in M 27, to two types of substance.

40. Note Boethius' use of "*consistere in*" at PL 64:190CD: "Nam secundae substantiae de primis substantiis solum praedicantur, non in ipsis sunt. Animal enim de quodam homine tantum dicitur, non etiam in aliquo homine consistit, ut in subjecto."

41. PL 64:239B.

42. PL 64:168A.

43. PL 64:462D.

44. Note my previous discussion of this point on p. 46 above (Ch. II).

45. Cf. DV 13.

46. M 27.

47. The following two nonconsecutive passages from DV 13 make evident that *according with* something is not the same as participating in it: (1) Student: "I conceded previously that if there is more than one rightness simply because there is more than one thing in which rightness is seen to be, then it necessarily follows that these rightnesses exist and change *in accordance with* those things." (2) Teacher: "Moveover, if it is only when things are *in accordance with* what they ought to be that rightness is in those things which ought to have it. . . ."

48. "We speak improperly when we say 'the truth of this thing' or 'the truth of that thing.' For truth does not have its being *in* or *from* or *through* the things in which it is said to be. But when these things are in accordance with truth, which is always *present to* things which are as they ought to be, then we say 'the truth of this thing' or 'the truth of that thing' (for example, 'the truth of the will' or 'the truth of action')."

49. Anselm regards truth as a species of rightness; he defines "truth" as "rightness perceptible only to the mind." See DV 11.

50. Note DL 8.

51. See PL 64:401B, where Boethius declares that an affirmation and a

negation, equally, participate in truth and falsity — i.e., each of them may be either true or false.

52. In fact, Anselm does not at all move from the one statement to the other.

53. Question 24 (PL 40:17). Note also DT 14.12.15 (PL 42:1048): the human mind is wise by participation in God.

54. Note my previous discussion in Ch. II, pp. 41–48.

55. This rejoinder is made by Kurt Flasch (AA II, 22 and 25).

56. Ch. II, p. 54.

57. M 9.

58. See the first sentence in M 10.

59. *Eighty-Three Different Questions* 46.2 (PL 40:30); *On the Gospel of John* 1.17 (PL 35:1387); *Literal Commentary on Genesis* 5.14.31 (PL 34:332).

60. See my Ch. II, p. 45.

61. E.g., in M 31 and 34.

62. Note M 66.

63. See M 66 (S I, 77:11–13).

64. Cf. M 9: "Therefore, although it is clear that before they were made, those things which have been made were nothing — with respect to the fact that they were not then what they are now and that there was not anything from which they were made — nevertheless they were not nothing with respect to their Maker's thought, through which and *according to* which they were made."

65. *On the Harmony of the Gospels* 1.23.35 (PL 34:1058); 1.35.53 (PL 34:1069).

66. I.e., the quotation cited on p. 59 above.

67. Others such as Maurice De Wulf, *Histoire de la philosophie médiévale*, Vol. I (Paris, 1925, 5th ed.), p. 104; B. Hauréau, *Histoire de la philosophie scolastique, Première Partie* (Paris, 1872), p. 250; Joseph Fischer, *Die Erkenntnislehre Anselms von Canterbury nach den Quellen dargestellt* (*Beiträge zur Geschichte der Philosophie des Mittelalters*, 10/3), (Münster, 1911), p. 71.

68. Hauréau, for instance, unequivocally states that, for Anselm, color is a universal substance. See Hauréau, *op. cit.*, p. 281. Cf. Cousin, *op. cit.*, p. 120.

69. Note DG 14 (S I, 160:7–8).

70. Of course, Anselm is *not* implying that the divine persons are one God *in species*.

71. See n. 10 of this chapter.

72. S II, 77:10–13. A better example can be found in *A Meditation on Human Redemption:* "Thus, in that man [viz., Jesus] human nature freely and out of no obligation gave to God something its own, so that it might redeem itself in others in whom it did not have what it, as a result of indebtedness, was required to pay" (S III, 87:99–101). Note the discussion on pp. 6–7 of Ch. I above.

73. Even in his early work DL Anselm had used the singular form "*humanitas nostra*" in alluding to the powerlessness which our human nature sometimes feels in the face of temptation (DL 6). And in his last treatise, DC, he continued to make the point that "in all infants who are begotten by natural means human nature is born with sin and its penalty" (DC III, 9. S II, 278:4–5).

74. Anselm of Canterbury, *Why God Became Man and The Virgin Conception and Original Sin*. Trans. and intro. Joseph Colleran (Albany, N. Y.: Magi Books, 1969), pp. 50–51 and 244, n. 109.

75. DCV 23 (S II, 165:12–13).

76. DCV 27 (S II, 170:12–14).

77. Viz., "*Siquidem quidquid peccati super illud additur in homine, personale est*."

78. See Ch. I, pp. 8–9 above.

79. Similarly, at CDH II, 14 (S II, 114:11) Anselm writes "*in persona eius*." But elsewhere "*eius*" drops out. Cf. S I, 101:9 with 101:14.

80. E. g., in this very translation of the disputed passage in DCV 27. Also note his translation of DCV 20. See, too, his translation of Boso's first speech in CDH II, 16, where "*hominis eiusdem*" is translated as "of this individual human nature." This latter translation renders his discussion of Anselm's alleged ultra realism, or Platonic realism, all the more unclear.

81. N. B. CDH II, 3: "The whole man (i.e., consisting in a soul and a body) . . . ."

82. DCV 2: "And because the whole of human nature was in Adam and Eve, no part of it being outside of them, human nature as a whole was weakened and corrupted."

83. N. B. Elsewhere (DCV 10. S II, 152:23) Anselm says, without reference to Eve, that the whole of human nature was in Adam. But this practice is consistent with his rule, in DCV 9, of using "Adam" to refer to both Adam and Eve, except where his argument requires distinguishing between them.

84. See n. 72 above.

85. "So, then, he bears his own iniquity and not Adam's, even though *he is said* to bear Adam's iniquity because the iniquity of Adam was the cause of his own sin."

86. Cf. the relevant passages in DCV 3, 7, 8, and 29.

87. DCV 7 (S II, 149:9–13).

88. S I, 235:20–22.

89. DL 6 (S I, 218:3).

90. DC III, 6 (S II, 272:29).

91. DL 6 (S I, 218:9–10).

92. DCD 1 (S I, 235:10–12).

93. PL 64:82ff.

94. Cf. the interchangeability of "*unum*" and "*idem*" in M 1–4. See p. 38 of my Ch. II above.

95. PL 64:1249D.

96. PL 64:93D.

97. Re two further uses of "participate," see CDH II, 19 (S II, 131:8) and CDH II, 12 (S II, 112:7–8).

98. Fischer, p. 41. See also De Wulf, *op. cit.*, p. 117.

99. Adams, p. 13.

100. Friedrich R. Hasse, *Anselm von Canterbury* (Leipzig, Vol. II, 1852), p. 98.

101. (1) Etienne Gilson, "Sens et nature de l'argument de saint Anselme,"

Archives d'histoire doctrinale et littéraire du moyen-âge, 9 (1934), p. 11. (2) Joseph Fischer, *op. cit.*, p. 74.

102. Siegfried Dangelmayr, "Anselm und Cusanus. Prolegomena zu einem Strukturvergleich ihres Denkens," AA III, 115.

103. B. Hauréau, *op. cit.*, p. 281.

104. Joseph Colleran, *op. cit.*, p. 208.

105. Victor Cousin, *op. cit.*, p. 119.

106. F. S. Schmitt, "Anselm und der (Neu-)Platonismus," AA I, 41.

107. D. P. Henry, "Was Saint Anselm Really a Realist?," *op. cit.*, p. 183.

108. Maurice De Wulf, *op. cit.*, p. 118.

109. Xavier Rousselot, *op. cit.*, p. 215.

Chapter IV: Anselm's Debate with Gaunilo

*I am grateful to Richard R. La Croix, William E. Mann, Gareth B. Matthews, and C. Wade Savage for their helpful comments on an earlier draft of this chapter. Unfortunately, I cannot be certain that any one of them would agree completely with the present version.

1. *The Life of St Anselm by Eadmer*, ed., intro., and trans. R. W. Southern (New York: Thomas Nelson and Sons, 1962), 31 n.

2. Charles Hartshorne, *Anselm's Discovery: A Re-examination of the Ontological Proof for God's Existence* (La Salle, Ill.: Open Court, 1965), 20. See also p. 151.

3. Hartshorne complains that Gaunilo, and others like him, neglected the principle of *Proslogion* 3 that *to exist without conceivable alternative of not existing is better than to exist with such alternative. Anselm's Discovery*, 88 (verbatim).

4. *Anselm's Discovery*, 18.

5. F. S. Schmitt, "Der ontologische Gottesbeweis und Anselm," in AA III, 81–94.

6. S I, 126:30; 127:23. Gaunilo employs the phrase "*aliquid omnibus maius*" (S I, 127:11–12) in the middle of this same section. Cf. the end of Section 3 (S I, 126:26–27).

Even those who would deny that Gaunilo intended "*maius omnibus*" as an abbreviation would still have to translate this phrase as "that which is greater than all *others*" and not as "that which is greater than all." To omit the word "others" — on the ground that the Latin term "*aliis*" does not appear in the text — would have the consequence that that which is greater than *everything* would be greater than itself. And this is surely not an accurate expression of Gaunilo's point.

However, in Section 4 of *On Behalf of the Fool "illud maius omnibus quae cogitari possunt"* could admittedly be read as "that which is greater than all that can be thought." Now, the sentence "God is that which is greater than all that can be thought" entails that God cannot be conceived. Although in Section 4 Gaunilo does argue that God cannot be conceived, he does *not* do so by claiming that "God is *illud maius omnibus quae cogitari possunt*" entails that God is inconceivable — something he could hardly have failed to do on the above reading. Moreover, he is using this Latin phrase to identify Anselm's position. And he knows that in *Proslogion* 2 (where Anselm says that God is something than which nothing greater can be thought) Anselm neither means nor implies that God cannot be thought. The intent of Gaunilo's Latin expression, therefore, is that God is greater than all *others* that can be thought. Accordingly, in Section 4 he challenges Anselm's belief that God *can* be conceived. Thus, he maintains that one reason God can be supposed not to exist is that He *cannot at all* be conceived *secundum rem*. Gaunilo's Section 4 is addressed to *Proslogion* 4 and not to *Proslogion* 15, where Anselm allows that God *can be thought* (i.e., can be apprehended) even though He is greater than can be thought (i.e., greater than can be comprehended).

Moreover at S I, 128:22 Gaunilo obviously means an "island which is more excellent than all *other* lands," though he writes only "*insulam illam terris omnibus praestantiorem*." Where the context suffices to imply "*aliud*" Anselm himself sometimes does not bother to insert this word. E.g., cf. M 64 (S I 75:7) with M 65 (S I, 76:3), and DCD 4 (S I, 241:31) with DCD 4 (S I, 242:1).

To be sure, there is a *prima facie* difference between (1) "God is that which is greater than all others that can be thought" and (2) "God is that than which nothing greater can be thought." For the former entails that God can be conceived, whereas the latter seems to entail neither that God can be conceived nor that He cannot be conceived. Nonetheless, Gaunilo's use of *1* is not a *distorted* substitute for Anselm's use of 2, given Anselm's insistence on the conceivability of that than which no greater can be thought. At any rate, "*maius omnibus*," as Gaunilo uses it, does not stand for "*maius omnibus quae sunt*," as Anselm supposes it does.

7. *Reply to Gaunilo* 5 (S I, 135:8–10). N. B. In our own day Anselm's long formula has been abbreviated by Sylvia Crocker, who speaks of Anselm as "proving that the *quo maius* exists." See "The Ontological Significance of Anselm's *Proslogion*," *Modern Schoolman*, 50 (November 1972), p. 33. She employs this formula throughout her article; and, in doing so, she is motivated by the same desire for conciseness as was Gaunilo.

8. N = something than which no greater can be thought = that than which a greater cannot be thought = a necessary being.

9. See pp. 114–115 below for an interpretation of this premise.

10. Gaunilo's recapitulation occurs in *On Behalf of the Fool* 1: "To one who doubts whether there exists or denies that there exists a nature than which nothing greater can be thought, the claim is made that the existence of this nature is proven from two considerations: first, from the fact that the very one who doubts or denies the existence of this nature already has this nature in his understanding when, upon hearing it spoken of, he understands what is said; and, secondly, from the fact that, necessarily, what he understands exists not only in his understanding but also in reality. This second consideration is [allegedly] established by the following reasoning:

> To exist also in reality is greater than to exist solely in the understanding. Now, if this thing existed solely in the understanding, then whatever existed also in reality would be greater than it. Thus, that which is greater than all others would be less than some other and would not be greater than all others — surely a contradiction. Therefore, it is

necessary that that which is greater than all others (having already been shown to exist in the understanding) exist not only in the understanding but also in reality. For otherwise it could not be that which is greater than all others (S I, 125:3–13).

11. *"In intellectu"* ("in the understanding") is as idiomatic for Anselm as "in mind" is for us. McGill worries that "in the understanding" sounds too spatial, and consequently he prefers the translation "in relation to the understanding." Yet, on p. 19 McGill reverts to "in the understanding of the painter." Surprisingly, he finds no analogous problem with "held in thought" and "in his imagination" (p. 17, p. 19). Why should "in the understanding" sound more spatial than "in the imagination"? McGill's distinction seems invidious; and his worry is unnecessary. See John Hick and Arthur McGill, eds., *The Many-faced Argument* (New York: Macmillan, 1967), 4, n. 10.

12. *On Behalf of the Fool* 2. "Regarding the fact that this thing is said to exist in my understanding simply because I understand what is said, I ask. Could I not similarly be said to have in my understanding — because if someone were to speak of them I would understand whatever he said — all manner of unreal things that in no way actually exist? But suppose that this thing [than which nothing greater can be thought] were proven to be such that it is not able to exist in thought in the same way as any unreal and doubtfully real things do. And, accordingly, suppose that when I have heard of it I am not said to think it (or to have it in thought) but am said to understand it (and to have it in the understanding) since I could not think it except by understanding (i.e., by apprehending with certainty) that it really exists" (S I, 125:14–126:1).

13. Literally: "This being is such that as soon as it is thought of it can only be perceived with certain understanding of its own indubitable existence" (S I, 126:8–9).

14. N. B. *Reply to Gaunilo* 4 addresses itself to *On Behalf of the Fool* 7; *Reply to Gaunilo* 6 takes issue with *On Behalf of the Fool* 2.

15. This change begins at S I, 129:10 with the sentence "*Cum autem dicitur* . . ."

16. In the *Proslogion* Preface Anselm explains why at first he did not append his name to his manuscript. "Modesty" of the same sort probably induced Gaunilo to publish his objections anonymously.

17. *The Life of St Anselm by Eadmer*, 31.

18. For this division see the opening sentences of *Reply* 5.

19. As do Hick and McGill.

20. Hick and McGill, 9. Cf. Barth's label "*eine Notizensammlung*." Karl Barth, *Fides Quaerens Intellectum*, ix, n. 1 (English ed., 14, n. 2).

21. DIV 1 and CDH preface. Note also the one preface for the three dialogues DV, DL, and DCD.

22. See Hick and McGill, 25, n. 13. N.B. It would be a mistake to infer from the fact that the section divisions are *not* found in the early mss. that the *Reply* was originally an unordered series of notes loosely strung together. Although Hick and McGill come to the "series of notes" conclusion, they do *not* utilize this mistaken inference. See their p. 9.

23. Gaunilo can be interpreted as discussing a thing (viz., an island) than which no greater *island* can be thought — whereas Anselm discusses a

thing than which *nothing* greater can be thought. To effect a legitimate counterargument, Gaunilo would have to talk about an island than which *nothing* greater can be thought. But no contradiction results from denying that such a thing exists — whereas a contradiction does result from denying that something than which nothing greater can be thought exists (given the presupposition that existence is a perfection).

In the argument (interpreted as being) about an island than which no *greater* island can be thought, Gaunilo seems to accept Anselm's construal of "greater" as "better." Thus, he mentions that the island "abounds with countless riches and delights of all sorts." He shows no sign either of restricting "greater" to *size* (e.g., an island 1,000 miles in circumference is greater than one 200 miles in circumference) nor of supposing that the island *with its delights* would be better (i.e., greater) in proportion to its size. For Gaunilo the claim "The bigger the island the better" would be as counterintuitive as for us is the assertion "The bigger the flower the better." So no one is entitled to object to the logic of Gaunilo's counterexample on the ground that, like "the positive integer than which no greater positive integer can be conceived," the notion "the island than which no greater island can be conceived" is unintelligible.

24. See Hick and McGill, 15–16. Here they present S I, 125:14–126:4 and 126:8–13. That is, they have elided 126:4–7 simply to suit themselves editorially.

25. Hick and McGill, 4, n. 10.

26. Not even McGill reads this passage as telling us that the Fool has no "*act* of understanding."

27. (1) M. J. Charlesworth, *St. Anselm's Proslogion* (London: Oxford University Press, 1965), 175. (2) Hick and McGill, 21. (3) John Wippel and Allan Wolter, eds., *Medieval Philosophy: From St. Augustine to Nicholas of Cusa* (New York: Free Press, 1969), 166. (4) S. N. Deane, trans., *St. Anselm: Basic Writings* (La Salle, Ill.: Open Court, 1962, 2nd ed.), 158, N. B. At S I, 132:14–15 "*in nullo intellectu*" seems best rendered as "not at all in the understanding." Cf. M 19 (S I, 34:19–21).

28. *Reply to Gaunilo* 1 (S I, 130:12–18).

29. *Meditatio Redemptionis Humanae* (cf. S III, 88:110 with 88:114). Cf. Gaunilo, *On Behalf of the Fool* 7 (cf. S I, 129:14–15 with 129:16).

30. *Reply to Gaunilo* 7 (S I, 136:28–137:1).

31. Cf. 42:32–33 with 43:14–15. N. B. Gaunilo makes the same substitution in *On Behalf of the Fool* 6 (S I, 128:30).

32. Note also S I, 131:10; 114:20–21. Cf. S I, 104:3–4.

33. E.g., translating "*essentia*" always as "essence."

34. E.g., translating "*existere*" as "to exist" and "*subsistere*" as "to subsist," thereby implying that Anselm was making a distinction between existing and subsisting.

35. "*Aliter enim cogitatur res cum vox eam significans cogitatur, aliter cum id ipsum quod res est intelligitur*" (S I, 103:18–19).

36. Cf. M 10: "For in ordinary usage we recognize that we can speak of a single object in three ways. For we may speak of it either (1) by perceptibly employing perceptible signs (i.e., signs which can be perceived by the bodily

senses) or (2) by imperceptibly thinking to ourselves these same signs, which are perceptible outside us, or (3) neither by perceptibly nor by imperceptibly using these signs, but by inwardly and mentally speaking of the objects themselves by imagining them or by understanding their respective definitions, depending upon the type of object. For in one way I speak of a man when I signify him by the name 'man.' In another way [I speak of him] when I think this name silently. In a third way [I speak of a man] when my mind beholds him either by means of an image of his body or by means of his definition — by means of an image of his body, for instance, when [my mind] imagines his visible shape; but by means of his definition, for instance, when [my mind] conceives his universal being, viz., *rational, mortal animal*'' (S I, 24:29–25:9).

Gaunilo may have had this passage in mind when he mentioned the possibility of conceiving of a nonexistent man by conceiving of the generic concept *man* (*On Behalf of the Fool* 4).

37. These terms occur in Section 4 (e.g., S I, 127:12–13).

38. *De Divisione Naturae* (*Patrologia Latina* 122:459D, 463D, 464A).

39. See Anselm's preface to the *Proslogion*. In some contexts ''*argumentum*'' means ''premise.'' Note Anselm's use of ''*pro argumentis*'' = ''as premises'' in S II, 177:16 (DP 1).

40. Note my Section 7. In P 2 Anselm *assumes* that God is identical with N since ''N'' entails the list of attributes traditionally ascribed to God. (This assumption is made more explicit in *Proslogion* 4.) Then he goes on in *Proslogion* 2 to prove, to his own satisfaction, that N exists. Chapters 5 and following *demonstrate* what was assumed — viz., that N is God — by exhibiting the list of attributes derivable from ''N.'' Hence, the proof of *God's* existence in *Proslogion* 2 depends, in some final sense, upon the further proofs in Chapters 5 and following, as Richard La Croix rightly recognizes (*Proslogion II and III: A Third Interpretation of Anselm's Argument*. Leiden: E. J. Brill, 1972).

41. *Reply* 10 (S I, 138:30–139:3). La Croix is misled by Charlesworth's translation of ''*prolatio*'' as ''proof,'' instead of as ''utterance.'' See La Croix, 38.

42. Kant, of course, in rejecting the soundness of the ontological argument, is dealing with the construals of Leibniz and Wolff.

43. [1.] ''With confidence I assert that if N can be even thought to exist, it is necessary that it exist. For N can only be thought to exist without a beginning. Now, whatever can be thought to exist but does not exist can be thought to begin to exist. Thus, it is not the case that N can be thought to exist and yet does not exist. Therefore, if it can be thought to exist, it is necessary that it exist.

[2.] ''Furthermore: if indeed it can be even thought, it is necessary that it exist. For even one who doubts or denies the existence of N admits that if this being were to exist it would neither actually nor conceivably be able not to exist. For otherwise [i.e., if it existed but were able not to exist] it would not be N. Now, as for whatever can be thought but does not exist: if it were to exist, it would either actually or conceivably be able not to exist. Therefore, if N can be even thought, N is not able not to exist.

[3.] ''But let us suppose that it can be thought and yet does not exist. Now, whatever can be thought and yet does not exist would not, if it were to exist, be N. Hence, if N [assumed for the sake of argument not to exist] were to exist, it would not be N — an utterly absurd consequence. Therefore, it is false [to suppose] that N can be thought and yet does not exist."

44. Anselm never mentions the possibility of a counterargument in support of the Fool:

	(1)	Either N is able to begin to exist or N is not able to begin to exist. (premise)
Assume:	(2)	N is able to begin to exist.
	(a)	What is able to begin to exist can be thought to begin to exist. (premise)
	(b)	What exists without beginning is greater than what exists through a beginning. (presupposition)
So:	(c)	N can be thought to be greater than it is. (impossible)
Hence:	(3)	It is not the case that N is able to begin to exist. (2) (b)
Hence:	(4)	N is not able to begin to exist. (1) (3)
	(5)	If anything does not exist but it is able to exist, then it is able to begin to exist. (premise)
Hence:	(6)	If N does not exist but N is able to exist, then N is able to begin to exist. (instance of (5))
Thus:	(7)	It is not the case that N does not exist and N is able to exist. (4) (6)
Thus:	(8)	Either N exists or N is not able to exist. (7)
Assume:	(9)	N does not exist.
Then:	(10)	N is not able to exist. (8) (9)
So:	(11)	If N does not exist, N is not able to exist. (9) (10)

N.B. N can, nonetheless, be thought to exist (because whatever can be thought can be thought to exist); i.e., "N exists" is not self-contradictory.

N.B. "N does not exist and N is able to exist" is inconsistent.

45. The same is true of the text of Arguments 1 and 2 and my representations of them.

46. By truncating the sequence of these two arguments, Hick and McGill bury the noteworthiness of this shift, so that for them it is not an issue. They place the one argument at the top of p. 22 and the other at the bottom of p. 25. Anselm is allegedly responding to two *different* criticisms made by Gaunilo!

47. The ambiguity of "thinking" (conceiving vs. knowing) is partially indicated by Anselm in *Reply* 4.

48. See William Mann, "The Ontological Presuppositions of the Ontological Argument," *Review of Metaphysics*, 26 (December 1972), 260–277.

49. "So even the Fool is convinced that something than which nothing greater can be thought exists at least in his understanding; for when he hears of this being, he understands [what he hears], and whatever is understood is in the understanding. But surely that than which a greater cannot be thought cannot be only in the understanding. For if it were only in the understanding, it could be thought to exist also in reality — which is greater [than existing only in the understanding]. Therefore, if that than which a greater cannot be thought existed only in the understanding, then that than which a greater *cannot* be thought

would be that than which a greater *can* be thought! But surely this conclusion is impossible. Hence, without doubt, something than which a greater cannot be thought exists both in the understanding and in reality.

50. For a different view see D. M. Lochhead, "Is Existence a Predicate in Anselm's Argument," *Religious Studies*, 2 (October 1966), p. 124. Lochhead maintains that Anselm subscribed only to *6 b* and not to *P*.

In "Existence as a Perfection: A Reconsideration of the Ontological Argument," *Religious Studies*, 4 (October 1968), p. 97, L. T. Howe contends that "Whatever exists in the understanding and outside the understanding is more perfect than whatever exists in the understanding alone" is false. As a counterexample he mentions secrets. But this example is not really to the point since in *Proslogion* 2 and *Reply* 1 Anselm's universe of discourse is "substances." He is not dealing with dreams, illusions, or secrets — none of which can exist independently of the mind. I may, to be sure, wonder whether tonight I shall have such and such a recurrent dream. If I do have this dream, then (Anselm could say) the dream as it occurs is more perfect than the dream as merely surmised. But the dream would exist in the way that dreams do, viz., in the mind. Anselm recognizes that the notion of reality is context-dependent. The very fact that in *Proslogion* 2 he contrasts *esse in re* with *esse in intellectu* shows that he has restricted his domain of reference to things which *can* exist extramentally. He further indicates the context of his discussion by taking as his example the case of an artist and his painting.

Not even Lochhead's comment that a real slum is worse than an imaginary one (p. 122n.) overthrows *P*; for a real slum is a better slum than is an imaginary one.

The main motive for wanting to deny that Anselm subscribed to *P* is that, given *P*, he has no way to fault one interpretation of Gaunilo's perfect-island argument. For if the island than which no greater island can be conceived did not exist in reality, it would be an island than which a greater island could be conceived, etc. Anselm failed to recognize the forcefulness of Gaunilo's reasoning. He failed not because he did not regard existence as a perfection for any being other than N (as Lochhead suggests) but because of the considerations alluded to in n. 23 above.

The closest Anselm comes, elsewhere, to comparing a thing *as thought* with that thing *as existing in reality* is *Monologion* 36: "For no one doubts that created substances exist in themselves much differently from the way they exist in our knowledge. In themselves they exist in virtue of their own being; but in our knowledge their likenesses exist, not their own being. It follows, then, that the more truly they exist anywhere by virtue of their own being than by virtue of their likenesses, the more truly they exist in themselves than in our knowledge." Also note *Reply* 5 (S I, 135:14–16).

51. Moreover, the logical structure of this argument is not subject to La Croix's counterinterpretation, which entails the conclusion that N does not exist (p. 126).

52. La Croix, Chapter 3 — especially 99–100; 106–107. La Croix interprets *S* by reference to the principle of *Reply* 5 which states: "What does not exist is able not to exist; and what is able not to exist is able to be thought not to exist." This principle is implicit in *Reply* 1.

53. Anselm nowhere teaches, and indeed always denies, that N can be thought not to exist in the sense that something can be thought not to exist because it is able not to exist (à la *Reply* 5); for it is never the case that N is able not to exist. He does allow that we can *assume* (a Pickwickian sense of "think") N not to exist — just as in a logical proof we might assume a premise which we do not realize to be self-contradictory. We can think this schema in the sense of premising it; but we cannot think it *consistently*. By comparison, Anselm regards "N does not exist" as self-contradictory and therefore as unable to be thought (consistently), though able to be assumed as a step in a proof.

54. (F) ≡ (F′):

(1) Let x be any predicate such that to be x is greater than not to be x.

(2) Either N is x or N is not x.

Assume: (3) N is not x.

(a) N can be thought to be x.

So: (b) N can be thought to be greater than it is (and so N is that than which a greater *can* be thought). (impossible)

So: (4) N is x.

55. E.g., pp. 133, 178, 236, 286, 298.

56. *Anselm's Discovery*, 13. Note also p. 98.

Chapter V: Some Alleged Metaphysical and Psychological Aspects of the Ontological Argument

1. R. Brecher, "'Greatness' in Anselm's Ontological Argument," *Philosophical Quarterly*, 24 (April 1974), p. 103.

2. Lewis S. Feuer, "God, Guilt, and Logic: The Psychological Basis of the Ontological Argument," *Inquiry*, 2 (Autumn 1968), p. 259.

3. Brecher, p. 97.

4. Brecher, p. 98.

5. Re "*melius*" note the following comments of Brecher: (1) "In Ch. 9, Anselm discusses God's moral goodness, his *bonitas* . . ." (p. 98); (2) ". . . the idea of the creature's thinking of something (morally) better, as opposed to something greater . . ." (p. 98); (3) "Hitler could not be better or worse than King Arthur, since the latter, being nonexistent, could have no moral qualities at all attaching to him" (p. 99); (4) "If it [viz., 'more perfect'] means simply 'better', that is, 'morally better', then that, as we have seen, solves nothing" (p. 100).

6. Brecher, p. 103.

7. Brecher, p. 102.

8. *Loc. cit.*

9. "Degrees of Reality in Plato," in *New Essays on Plato and Aristotle*, ed. Renford Bambrough (New York: Humanities Press, 1965), pp. 1–19.

10. Brecher, pp. 104–105.

11. Brecher, p. 97.

12. P 14 (S I, 111:9) and P 18 (S I, 114:21–22).

13. Brecher, p. 98.

14. N. B. In M 2 Anselm states that only what is supremely good can be supremely great. Because of this metaphysical view he can interchange talk about God's goodness with talk about His greatness — even though "great" and "good" have different definitions. By "God's goodness" Anselm signifies both God's moral perfections and His nonmoral perfections.

15. *Reply to Gaunilo* 8.

16. Brecher, p. 99.

17. Brecher, p. 98.

18. E.g., in P 5.

19. M 31.

20. It is not clearly the case, for example, that (for Anselm) God's existence is cognitively more reliable than the truth that something has existed in the past. But even if Anselm would have asserted such a greater reliability, his argument in *Proslogion* 2 does not depend upon or employ such a premise.

21. Ep. 204 (PL 33:941).

22. Similarly, "*oratio*" and "*enuntiatio*" are not synonymous. But Anselm uses them interchangeably in DV 2. Boethius distinguishes five different kinds of *oratio* — of which *oratio enuntiativa* is one. See PL 64:296C.

23. Note DCD 1.

24. See pp. 33–34 of my Ch. II.

25. Note M 4 (S I, 17:1–2), where Anselm interchanges "*melior*" and "*praestantior*." Jonathan Barnes is wrong in asserting flatly that Anselm construes greatness as moral goodness (*The Ontological Argument*, p. 82).

26. See Sylvia Crocker's interesting article "The Ontological Significance of Anselm's *Proslogion*," *Modern Schoolman*, 50 (November 1972), 33–56. Crocker, who believes that in P 2–4 "greater" properly means "more real," recognizes that it does not bear this one meaning throughout the *Proslogion*. However, I deem it more accurate to say that in P 2–4 "greater" *includes* the meaning "more real." For it also includes the meanings "more excellent," "more perfect," "ontologically better": A being which exists both in the understanding and in reality is a more excellent *being* than it would be if it existed only in the understanding. (In this respect, it is also a more perfect being, a better being.) Perhaps Crocker would concede this point; for later she switches from saying "the proper meaning" (p. 33) to saying the "primary meaning" (p. 35).

Note M 36, where Anselm teaches that a being exists more truly (really) outside the human mind than it exists in our knowledge. M 31 shows that Anselm links degrees of existence and degrees of excellence. Thus, there is a sense in which, according to the *Monologion*, a being that exists outside the human mind is both a more real being and a more excellent being than its "likeness" in our mind — as strange as either of these comparisons may seem to us. (And to me they seem equally strange.) Similarly, in P 2 Anselm's argument is formulated in terms of an ontology where degrees of reality and degrees of excellence are exactly correlated to each other. By using the phrase "*aliquid quo nihil maius cogitari potest*," Anselm captures both the notion of *res quae magis est* and the notion of *res quae praestantior est*.

27. Note Ch. I, pp. 1–2 above.

28. "An emotional base underlying a mode of philosophical argument is, of course, best grasped in the complexities of the philosopher's personal life" (Feuer, p. 259).

29. Feuer, p. 259.

30. Feuer, pp. 260–261. His quotations are from P 1.

31. Note also the end of CDH II, 13, where Boso says: "Although I did not doubt that this was always the case with Christ, nevertheless I asked to hear the reason for it. For often we are certain that something is the case but nevertheless do not know how to prove it rationally."

32. Feuer: "It was precisely during an intense experience of guilt that Anselm's logical resistances gave way, and he yielded to the validity of the onotological argument" (p. 260).

33. Feuer, p. 261.

34. *Proslogion* Preface.

35. Feuer, p. 260.

36. See DCV 24.

37. Feuer, p. 260.

38. Cf. *Meditatio* III (S III, 86:75ff.). N.B. John McIntyre, "Cur Deus-Homo: The Axis of the Argument," in *Sola Ratione* (ed. Helmut Kohlenberger. Stuttgart: F. Frommann Press, 1970), 111–118. [Also note McIntyre's insight about how to translate the title "*Cur Deus Homo*." See *St. Anselm and His Critics: A Re-Interpretation of the Cur Deus Homo* (London: Oliver and Boyd, 1954), p. 117.]

39. S II, 115:17–18.

40. DCV 26.

41. CDH I, 22.

42. DCV 24.

43. Anselm does not distinguish orders of infinity as does a post-Cantorian mathematician. In DIV 15 he does, however, remark that an eternity together with an eternity would still be one eternity, just as a point together with a point would still be one point. Note Boso's first question in CDH II, 15.

44. Feuer, p. 260.

45. *Loc. cit.* See *Oratio* 10 (S III, 40:197ff.). Feuer quotes this paraphrase from M. J. Charlesworth, *St. Anselm's Proslogion* (Oxford: Clarendon Press, 1965), p. 16.

46. *Exposition of Ps.* 26.2.18 (PL 36:208).

47. Isa. 66:9: "Shall not I that make others to bring forth children, myself bring forth, saith the Lord? Shall I, that give generation to others be barren, saith the Lord thy God?" (Douay version). Isa. 66:13: "As one whom the mother caresseth, so will I comfort you: and you shall be comforted in Jerusalem" (Douay version). Regarding others, after Anselm, who used the mother-imagery, see Benedicta Ward, ed. and trans., *The Prayers and Meditations of Saint Anselm* (Baltimore: Penguin Books, 1973), p. 67.

48. Matt. 23:37: "Jerusalem, Jerusalem, thou that killest the prophets and stonest them that are sent unto thee, how often would I have gathered together thy children, as the hen doth gather her chickens under her wings, and thou wouldst not?" (Douay version). In his prayer Anselm alludes to this verse.

49. Job 17:14.

50. Martin Rule, *The Life and Times of St. Anselm*, two vols. (London: Kegan Paul, Trench, and Co., 1883).

51. Rule, *op. cit.*, Vol. I, pp. 104–105. My italics.

52. Rule, Vol. I, pp. 115–116.

53. *The Idea of History* (Oxford: Clarendon Press, 1946), p. 240. N. B. Collingwood's fuller statement: "The act of interpolation . . . is in no way arbitrary or merely fanciful: it is necessary or, in Kantian language, *a priori*. If we filled up the narrative of Caesar's doings with fanciful details such as the names of the persons he met on the way, and what he said to them, the construction would be arbitrary: it would be in fact the kind of construction which is done by an historical novelist. But if our construction involves *nothing that is not necessitated by the evidence*, it is a legitimate historical construction of a kind without which there can be no history at all" (pp. 240–241, italics mine).

54. Rule, Vol. I, p. 213.

55. Feuer, p. 259. Feuer quotes Martin Rule, *The Life and Times of St. Anselm*, pp. 57–58. I should think that a more plausible case could be made for inferring that Anselm's chief joy was understanding. See, for example, CDH II, 15 (S II, 116:11–12) and Ep. 136 (S III, 280:34–281:41). Also note DCD 3 (S I, 237:7).

56. Rule, Vol. I, pp. 57–58. Italics mine.

57. Eadmer: "He gradually turned from study, which had formerly been his chief occupation, and began to give himself up to youthful amusements. His love and reverence for his mother held him back to some extent from these paths, but she died and then the ship of his heart had as it were lost its anchor and drifted almost entirely among the waves of the world." See Eadmer, *The Life of St Anselm, Archbishop of Canterbury*. Ed. and trans. R. W. Southern (London: Thomas Nelson and Sons, 1962), p. 6.

58. Eadmer, *op. cit.*, pp. 4–5.

59. Rule, *op. cit.*, Vol. I pp. 13–14.

60. I. e., Anselm's father.

61. Feuer, p. 260.

62. Feuer, p. 271.

63. E.g., A. Nemetz writes: "St. Anselm did not intend to make a formal proof for the existence of God. He was not concerned with making a scientific demonstration for the existence of a necessary being, or for the possibility of a necessary being, or for the non-contradictoriness of the existence of a necessary being. Instead, St. Anselm intended his argument to exemplify a method through which the understanding can find an expression for the certitude of faith or through which reason can find a way to articulate the 'reasonable solidity of Truth.' From this perspective the argument can be regarded as valid." *New Catholic Encyclopedia* (New York: McGraw-Hill, 1967), Vol. X, p. 701 ("Ontological Argument").

Chapter VI: What Is a Translation?

1. By way of further illustrating this point: Richard Campbell takes the second sentence of P 3 to mean: "it (i.e. that-than-which-a-greater-cannot-be-thought) can be thought to be something which cannot be thought not to be

. . . .'' (See R. Campbell, *Theology*, 78(August 1975), 442–443.) By contrast, I believe that the sense of the reasoning is: ''For there can be thought to exist something whose non-existence is inconceivable . . . .'' (Or more literally: ''For there can be thought to exist something which cannot be thought not to exist'': Nam potest cogitari esse aliquid, quod non possit cogitari non esse. . . .) Cf. the Latin construction in P 15: Quoniam namque valet cogitari esse aliquid huiusmodi: si tu non es hoc ipsum, potest cogitari aliquid maius te; quod fieri nequit: ''For since there can be thought to be something of this kind: if You were not this thing, then something greater than You could be thought — a consequence which is impossible.''

Cf. Proposition F on p. 116 above.

Of course, considered from a purely grammatical standpoint ''*potest*'' can be translated either as ''it can'' or as ''there can.''

2. Of course, where a code-book does not exist, decoding becomes deciphering, and the contrast between deciphering and translating will be even less sharp. One thinks of the problems accompanying Ventris' ''breaking the code'' of Linear B.

3. Thus, in P 2 Schmitt accepts the reading ''Nam cum pictor praecogitat, quae facturus est, habet quidem in intellectu, sed nondum intelligit esse quod nondum fecit,'' even though the principal ms. has ''Nam cum pictor praecogitat quae facturus est, habet quidem rem in intellectu et intelligit quam intelligit nondum esse.'' Cf. p. 64*–65* (i.e., of the Prolegomena) in Vol. I of *Sancti Anselmi Opera Omnia* (ed. F. S. Schmitt) as republished by Frommann Verlag, 1968.

4. See Ch. IV, p. 108 above.

5. See Ch. I, p. 9; Ch. II, pp. 14–15; Ch. IV, p. 191, n. 6 above.

6. Note, for instance, the practical limits encountered by Michael Loux in his translation entitled *Ockham's Theory of Terms*: *Part I of the Summa Logicae* (South Bend, Ind.: University of Notre Dame Press, 1974): (1) ''Early in the project I realized that a *literal* translation in readable English would be difficult if not impossible. I opted for readability . . .'' (p. xi). (2) ''The examples Ockham employs also provide some difficulty. Upon occasion, these examples depend upon grammatical features of Latin that have no parallel in English, so that it is impossible to translate these examples into English while retaining their point in the text. Where such examples were essential I retained the Latin, where non-essential I eliminated them'' (p. xii). (3) ''In some cases it was difficult to determine whether Ockham is using a term in material or simple supposition. In those cases I opted for single quotes. In a few places, especially the section on the predicables, this convention forced arbitrary choices upon me; but alternative conventions would have involved considerable semantical and syntactical awkwardness'' (p. xii).

7. One may, of course, legitimately wonder how well Anselm understood himself.